iBPMS

Intelligent BPM Systems
Impact and Opportunity

BPM and Workflow
Handbook Series

iBPMS

Intelligent BPM Systems: Impact and Opportunity

Foreword by
Jim Sinur

BPM and Workflow Handbook Series

Published in association with the
Workflow Management Coalition

Workflow Management Coalition

20 Years of Thought-Process Leadership

Edited by
Layna Fischer

Future Strategies Inc., Book Division
Lighthouse Point, Florida

iBPMS
Intelligent BPM Systems: Impact and Opportunity

Copyright © 2013 by Future Strategies Inc.

ISBN-13: 978-0-9849764-6-1

Published by Future Strategies Inc., Book Division

3640-B3 North Federal Highway #421
Lighthouse Point FL 33064 USA
954.782.3376 fax 954.719.3746
www.FutStrat.com; books@FutStrat.com

Publisher's Cataloging-in-Publication Data

Library of Congress Catalog Card LCCN No. 2013944612

iBPMS
Intelligent BPM Systems: Impact and Opportunity

/Layna Fischer (editor)

p. cm.

Includes bibliographical references, appendices and index.

ISBN 978-0-9849764-6-1

1. Business Process Management. 2. Intelligent Systems. 3. Big Data. 4. Business Intelligence. 5. Business Process Technology. 6. Adaptive Case Management. 7. Machine Intelligence. 8. Predictive Analytics 9. Business Process Technology. 10. Electronic Commerce. 11. Process Mining

Palmer, Nathaniel; Swenson, Keith; Shapiro, Robert *et al* (authors)

Fischer, Layna (editor)

Table of Contents

Section 1

Section 2: Appendices

Foreword

The need for Intelligent Business Operations (IBO) supported by intelligent processes is driving the need for a new convergence of process technologies lead by the iBPMS. The iBPMS changes the way processes help organizations keep up with business change.

Change to Rich Outcome/Goal Directed Processes:

One of the major differences with an intelligent process is that it can seek out business outcomes and suggest or automatically make changes to stay on track or respond to business changes. This implies that processes have knowledge of conflicting outcomes and can dynamically balance them, with or without the assistance from a process manager or participant, to attain blended and dynamic outcomes. This can be accomplished through static or dynamic goal models in an iBPMs.

Change to Rich Policy/Business Rule Management:

Traditional processes can deal with small scale rule changes to enable agility, particularly around navigation, work environments, dashboards and work load assignments, but sophisticated coordinated and managed change around business polies and scenarios can only be supported by true rule management; not just a rules engine alone. Rule management that impacts the end to end processes is the hall mark of an iBPMS.

Change to Rich On-Demand Analytics:

Typical processes have been quite restricted in their use of analytics. In order to deal with modeling potential actions and changes in behavior, processes must possess deep pol-analytics that can be called upon by business process managers and participants to respond to changing conditions and difficult process instances/cases. These analytics should be tuned to run in a real time environment leveraging big data. This is normally only found in an iBPMS or a separate, but linked decision focused stack. Quite often and automated business process discovery set and/or social network analytics are included in this component.

Change to Rich Active Analytics:

This is a brand new area for process suites. This includes real time event and complex event recognition. These are running in an "always on" fashion sniffing for expected and unexpected events and patterns. These usually leverage rules and poly-analytics for complex patterns, but there is room to sense simple an interesting events. The iBPMS is typically event sensitive, but may be completely event driven.

Change to Rich Social/Collaborative Human Interactions:

Intelligent processes must enable great knowledge worker collaborations. Process instances/cases, emerging patterns, decisions and potential actions all can use assists from technologies such as event, business rules, analytics and goals, but leveraging human resources optimally is key to intelligent processes. Skills and knowledge-driven approaches are helpful, but so are better practice pattern discovery and analysis are typically in an iBPMS.

Jim Sinur, Independent Consultant and Gartner Emeritus

iBPMS

Introduction and Overview
Layna Fischer, Future Strategies Inc.

"The need for Intelligent Business Operations (IBO) supported by intelligent processes is driving the need for a new convergence of process technologies lead by the iBPMS. The iBPMS changes the way processes help organizations keep up with business change," says Jim Sinur in his Foreword to this book.

Intelligent business process management is the next generation of enterprise BPM, leveraging recent technological advances to attain a degree of operational responsiveness not possible with yesterday's business process platform.

Today, companies of all types want faster and better insight into their operations. This growing demand for operational intelligence has given rise to a new, "smarter" variety of business process management suites (BPMSs).

Dubbed 'iBPMS" by Gartner Group, who describes the intelligent BPM Suite as having 10 core components:

- A process orchestration engine
- A model-driven composition environment
- Content interaction management
- Human interaction management
- Connectivity
- Active analytics (sometimes called continuous intelligence)
- On-demand analytics
- Business rules management (BRM)
- Management and administration for the suite's technical aspects
- A process component registry/repository

An intelligent BPM suite provides the functionality needed to support more intelligent business operations, including real-time analytics, extensive complex event processing (CEP) and business activity monitoring (BAM) technologies and enhanced mobile, social and collaborative capabilities.

The co-authors of this important book describe various aspects and approaches with regard to impact and opportunity.

THRIVING ON ADAPTABILITY: HOW SMART COMPANIES WIN IN A DATA-DRIVEN WORLD.

Nathaniel Palmer, Business Process Management, Inc. (BPMI) and WfMC

Whatever business you are in today, inevitably you face an environment defined by growing uncertainty and unpredictability, where advantage favors not the best plans but the speed of change. Yet in the face of constant change, competitive advantage is derived not simply from the flexibility to move with the tide, but rather from having the intelligence to interpret the signals that indicate where the tide is headed, and the capability to proactively move in that direction. In this way, we see the much-lauded trait of "agility" (defined generally as "the ability to change") as being necessary yet insufficient. Rather it is "adaptability" which enables sustainable competitive advantage – the ability to not only do new things well, but also identify what to do and how to do it.

AVOIDING FRAGILITY IN INNOVATIVE LEARNING ORGANIZATIONS

Keith Swenson, Fujitsu America Inc.

Do you conceptualize your organization as a machine? If so, you may be led down the wrong path for optimizing business processes. Machines are complicated, but truly complex systems, like an organization, a marketplace, an ecosystem, are not like machines. Evidence for this is both familiar and surprising. It is the "Enlightenment Bias" which blinds us to the true nature of organizations. If you want your organization to excel, you need to understanding the true nature of organizations, and the new generation of tools that are becoming available to support them.

ADAPTIVE CASE MANAGEMENT FOR RAILWAY FREIGHT OPERATIONS

Helle Frisak Sem, Steinar Carlsen, Gunnar John Coll and Thomas Bech Pettersen, Computas AS, Norway

CargoNet AS is the primary Norwegian freight train operator, and GTS is their system for logistics-handling. GTS adaptively unifies contributions from knowledge workers across the organization, from marketing and sales to train configuration and composition, scheduling, real-time monitoring, handling of dangerous goods, truck operations and container quality assurance. It is an ACM system, multiplying as an ERP solution. GTS is a mission critical system used by most employees involved in the primary value chain, fully integrated with CargoNet's internet customer portal. Since going online in 2002, GTS has been gradually enhanced in terms of end-user functionality.

Showcasing a non-traditional application of case management technologies, the GTS architecture is information centric. A range of tasks and tools operate on shared work folder contents. The integrated customer portal for placing orders contributes to the contents of work folders. A ruggedized mobile client is deployed in cargo handling trucks, used for container reception, placement and depot management. Another mobile client handles container damage assessment.

CREATING AN INTEGRATED PLATFORM FOR ENTERPRISE-WIDE PROCESS INTELLIGENCE

Roy Altman, Peopleserv, Inc.

What does it take to make BPM strategic to the organization? BPM systems have traditionally focused tactically on individual processes. A platform integrating a range of BPM technologies is required to scale BPM to orchestrate processes and tasks across the entire extended enterprise, thus providing strategic value.

BPM technology is advancing rapidly, encompassing structured workflow, tools for the knowledge worker, mobile, social, and machine intelligence. We need to take an "all of the above" approach to leverage these technologies to assist with the dynamically changing nature of business. To accomplish this requires a platform that enables one to "plug in" technology components which can interact as an integrated whole, leveraging the tool that's appropriate for each problem.

By taking this holistic approach and creating an end-to-end process platform, BPM can provide strategic value to the organization by allowing seamless use of various technologies to address business needs.

An intelligent BPM platform requires deep technical integration for the software components, as well as Relationship Management to provide functional integration for the interactions between people involved in the processes. Only through functional as well technical integrations can we provide a fully integrated environment to make full use of the powerful BPM technologies of the present and the future.

PROCESS OF EVERYTHING

Setrag Khoshafian and Don Schuerman, Pegasystems Inc.

The Internet of Everything will involve billions "things" or devices connected over the Internet: generating data, being controlled, and pro-active in innovations that will transform both individual lives as well as businesses. These things or devices will be intelligent. Increasingly, the Internet of Things will extend beyond traditional electronic devices to include everything from food products to cars to the houses we live in. In the next decade, digital-enabled things will generate more Internet traffic than people. They will be the main source of Big Data – characterized by enormously large volume, velocity, and complexity. Through embedded intelligence, the things will be semi-autonomous agents.

Intelligent BPM will provide the context to coordinate these events. It will instantiate, complete, and resolve work created from these devices and serve as a bridge to connect these devices to human participants. It will mine the events in real-time. Intelligent devices will execute business rules and decisions. They will learn and adapt – while being "process" connected to other devices or humans.

This is a natural evolution of BPM: human participants in Intelligent Business Process Management solutions are already augmented with guided interactions and decisioning intelligence. When associated with "things," the process automation extends from the confines of humans and includes intelligent devices over the Internet: The Process of Everything.

THE iBPM ECOSYSTEM: MORE HUMAN THAN SYSTEM

Gianpiero Bongallino, openwork

Similar to the human nervous system, the iBPM is a system that allows us:
- to process the inputs from external or internal systems (Events),
- to correlate them in order to obtain a more meaningful signal (CEP),
- to send the pre-processed impulses to the brain (Event Channel), which further processes them and triggers a reaction, according to pre-established patterns (BPM and business rules),
- to adapt them to different situations (ACM), according to the contingency and previous memory (BAM and Recommender System).

Each sub-system has unique characteristics and can adapt to different business needs in different domains, thus enabling it to solve complex problems, in real-time or even before the issue arises. A healthcare scenario will be also examined, illustrating how these technologies can be used in some phases of the management of a healthcare organization.

MARKETING INTELLIGENT BPM TO HEALTHCARE INTELLIGENTLY

Charles Webster, EHR Workflow Inc.

Health information technology (HIT) professionals who learn about business process management (BPM) technology are usually impressed. Nonetheless, BPM has been slow to diffuse into healthcare. HIT has technologies corresponding to some BPM suite core components. But process orchestration engines remain rare. Fortunately, there are signs that the HIT market is entering a period of greater need and appreciation for BPM ideas, products, and services. I describe the current state of affairs within the health IT industry and suggest how BPM vendors can engage, educate, and communicate, about BPM's unique value to healthcare and health IT.

HOW TO MAKE MOBILE BPM ROBUST AND INTELLIGENT

Dirk Draheim, University of Innsbruck, Austria, Theodorich Kopetzky, SCCH GmbH, Austria, Josef Küng, FAW GmbH, Austria

We represent a workflow management system that realizes a sweet spot between the robustness of a centralized master workflow enactment service and the flexibility of distributed disconnected workflow management services. The architecture emerged in a concrete scenario with the requirement that traveling business agents can continue to work with their supporting enterprise applications even if they are disconnected from the Internet and therefore disconnected from their enterprise IT infrastructure. Key characteristics of the solution are mobile and intelligent data and workflow state synchronization mechanisms. The system was implemented at the largest Austrian insurance company AUVA. There is still no single systematic BPM suite available that handles the problem of disconnecting and reconnecting clients in a smart way. As we now from many discussions in CIO cycles, in practice only ad-hoc solutions based on ECM systems or public mail folders are used to deal at least with the data facet of the described problem. However, with these ad-hoc solutions a smart treatment of distributed workflow state is nigh on impossible. The presented system shows a way out of this dilemma.

DECISION SUPPORT FOR INTELLIGENT BPM

Pieter Van Schalkwyk, XMPro

This chapter covers the introduction of decision support for BPM to create Intelligent BPM. It describes the evolution on BPM from a machine economy to a knowledge economy where human capital is now the biggest asset. Business and processes rely on people's knowledge, experience and intuition to get much of the work in modern businesses done. Decision support can take many forms. It can be based on analytics where information is made available to processes in real time to create Operational Intelligence (and it is contrast with more strategic BI). It can be in the form of external data that help guide process decisions, like weather web-services that support logistics routing processes. It can be algorithmic decision trees that help guide the decision process.

Intelligent BPM without in-built decision support doesn't aid knowledge workers to drive process outcomes to KPIs or goals. Decision support is the GPS of Intelligent BPM.

EMERGING STANDARDS IN DECISION MODELING—AN INTRODUCTION TO DECISION MODEL & NOTATION

James Taylor, Decision Management Solutions; Alan Fish, FICO; Jan Vanthienen, KU Leuven; Paul Vincent, TIBCO

Written by four members of the submission team (representing FICO, TIBCO, Decision Management Solutions and the University of Leuven), this paper introduces the Decision Model & Notation.

The BPM market has expanded and matured in recent years, driven in part by the growing acceptance and broad use of process standards and common modeling notations. As companies transition to intelligent BPM, however, there is a need to focus on decision-making as well as process execution and workflow. Decision-making is important in intelligent processes, making them simpler and more agile as well as increasing the rate of straight through processing. However existing standards and notations do not readily support the modeling and specification of decision making. To address this need a new standard is being developed at the OMG, the Decision Model and Notation (DMN) standard.

A RELIABLE METHODOLOGY FOR BPM PROJECT IMPLEMENTATION

Josip Brumec and Slaven Brumec, KORIS d.o.o., Croatia

The methodology for the implementation of BPM project is presented as a set of mutually related activities performed by business experts, process designers and software engineers, and their collaboration while performing BPM projects. The roles of the participants are different: business experts must participate in As Is modeling, define the KPIs to measure the effects of BPR, estimate To Be models and prepare the company for implementation of improved business processes. Business process designers must define the optimal solutions for future business processes and to prove their performance that match predefined KPIs and define ICT infrastructure for BPM. Software engineers need to develop a process-oriented applications, test them and prepare for the implementation.

The methodology itself is defined as a business process model with more than 25 activities and sub-processes, arranged in three lanes. Procedures for each participant were determined by sequence flows, events and decisions, and collaboration among the participants is presented as information flows. The methodology is graphically presented in accordance with the BPMN 2.0 standard and the meaning of all steps and symbols is described in details.

The proposed methodology is practically validated through several implemented projects, and has also confirmed as an excellent manager's tool to control the realization of BPM project.

COMPOSING SERVICES IN THE FUTURE INTERNET: CHOREOGRAPHY-BASED APPROACH

Marco Autili, University of L'Aquila, Italy; Amira Ben Hamida, Linagora GSO, France; Guglielmo De Angelis, CNR-ISTI, Italy; Darius Silingas, No Magic Europe, Lithuania

In this chapter, we will discuss emerging technology that enables intelligent business processes enacting services based on choreography specifications. This technology was produced by CHOReOS research project funded under European research program FP7 (CHOReOS 2013).

Today service-based software engineering is heavily based on service orchestrations that can be specified in various formats, such as BPEL (OASIS 2007) or BPMN 2.0 (OMG 2011). Service orchestration is a centralized approach to composing multiple services into a larger application. It works well in static environments where services are predefined and environment changes are minimal. Alas, this is a wrong assumption for the Future Internet, which envisions an ultra large number of diverse service providers and consumers that are impossible to coordinate using centralized manner.

MAKING SOA WORK—A PRACTICE-ORIENTED OVERVIEW

Gerhard Rempp & Martin Löffler, MID GmbH, Germany

Services represent the pivotal feature of service-oriented architecture. This paper highlights how a service evolution can take place within a SOA service lifecycle, from the specialized process and defining business services all the way to technical service implementation.

SOA has often been declared a failure. But, in fact, we can see that SOA use has now become a reality! After all, those who have been declared dead often live the longest, and many prophets are later revealed to be naysayers.

There are active SOA projects in every large company, and "SOA-ification" is forging ahead. Still, there is no longer any huge hype surrounding it. And that's a good sign! SOA and the associated standardization has become part of our everyday lives.

Still, there are some unresolved issues. The authors discuss why, in order to lay the right foundations for a successful SOA project, services need to be developed on the basis of specialized knowledge.

SMART TOOLS AND VISUAL ANALYTICS

Hartmann Genrich, Process Analytica, Germany; Robert Shapiro, Process Analytica, USA

Smart tools of PA Optima support fast optimization by simulation and analysis using only that subset of the analytics required by the particular optimization technique. They are rather 'autistic' and focus on efficiency rather than interaction and generality.

So far two such tools are available: Smart Resource Allocation and Smart Productivity Improvement. We briefly describe Smart Allocation because the optimization algorithms in it are also used in Smart Productivity. The Smart Productivity Improvement tool is novel and different from all other components of Optima. It goes one step beyond identifying potential improvement. It combines functionality of existing applications for cost/benefit and return-on-investment analysis with the Visual Analytics power of PA Optima; it facilitates the quick assessment of proposed improvement measures.

Section 1

Thriving on Adaptability: How Smart Companies Win in a Data-Driven World

Nathaniel Palmer
Business Process Management, Inc. (BPMI)

Whatever business you are in today, inevitably you face an environment defined by growing uncertainty and unpredictability, where advantage favors not the best plans but the speed of change. Yet in the face of constant change, competitive advantage is derived not simply from the flexibility to move with the tide, but rather from having the intelligence to interpret the signals that indicate where the tide is headed, and the capability to proactively move in that direction. In this way, we see the much-lauded trait of "agility" (defined generally as "the ability to change") as being necessary yet insufficient. Rather it is "adaptability" which enables sustainable competitive advantage – the ability to not only do new things well, but also identify what to do and how to do it.

INTRODUCTION

Adaptability is not a feature or a capability offered by any single system, but an outcome of how the right combination of IT-capabilities and business practices are leveraged. In a ground-breaking book by noted innovation strategist Max McKeown (*Adaptability: The Art of Winning*, Kogan Page 2012) the notion of adaptability within the business environment is distilled into a three-step model represented by the acronym "RUN" – Step 1: Recognition of required adaptation; Step 2: Understanding of adaptation required; and Necessary adaptation. In basic terms, you must first identify what do, then how to do it, then ultimately execute on one and two. In the context of IT systems and technology led innovation, the framework best able to facilitate this is Business Process Management (BPM).

In the decade since BPM first emerged as an identifiable software segment, the center of gravity for the competitive landscape has shifted from automation and integration, to orchestration and coordination. The first of BPM (let's call it "Phase One") offered one of the first real opportunities for enabling the separation of business management from systems management; enabling the abstraction of business and application logic. This has provided significant gains in how organizations manage work and respond to change, yet also best suited to a relatively stable and predictable business environment. Firms have invested in BPM to realize sustainable competitive advantage by exploiting scale, throughput and repeatability—finding what works and doing more of it.

Yet the impact of new technologies, the mandate for greater transparency, and the ongoing aftershocks of globalization have collectively removed nearly any trace of predictability within the business environment. As a result, sustainable competitive advantage no long comes from scale and efficiency but adaptability—the ability to read signals (data from many sources)—make sense of these, and rapidly translate these into effective responses designed for precision rather repeatability.

This chapter focuses on the role of BPM in fostering adaptability and adaptable business models. Specifically, however, it is not the "Phase One" BPM or even the "Phase Two" but rather a third phase now known as *Intelligent BPM Systems*" or *iBPMS*, which builds upon the previous generations yet extends into directions previously out of reach. "Intelligent," you may ask, "as opposed to Dumb BPM?" No, not dumb, per se, but *blind*. Whereas previous generations of BPM offered limited ability to make sense of external signals, iBPMS is distinguished foremost by a "sense and respond" orientation. This notion frames the Phase Three of BPM in terms of the synergistic combination of three groups of capabilities:

- **Phase One** – separating systems (application logic) from the processes (business logic) which they support;

- **Phase Two** – presenting a flexible architecture that supports adaptable, goal-driven process models by maintaining the intelligence for how to access information and application resources without having the bind this into a rigid process model; and

- **Phase Three** – building on the first two sets of capabilities while delivering visibility and feedback which shows what is going on within a process, as well as what will likely occur in the near future.

The first two phases of BPM have set a solid foundation for enabling adaptable systems, allowing BPM adopters to respond with far greater agility than ever before – moving away from the command-and-control structure which has defined management systems for the last 30 years.

For the first several years of the BPM market, these sorts of applications dominated. This also limited the potential market for BPM software, however, because for most firms the exception is the rule. The vast majority of business processes are dynamic, not standardized, and thus require the business systems (e.g., deployed software) that support them to adapt quickly to changes within the business environment. As a business technology, the greatest value of process management software is delivered not through automation and integration alone, but by introducing a layer between users and existing IT infrastructure to allow business systems to adapt and keep pace with the constant found in most business environments. Fully realizing the ability offered through orchestration, however, requires the 'situational awareness' necessary to adapt business systems to a changing business environment – the ability to sense and respond. By taking the lid off the black box of automation, the Phase Three of BPM offers a framework for continuously validating and refining an understanding of business performance drivers, and adapting business systems accordingly.

This will require a new level of transparency of processes and operations that is sure to present cultural and human factors challenges. But this is nothing new for BPM. At the end of the day BPM is only slightly about technology. It is, instead, mostly about the business and the people. What is indeed new, however, and at the center of the Phase Three opportunity, is the ability now to adapt systems continuously to match the ever-changing business environment. The model most frequently referenced throughout this chapter, this continuous loop of visibility and adaptability offers one of the first real leverage points for transforming business through adaptability.

THE EVOLUTION OF INTELLIGENT BPM

To understand the opportunities offered by Intelligent Business Process Management, it's helpful to consider the phases of maturation solutions have gone through over the last decade. During technology expansion of the mid- to late-1990s, the management of business processes was typically limited to the repetitive sequencing of activities, with rigid, "hard-wired" application-specific processes such as those within ERP systems. Any more sophisticated degree of workflow management generally imposed a significant integration burden, frequently accounting for 60-80 percent of the project cost with little opportunity for reuse. Still, integration was typically limited to retrieval of data or documents, similarly hard-wired with one-to-one connection points.

These early process management initiatives often focused on integrating and automating repetitive processes, generally within standardized environments. Whether focused on Straight-Through Processing transactions or a discrete process such as Account Activation, these are applications where the flow and sequence of activities is predetermined and immutable. The role of exception handling here is to allow human intervention to quickly resolve or correct a break in the flow of an otherwise standard process.

By the end of the 1990s, however, BPM had emerged as an identifiable software segment, a superset of workflow management distinguished in part by allowing process management independent of any single application. This was enabled by managing application execution instructions separate from process flows, so processes could be defined without limitation to single application, as well as through support for variable versus hard-wired process flow paths.

The first wave of BPM deployments were typically aimed at bridging the island of automation described above, such as closing gaps in existing ERP deployments. Early BPM solutions were differentiated by integration-centric functionality, such as application adapters, data transformation capabilities and product-specific process definitions (e.g., an order-to-cash process). Eventually, the introduction of standards such as Web Services and advances in the development tools within BPM suites lowered the cost and complexity of data integration. This began to shift the fundamental value proposition of BPM from discrete capabilities to enabling the management of business logic by business process managers, without threatening the integrity of the application logic (the infrastructure that is rightfully managed and protected by IT personnel).

The availability of standards-based protocols significantly lowered the burden on BPM adopters for building and maintaining integration infrastructure, freeing time and resources to focus on the process and business performance, rather than being consumed with plumbing issues. Over time this facilitated a refocus of process management software from that of automation and integration to orchestration and coordination, bringing BPM into the realm of business optimization. Business environments are dynamic, requiring the business systems that support them to be so as well. This means that systems must be able to easily adapt to changing business circumstances. Phase Two of the BPM opportunity was presented through making orchestration a reality—the ability to connect abstracted application capabilities across orchestrated business processes, thereby transforming existing automation infrastructure into reusable business assets. What separates orchestration from automation is presented by a fundamental shift in perspective, from thinking of processes as a flow of discrete steps, to understanding processes in terms of goals and milestones.

FROM AUTOMATION TO ORCHESTRATION: THE REALIGNMENT OF BPM AROUND SOA

Orchestration allows systems to mirror the behavior of the rest of the business environment (one defined in terms of objectives rather than scripts). Over the last decade, orchestration has introduced a visible shift in the axis of business computing. As firms realize the opportunities presented by orchestration, it offers (arguably mandates) a wholesale rethinking of the role of applications and information systems.

Orchestration has already had a visible impact on the direction of the BPM market, enabled by standards protocols (notably XML and the core Web Services stack of SOAP, UDDI, and WSDL), the emergence of Service-Oriented Architectures (SOA) has provided a new level flexibility and simplicity in resolving integration issues. In fact it has to such an extent that it almost seems redundant to discuss in the context of forward-looking perspective of modern BPM.

Indeed, most 'adaptability pundits' would find the discussion of SOA as a propeller-head anathema, something only the geekiest techies and such worry about. Yet, that is why it is so relevant to the adaptability discussion, since previously (e.g., prior to SOA) performing the most basic changes to underlying integration configurations, such as a change in the structure of a document by its sender or the set of information required by the requester, would require taking running processes and/or systems offline, then having a programmer manually code each of the changes.

Now we can nearly take for granted that the underlying systems of record are decoupled from how we access them—that access is enabled through a services layer rather than a programmatic interface which requires integration at the code level (i.e., "tightly-coupled"). What SOA provides for BPM and other software environments is a common means for communicating between applications, such that connections do not need to be programmed in advance—as long as the BPM environment knows where to find information and how to access it. This is critical to dynamic processes where the specific information, activities and roles involved with a process may not be predetermined but identified as the process progresses.

Of course this does require, however, that the information and infrastructure sought to be accessed is exposed as services. For example, core system capabilities can be exposed as containerized Web services with a WSDL description, able to be invoked by any Web services compliant application, or increasingly with a RESTful interface allowing integration points and data variables to be defined at design time, but resolved at run-time, eliminating the inherent problems of hard-wired integration.

APPLY SOA STRATEGIES TO INTEGRATING UNSTRUCTURED INFORMATION

While the evolution of Service-Oriented Architecture has dramatically improved the accessibly of structured information through standardized interfaces, access to unstructured information can be far more challenging. Consider for a moment where customers reside in your firm. The answer is most likely "everywhere"; records, transactions, profiles, project data, recent news, and other sources of structured and "semi-structured" information (such as correspondence and other documents without uniform representation). For many firms it would take years to rationalize all the places where customer data might be found. But by instead knowing where to find it and how it is described, it can be left intact yet used for multiple purposes.

Leveraging Content as a Service

Following the same strategy as is presented by SOA for accessing structured information, a relatively new standard called "Content Management Interoperability Services" or more commonly "CMIS" enables a services approach to "content middleware" by exposing information stored within CMIS-compliant content repositories, both internally and externally managed sources. As content is captured or otherwise introduced to a process, it can be automatically categorized and indexed based on process state and predefined rules and policies.

This presents a virtual repository of both content and meta-data that describes how and where content is managed at various stages of its lifecycle. Meta-data is exposed to the system and process nodes, but invisible to users who instead are presented with the appropriate content and format based on their identity the current state of the process.

REALIZING ADAPTABILITY: SHIFTING FROM EVENT-DRIVEN TO GOAL-DRIVEN

The notion of orchestration has changed the role of BPM from that of a transit system designed to shuttle data from one point to another over predefined routes, to that of a virtual power user that "knows" how to locate, access and initiate application services and information sources. In contrast with more easily automated system-to-system processes and activities, "knowledge worker" processes characteristic of manual work involve a series of people-based activities that may individually occur in many possible sequences.

This transition in computing orientation can be described as the shift from *event-driven* where processes are defined in terms of a series of triggers, to *goal-driven* where processes are defined in terms of specific milestones and outcomes (goals) and constant cycles of adaptations required to achieve them. In event-driven computing, systems respond to a specific event—a request for information is received and the appropriate information is sent, or a process step is complete and so the results are recorded and the next step is initiated. In most cases, the nature of event-driven computing requires explicit scripting or programming of outcomes.

Goal-driven processes, however, are far more complex. A process that has only 20-30 unique activities, a relatively small number for most knowledge worker processes, may present over 1,000 possible permutations in the sequencing of activities. This of course presents too many scenarios to hard-code within linear process flows in advance, or to create a single process definition, which helps explain the difficulty traditionally faced in the automation of these types of goal-driven processes. Rather, this capability is enabled through the application of goals, policies and rules, while adjusting the flow of the process to accommodate outcomes not easily identifiable.

Goal-Driven Scenarios

In many cases each subsequent step in a process is determined only by the outcome and other circumstances of the preceding step. In addition, there may be unanticipated parallel activities that occur without warning, and may also immediately impact the process and future (even previous) activities. For these reasons and the others described above, managing goal-driven processes requires the ability to define and manage complex policies and declarative business rules; the parameters and business requirements which determine the true "state" of a process. Goal-driven processes cannot be defined in terms of simple "flow logic" and "task logic" but must be able to represent intricate relationships between activities and information, based on policies, event outcomes, and dependencies (i.e, "context.")

Such a case is the admission of a patient for medical treatment. What is involved is in fact a process, yet the specific sequence and set of activities most does not follow a specific script, but rather is based on a diagnostic procedure which likely involves applying a combination of policies, procedures, other rules, and the judgment of healthcare workers. Information discovered in one step (e.g., the assessment a given condition) can drastically alter the next set of steps, and in the same way a change in 'patient state' (e.g., patient goes into heart failure) may completely alter the process flow in other ways.

The patient admission scenario described earlier is an example of this. What is needed to successfully execute an admission process is a super user who knows both the medical protocols to make a successful diagnosis and the system protocols to know where and how to enter and access the appropriate information. Alternatively, BPM can exist as the virtual user layer, providing a single access point for the various roles involved, while assuming the burden of figuring out where and how access information.

Yet what really differentiates this as a goal-driven system is the ability to determine the sequence of a process based on current context. For example, a BPM system can examine appropriate business rules and other defined policies against the current status of a process or activity to determine what step should occur next and what information is required.

Facilitating Better Decisions vs Mandating Actions

Often the flow and sequencing of a goal-driven process is determined largely by individual interpretation of business rules and policies. For example, a nurse who initiates a patient admitting process will evaluate both medical protocol and the policies of the facility where the healthcare services are administered. Similarly, an underwriter compiling a policy often makes decisions by referring to policy manuals or his own interpretation of rules and codes. As a result, what may be an otherwise 'standard' process will be distinguished by exceptions and pathways that cannot be determined in advance, but at each step each activity must nonetheless adhere to specific rules and policies.

PHASE THREE: INTELLIGENT BPM

The first two phases of BPM laid a solid foundation for enabling adaptable business systems, by allowing business logic (processes, policies, rules, etc.) to be defined and managed within a separate environment, as well as using an open approach to communicating with other systems (Web Services). This has provided a level of adaptability that allows BPM adopters to respond to changes in the business environment with far greater agility than ever before.

This shift toward goal-oriented computing has laid the path for Phase-Three BPM, which combines integration and orchestration with the ability to continuously validate and refine the business users' understanding of business performance drivers, and allowing them to adapt business systems and process flows accordingly. The effect of Phase Three BPM is to 'take the lid off' what has for years been a black box shrouding automation.

With the third phase of BPM, visibility combines with integration and orchestration to enable business process owners and managers to discover the situation changes which require adaptation. Phase Three of BPM offers a framework for continuously validating and refining an understanding of business performance drivers, and adapting business systems accordingly. This should represent in a new and significantly greater level of interest and adoption of BPM software, by attracting firms seeking to optimize business performance, rather than integrating and automating systems and tasks.

Part of the recent evolution towards iBPMS technology is inclusion of more sophisticated reporting capabilities within the BPM environment itself. This is both enabled and in many way necessitated by the greater flexibility of the architectures introduced with the BPM suites that define Phase Two. With these environments, the ability to support non-sequential, goal-driven models is greatly increased, requiring more feedback (reporting) to enable success execution of this type of less deterministic process models.

With few exceptions, reporting on process events and business performance was previously done only after a process had executed, or otherwise within a separate environment disjointed from the process. This obviously prevented any opportunity to impact the direction or a process, but was based on a limitation of system and software architectures. Specifically with regard to BPM, process models were most commonly defined as proprietary structures, and in many cases compiled into software. Thus, changes either required bringing down and recompiling an application, or were otherwise limited to discrete points in the process (such as exceptions and yes/no decision points).

Adaptability Begins With Reading Signals

Successful adaptation, to move in the right direction, requires the ability to accurately assess the full and relevant context of the current status. Indeed, the more flexible and adaptable the systems are, the greater the requirement for visibility. In the same manner, the greater the ability to monitor the signals which define business performance, the more value can be found in the ability to adapt processes and systems accordingly. To illustrate the distinction of orchestration over automation the metaphor of rail transportation – which moves across a predictable path and direction (quite literally "hardwired") has been used (arguably overused) to illustrate *automation*, contrasted with *orchestration* described in terms of a car or other personal transportation. The latter offers a vehicle to deliver passengers to a desired destination by understanding the rules of the road and milestones along the way, but does not require scripting every single inch along the way. In fact it would be nearly impossible to do so given the unpredictably of such factors as traffic and road conditions. Driving through traffic is entirely about *sense-and-respond* where adaptation is happening real-time – you brake, accelerate, steer left, and so forth. All of these actions are in response to a constant stream of signals and event data.

Thus what separates personal transportation from rail travel is not only the ability to deviate from the hardwired path, but also the need for visibility. This is an overly simplified, and again arguably overused metaphor, but it nonetheless offers a tangible concept for why "Intelligent BPM" is indeed a different animal. If you cannot see what is ahead of you, you cannot respond accordingly. Driving is an immensely data-driven exercise, even if it is largely tactile and observational data. At least this is the case today, in the absence of widespread adoption of *Google's driverless car*. Yet of course there too, it would be extremely data-intensive and literally data-driven, even if then majority of this data is visible only on a machine-to-machine basis.

In fact, as we see the rapidly growing intersection between Intelligent BPM and the *"Internet of Things"* we see already the reality of automobiles as participants in iBPMS managed processes. Specifically, sensor data generated by devices within the vehicles is used in a variety of consumer and commercial scenarios, ranging from the logistics optimization (determining routes, etc.) to user-targeted services such as communicating the expected arrival time to a building automation system to turn on lights and otherwise welcome the driver home. These are scenarios already underway, but this trend will only continue to expand as more event-data generating devices are leveraged to provide input into Intelligent BPM processes. Adaptability and adaptation requires visibility into process and business performance, as well as the ability to accurately assess the state of current events and circumstance, and the effect they may have on downstream process activities. This is why monitoring, reporting and simulation abilities are central to Intelligent BPM and iBPMS technology. Note that "simulation" snuck in there as well. While this may depart from the vehicle driving metaphor (albeit not entirely, if we follow the thread on GPS) simulation is indeed a critical iBPMS component.

ADAPTABILITY AND SIMULATION

In a recent *Harvard Business Review* article entitled *Adaptability: The New Competitive Advantage*, authors Martin Reeves and Mike Deimler of the Boston Consulting Group extend McKeown's *RUN* notion to describe four organizational capabilities as necessary to foster rapid adaptation. Specifically these capabilities are:

1. The ability to **read and act on signals** of change;
2. the ability to **manage complex and interconnected systems of multiple stakeholders**;
3. the ability to **experiment rapidly and frequently**—not only with products and services but also **with business models, processes, and strategies**; and
4. the ability to **motivate employees and partners**.

The *first* of these we have already discussed is what presents a critical distinguishing characteristic of the Intelligent BPM orientation. The *second* is also an essential precept of iBPMS technology, which necessarily involves connecting not just system-to-system integration points, but users and roles (stakeholders) engaged in the process, regardless of geographic or organizational boundaries. The *fourth* relates to organizational change and business motivation, which is of course essential to any successful transformation or sustainable business strategy. Yet the authors also rephrase the "ability to mobilize" and as we will discuss later in this chapter, this points to a significant need for social media and collaborative capabilities within iBPMS technology and Intelligent BPM processes. It is the ***third*** capability, however, *the ability to experiment rapidly and frequently*, discussed here in the context of business process simulation. To successfully leverage adaptable systems requires visibility into process state and business performance, such as the availability of resources, status of preceding activities, and the circumstances of related activities that impact decisions about a given process.

Similarly, it requires the ability to accurately assess the state of current events and their impact on downstream process activities; how will decisions made now effect business later, and what needs to be done now to accommodate likely events in the near future. For this reason, the integration capabilities that have continued to evolve within BPM suites must be able to present information and process state as actionable intelligence via dashboards and other reporting environments where business users can see the immediate cause-and-effect of business decisions (planned or implemented).

Ultimately this means the ability to engage in simulation within the process, not simply as part of the planning process (where it has traditionally been applied) but specifically within execution, e.g., as a core means by which the direction for adaptation is informed.

Which are the right signals to follow? What is the most likely result (impact and consequences) to a particular adaptation or change in strategy? What is the present relevance to corporate planning results now 6 months, or 1 year, or 5 years later? Answering these questions requires more than business forecasting (planning by another name) but rather the ability to generate, test, and replicate new innovative ideas (adaptations) faster, cheaper, and with less risk than the can otherwise be done in the materials world.

Beyond Trial and Error: Simulation as a Decision-enabler

As an example, Reeves and Deimler cite consumer products giant *Procter & Gamble* and their *Connect + Develop* model which leverages *InnoCentive* and other open-innovation networks to solve technical design problems, a virtual 3D walk-in store to run product placement experiments that are quicker and cheaper than traditional market tests, as well as *Vocalpoint* and similar online communities to safely introduce and test products prior to a full launch. As a result, P&G has been able to leverage a staff of ten skilled employees to generate over 10,000 design simulations in one year, at a fraction of the cost, time, and risk otherwise required for similar results without leveraging simulation.

In the face of constant and continuous change, the past is no longer prologue. What it does offer is a set of minable (e.g., data and processing mining) event data with detectable patterns and identifiable causalities that can be applied to current context for real-time, in-the-moment adaptation. With Intelligent BPM, simulations can be run continuously as part of the on-going monitoring and management of business performance. Whether it is part of the iBPMS system specifically or a separate environment (as in the P&G example) simulation provides an essential means for both validating assumptions, as well as understanding sensitivity and causality necessary to drive rapid and successful adaptation. To unearth both process model design problems, as well as to enable business model experimentation in an environment that optimizes results while minimizing risk.

INTELLIGENT BPM AS BUSINESS EVENT MANAGEMENT FRAMEWORK

Within Intelligent BPM processes, every business event has both a discrete lifecycle and ability to inform the larger process. In other words, Intelligent BPM processes are defined not specifically as a series of workflows, but as streams of events which both collectively and individually inform the direction of adaptation. This notion reframes iBPMS technology in terms of a business event management framework, leveraging event data from a variety of sources, including legacy systems or other transactional systems, social networks, as well as content—the ability to capture documents and pull content from various repositories and libraries (leveraging "content middleware" as described previously).

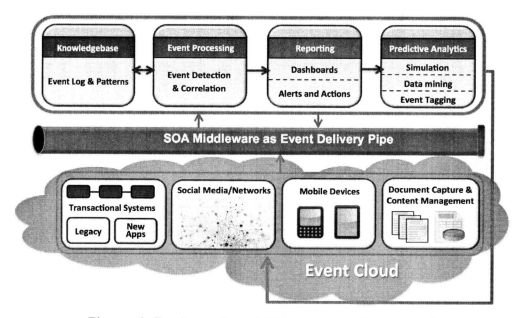

Figure 1: Business Event Management Framework

From a systems standpoint, we can envision SOA middleware as the connecting "pipe" for receiving and delivering event data from a broad group of sources, which are ultimately standardized for event processing, reporting, and simulation. Two key notions here are the event delivery network (for this purpose a SOA middle tier) and data standardization (in this context data normalization, however, this does not necessarily mean changes to data structures as has historically been the case.) For example, the events that define a customer may come from a heterogeneous mix of data sources, both internal and external, as well as structured and unstructured.

With event delivery network, events are received and managed across their lifecycle, value-added (data enrichment or "tagging" the event) allowing it to be understood in a larger context as well as both contributing to and benefiting from pattern detection. This standardization and enrichment are key to making sense of events as informative signals, and as to the inclusion of stakeholders (both intra- and inter-organizational) within the business process. Intelligent BPM is about enabling data-driven adaptability.

INTELLIGENT BPM LEVERAGES BIG DATA

Since its inception, IT has been defined by the architecture of the relational database (RDMS). The advances seen in computing, even in the evolution of Internet architecture, were essentially a derivative of the relational database. This has evolved over the last 40+ years, and everything from monolithic packaged software to comparatively simple and agile applications have been built on this model. Today, however, we are amidst an inflexion point, moving to the post-relational era, perhaps more aptly named the "Big Data Era."

The intelligence that comes from capturing event data (signal detection) as well as driving greater understanding and innovation through simulation, is a Big Data scenario. This cannot be done with a narrow lens on structured data, nor can it be limited to internal, single-company boundaries (nonetheless organizational or department constraints). Successful adaptation requires the ability to manage complex multi-enterprise systems, expanding the window of analysis for strategy beyond single company or business unit. Through partner value chains, customer interaction, outsourcing, offshoring, peer production, and other extended ecosystems of interdependent entities, Intelligent BPM processes often extend well beyond discrete transactions between suppliers or customers.

This level of collaboration requires standard conventions, mutually understood meaning of data exchanged between stakeholders, but without rigid structure or formalization. In this way, the post-relational shift to Big Data has largely paralleled, and in many ways is driven by the same conditions and requirements behind adaptability. The movement in both cases is to expand beyond the limits relational data structures and capture the richer context which define business events. One of the most frequently discussed Big Data initiatives is *Hadoop*, which is essentially a flat file document database or filesystem very reminiscent of the early database hierarchical architecture. It is parallel to the "*NoSQL*" movement, which while it might sound pointedly anti-SQL, actually stands for "Not Only SQL" in the spirit of post-relational flexibility for enabling greater reach and performance than otherwise possible with traditional relational databases.

A core driver behind Big Data is the vast growth of digitized information, in particular that which begins and exists throughout its lifecycle in digital format. It's not just that the data volumes are big, but that the broader spectrum of data must be managed differently. The data management goal is no longer about trying to create a monolithic structure, but rather to arrange data in ways such that the semantics—the understanding of the meaning of the data and the interrelationships within it—are accessible.

In an era when an aberrant Tweet can in a matter of minutes costs shareholders millions, it is the meta-context of business events across a spectrum of structured, unstructured, and semi-structured information that defines the larger perspective of business activity. The impact of mobile and social capabilities in enterprise systems, as well as external social networks is having a very real material impact on business. It has become critical (even if comparatively smaller but clearly growing) piece of the business event stream. It also has advanced the de-materialization of work as well as personal / professional demarcation. Is *LinkedIn* a "work tool" or personal site? Clearly it's both. Yet for most organizations an increasing amount of work is conducted through otherwise "unsanctioned" channels such as *LinkedIn*, *Twitter* and other social sources, offering either the potential wellspring of value-adding business events and event data, or otherwise process "dark matter" outside of the purview of the traditional business IT environment. Social media has allowed not only individuals, but also businesses and brands to connect directly to consumers. We now have volumes of case studies of missteps and miscalculations with the personas of corporate brands across social networks. These were clear and obvious failures of adaptability.

What is less visible, but arguably more important, is the leverage of these for successful adaptable business strategy and processes, as we saw with the P&G example. This comes back to the value of business event management and the speed of adaptation. All business events have an implicit half-life and utility curve. Whatever business you are in, the value represented by the response to an event diminishes over time. In every case, this is based on a utility curve, not a straight-line. Responding twice as fast is more than twice as valuable. The faster the response, the greater the business value realized.

Delays in response ("Latency") can be divided into two distinct groups: "Infrastructure Latency" or delay presented by the system in delivering notification of the event, and "Decision Latency" or the period of time between when the business event data is captured and when it is responded to. For example, the delay between the time from when a customer submits a complaint or (per the scenario above) tweets about a bad experience—from that moment until when it is within an actionable, reporting framework (e.g., when it becomes an actual *signal*)—that is Infrastructure Latency.

The time between when the signal is received until the moment someone responds, first deciding then acting, is Decision Latency. Recall the first organizational capability as necessary to foster rapid adaptation offered by Reeves and Deimler, *the ability to read and act on signals of change*, the speed of this is largely a matter of Decision Latency.

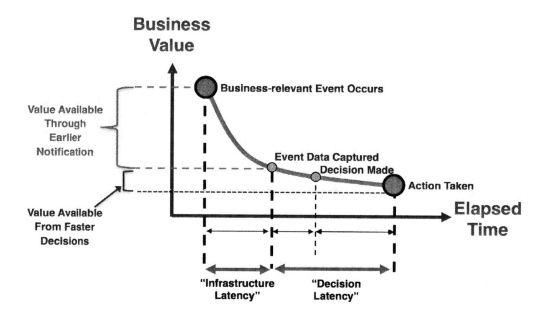

Figure 2: Time-based Value of Business Event Response

Regardless of the specific circumstances involved, the value of the response is greater closest to the moment of the complaint, diminishes over time and after a certain period in time, any response is going to be of little value. There is not a single set of hard metrics for all organizations, or all events, but in every case, there is predictable value gained from the ability to capture an event. It could be related to a sales opportunity, or field maintenance, or terrorist threat, in every case the faster the response the greater the value.

Faster Adaptation is Not Necessarily Faster Decisions

It can be assumed that the ability to take action on a specific event will always involve some delay. Yet there is a similar inevitability that the value lost as a result of that delay will follow a utility curve, not a straight line. Thus, the greatest source of value will always come from faster notification and action-ability, rather than faster decision-making.

The value of faster decisions (automating the function of knowledge workers in the decision-making process) offers little value, particularly when compared to the cost of poor decisions made in haste. Because of the greater the delay in notification and actionability, there is greater pressure on making decisions sooner rather than losing further value. Yet the opportunity lies in reducing Infrastructure Latency. By getting actionable information into the hands of knowledge workers sooner, iBPMS systems offer a predictable source of business value and clear differentiation from passive systems (i.e., notification only, without the ability to facilitate a response.)

THE VALUE OF SOCIAL MEDIA TO INTELLIGENT BPM

Understanding the time-based impact of business event response illustrates the critical capability and value offered by Intelligent BPM from the ability to move to signals and actions to the edge-points of interaction. The sooner signals are received and acted on, the tighter response loop, the greater the value derived from that business event. Yet this comes not simply as the ability to read events generated from within social media, but also the means or mode through which events are "socialized."

Consider the revolution of *Facebook* in recent years, which wasn't about enabling me to post stuff about myself for the world to see. That was an established set of capabilities and frankly the world hardly needed another outlet for this. If nothing else, *MySpace* sufficiently addressed this, which in 2009 far-exceeded *Facebook's* reach and community size. Rather, it was the introduction of the "Like" button, which rapidly transformed the site's orientation (and ultimately that of social networks overall) from self-publishing to collaboration. Within a few months of introducing the Like button *Facebook* overtook *MySpace* in community size, and soon after sealed its fate altogether.

The Like button was (and is) about tapping into an event pipeline and then enriching these events with personal contributions (if nothing else, indicating your like for them). For all intents and purposes, *Facebook* users are tagging that event, adding value to it across its lifecycle, just as presented in the notion of the business event management framework. This is the new model of collaboration that has transformed the now decades-old metaphor of threaded discussions. *Facebook* is now the collaboration metaphor for everything from *LinkedIn* to *Salesforce Chatter* to a growing number of iBPMS product vendors. Yet it is not merely a tribute to the success of *Facebook*, which while quite admirable in areas such as the leverage of agile software development methods and speed of community growth, has otherwise been a lackluster example of adaptability (note IPO struggles and user backlash, which would likely have been largely diminished following the strategies described in this chapter.)

Rather, the enduring success of the *Facebook Wall* metaphor for collaboration reflects the importance of business events and business event management to Intelligent BPM and enabling adaptability. The greatest value that social media offers to business processes is the ability to collaborate on events – including but not limited to spontaneous collaboration, but by also tagging and grouping events (e.g., "subscribing") across their lifecycle.

The Ability to Mobilize

Reeves and Deimler cite "the ability to mobilize" as a critical organizational practice for enabling adaptability. It was largely presented in the same context as described in the proceeding section, specifically for stakeholders to connect and collaborate within informal ways, but surrounding business events. Yet there is also a more literal interpretation as the ability to extend processes to mobile touch-points is a critical precept of Intelligent BPM.

Although the fact of the matter is that work is already mobile. The iPad, iPhones and other smartphones and tablets combined are reaching the point of saturation. Mobile is fast becoming the dominant means of personal computing, connected to the cloud and unleashing a flood of big data. This presents a well-spring of new opportunities for engaging customers and empowering knowledge workers, yet they can also quickly overwhelm existing IT resources.

Will you be able to evolve your enterprise applications fast enough to keep pace? Probably not. Yet this is where iBPMS is providing the ability to manage the event lifecycle across applications, offering both those connection points to existing applications and the ability to manage business events independently.

Beyond IT: The Economic Theory Behind Adaptability

As business and financial analysts alike seek to quantify the value of adaptive business models, considerable attention is given to the "lifetime value of a customer." In other words, once a customer has been successfully secured for the first time, what amount of business will he provide over the course of the relationship? At the root of this question is the notion that the cost of obtaining a new customer is greater than the cost of the retaining one. As a result, any business with an existing customer base has an apparent cost (and time) advantage over a competitor without. As such, businesses are driven to "lock-in" customers with economic incentives such as discounts for repeat business, as well as proprietary approaches which increase the cost of switching to competing alternatives, called "switching costs."

At its core, the notion of lock-in is premised on the idea that customers will stick with an inferior product, or if the cost or effort of switching outweighs the benefits offered by the alternatives. History is full such examples, including the now ubiquitous "QWERTY" keyboard layout. Invented by Christopher Latham Sholes and marketed by gun manufacturer *E. Remington & Sons* with the *Type Writer*, an eponymous product whose proprietary brand name evolved into a standard of its own, the QWERTY layout was designed not for its superiority but rather its inferiority; specifically to *slowdown typing speeds* in order to prevent jamming by the *Type Writer*'s clunky 19th century mechanics (albeit this notion remains a matter of debate among certain people who apparently still own typewriters).

Today known as the "Universal" format, the QWERTY layout has survived all would-be competitors, including the much-lauded *Dvorak* design, widely held as superior in both typing speed and user ergonomics. Given the relatively slow pace that average computer user types today, the prospect of a marginal increase in speed or comfort fails to counter the increased cost and effort required to re-learn a new keyboard layout. So in today's context, the switching costs inherent in the Dvorak design eliminate it as a serious contender to the Universal layout.

During the last century, however, this was definitively not the case. The economic benefit of increased typing productivity would have in nearly all cases outweighed the cost of mechanical conversion and personnel retraining needed for the Dvorak design. This was sufficiently demonstrated at the time to be accepted as a well-known fact. If so, why did the Universal design triumph? The enduring success of the Universal layout in the face of otherwise convincingly superior competition flies in the face of neoclassical economic theory, and indeed is often held up by economists as an example of market failure. To the contrary, however, it is an example of rational market behavior in the context of "*increasing returns*," an economic theory popularized by noted economist Dr. Paul M. Romer.

Increasing returns presents a lock-in scenario where switching costs are magnified beyond what is encountered in a discrete transaction, and are rather a function of community behavior as a whole. This is driven by demand and not monopolistic coercion. Only the market can create lock-in, by rallying around a preferred approach or product. But markets are dynamic rather than deterministic in their behavior, and as such are shaped by many different externalities (read "moments for adaptive response"). Seemingly random events reflect the changing circumstances that frame buyer behavior at specific points in time and often fly in the face of design superiority.

The Universal layout first persevered only marginally as the most common "standard" in a time of competing alternatives, and for decades remained only one of many choices. In a process referred to as "path dominance," a series of serendipitous events led to a greater number of users having been trained with the Universal layout, and in the interest of skills portability a tacit preference to the design. By the second half of the 20th century, the compound impact of these events meant that typists were far more likely to have trained on this format and unlikely to switch to without significant economic incentive—clearly more than was offered by the Dvorak design. In aggregate, there was value to switch, yet individually there was not, and the market was/is defined by a collection of individual decisions. Sound familiar? This is the essence of data-driven adaptability in the marketplace; responding in mass scale to individual buyer preference.

The lesson to learn from Universal vs Dvorak, as with *Facebook* vs *MySpace*, *Beta* vs *VHS*, DC vs AC power, and countless other examples throughout history, is that it is not necessarily superior advantage at outset but the ability to read signals and adapt accordingly (and continuously) which ultimately defines sustainable competitive advantage.

CONCLUSION

Change remains the one dependable constant in the business environment, yet the speed of change is greater now than perhaps any time before. Where the challenge may have once been simply to keep pace, today the megatrends of Social, Mobile, Cloud and Big Data collectively have redefined the IT landscape seemingly overnight. Effectively leveraged, these present a wellspring of new opportunities for engaging customers and empowering knowledge workers. Yet few enterprise systems in place today are positioned to support this. Rather, it is what we see with Intelligent BPM and iBPMS systems as the ability to support dynamic and adaptive work patterns is what will enable the type of collaborative work needed to thrive on adaptability in a data-driven work.

We conclude with five basic rules of thumb to follow in order to foster adaptability, to make mobile and cloud work for you today, and future-proof your IT investments for tomorrow. First, begin by considering the goal-driven processes within your business, and consider how current architecture both obstruct and support these processes (e.g., identify the obstructions to benchmark your need for adaptability.) Next, assess your ability to manage processes as collections of business events, and how to enable a business event management framework to quickly and effectively manage the ability to read and act on signals of change.

The third rule, a critical one, is the leverage of standards. Consider how you will take advantage of certain key standards, notably *CMIS*, *XPDL* and *BPMN*. You need to know that the assets that you're creating and managing today can be accessible and follow the same evolutionary curve as the systems that you're using to access them. Fourth, you must have the ability to understand social technologies and the means for tagging and adding value to business events and to understand the business event half-life and why responding to an event in a timely fashion is so critical.

Finally, look at the infrastructure within your organization that is increasingly commoditized, and prioritize where can leverage cloud and consumerization to offset future upgrades and maintenance. BYOD access is making it easy to get mobile devices in the hands of workers; because they're putting them in their own hands. Take advantage of this, and look to leverage Intelligent BPM as a framework for creating, delivering, and managing new capabilities to a larger network of stakeholders and process participants.

REFERENCES (H2)

(McKeown 2012) Max McKeown. *Adaptability: The Art of Winning.* Kogan Page, 2012.

(Reeves and Deimler 2011) Martin Reeves and Mike Deimler. *Adaptability: The New Competitive Advantage.* Harvard Business Review, 2011.

(Gurvis and Calarco 2007) Joan Gurvis and Allan Calarco. *Adaptability: Responding Effectively to Change.* Center for Creative Leadership, 2007.

(Fulmer 2000) William E Fulmer. *Shaping the Adaptive Organization: Landscapes, Learning, and Leadership in Volatile Times.* AMACOM, 2000.

(Haeckel 1999) Stephan H. Haeckel. *Adaptive Enterprise: Creating and Leading Sense-And-Respond Organizations.* Harvard Business Review Press, 1999.

Avoiding Fragility in Innovative Learning Organizations

Keith D Swenson, Fujitsu America

Do you conceptualize your organization as a machine? If so, you may be led down the wrong path for optimizing business processes. Machines are complicated, but truly complex systems, like an organization, a marketplace, an ecosystem, are not like machines. Evidence for this is both familiar and surprising. It is the "Enlightenment Bias" which blinds us to the true nature of organizations. If you want your organization to excel, you need to understanding the true nature of organizations, and the new generation of tools that are becoming available to support them.

1. ANTI-FRAGILE

An organization hires knowledge workers so that they will think outside the box. However, a BPM system that automates work is precisely the box they are hired to think outside of. This paper will deal with "BPM for intelligent workers" and particularly why an approach called adaptive case management (ACM) might be a good fit. Before concluding this, we need to understand some rather surprising things about human organizations. Let's start by exploring the concept of *anti-fragile*. This term was coined by Nassim Nicholas Taleb in his 2012 book "Antifragile: Things That Gain From Disorder."

We all know the meaning of 'fragile': When you stress something that is fragile, it might break. What is the opposite of fragile? Most people will readily suggest that the opposite of fragile is 'robust.' Something that is robust is something that, when you stress it, it does not break; it remains the same. You might call this robust, sturdy, resilient, but in all cases the idea is that the thing does not change at all when subjected to a disturbance or stress.

There exist things that are less fragile than robust. These are things that when subjected to stress, they not only resist change, they actually grow and get stronger. They actually get better when subjected to stress, and remain better after the stress is removed.

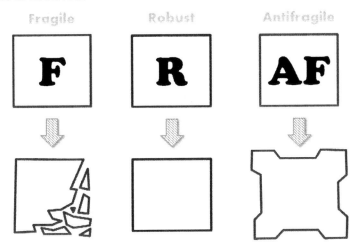

What kind of crazy notion is this? It is common sense that everything around you eventually wears out and breaks down. It may not happen all at once like a china teacup. Friction on the bearing of a wheel will eventually wear down and fail. Wind on a canvas tarp will eventually work the material and rip the weak spots. We simply know at an intuitive level that stress always causes things to wear out.

More sophisticated readers will point to the laws of thermodynamics which state that entropy of a system must always increase, and for something to get better might imply that entropy is decreasing, and therefore, antifragility is impossible, Q.E.D. Yet, on further consideration, there actually are many things around us that demonstrate antifragility.

Consider muscles. If you exercise, the result will be increased size and strength of the muscles used. To learn to play the piano, you practice. Reading a book on piano technique is not effective. Only by actually sitting at the keyboard and working through songs will you gain proficiency. To learn to play tennis, you have to get out on the court and start hitting balls.

Learning in general is antifragile. Quizzes and exams are purposeful stresses that help to prepare a student for when they will have to face real situations. Performing a fire drill is clearly an unwanted extra stress that takes people away from their main job, but the result will be an organization better prepared for such an emergency. A fire drill teaches these behaviors far faster and more effectively than any amount of textbook learning.

Things that actually get better as the result of stress are known as adaptive systems. Antifragility is a property that emerges from a complex adaptive system. Complex adaptive systems are all around us; ecosystems, biological systems, organizations, marketplaces, social networks, the economy, even our own muscles and brain. These do not behave like machines.

2. MACHINES

To create a good machine, you break the design into a set of discrete parts. Each part is made very precisely and accurately from a hard and durable material to perform a particular function. Parts fit together as perfectly as possible, with just the right gap to minimize friction and other degrading forces.

A good analogy for an idealized machine is a fancy mechanical watch. There are many gears, each made to fit precisely together with the other gears. The better watches have a jewel movement, which use a very hard stone at the pivot points. Built correctly, the watch will run for a very long time, and be very accurate.

It is rather obvious that machines are not adaptive systems. No matter how many

times you run out of gas, the car does not get better about conserving fuel! (However the driver might.) Less obviously, we should understand that organizations are not machines, even though we like to think of them as machines. Organizations can learn and flexibly adapt to situations. The introduction of a new CEO, with a different management philosophy, can have the effect of redefining many jobs in the company, without any explicit orders being given. The roles that people play are not like the parts of a watch. People routinely fill in for others while they are away on vacation. Organizations do not wear out; they may come to an end in many different ways, but they never simply wear out. Organizations routinely do many things that a machine could never do.

3. STABILITY

Stability is desirable because it allows us to anticipate and be prepared for things before they happen. In many ways, the purpose of an IT system is to help support the stability of the organization. A well-functioning IT system will help smooth out the peaks and valleys of the business environment, and allow the personnel to perform more effectively. The organization gets more done because it uses its existing resources better.

Organizations do not achieve stability the same way that machines do. Remember mechanical stability comes from designing parts very precisely and forming them from very hard materials. Even so, this stability is a temporary thing: the machine will eventually wear out.

An adaptive system achieves stability through what is called *homeostasis*; this stability comes from a balance between different adapting forces. In an ecosystem, good weather may cause an increase in vegetation. In response the population of grazers might increase. Later, the population of predators might increase as well. The next year weather might be less productive, and grazing populations would be down, and so would the predators. These population proportions are not maintained by any central plan, but instead by a balance of different adaptive forces working off each other.

Thinking that adaptive systems should be treated like machines is a large part of what I call "Enlightenment Bias." This is a way of viewing the world using ideas from Descartes, Newton, and other Enlightenment philosophers who promoted the idea that behind every complicated phenomenon is a set of simple rules that define the behavior. These ideas were revolutionary at the time and led to a tremendous expansion in understanding of natural laws. These ideas expanded into management with the advent of Scientific Management where large complicated operations are seen to be decomposable into smaller, simpler steps that can be precisely and rigorously defined. Scientific management is a part of our culture. We all learned that you should first plan, and then act. If you fail to act, then the fault can be attributed to poor planning. Plan better and you will act better in the future.

The ultimate expression of the Enlightenment Bias is in BPM systems where management attempts to define every possible detailed action that workers might make, and to find the optimal sequence of these actions. These designers are imagining the organization as a kind of machine. They are trying to define very precise and very durable parts for that machine. This works for automating routine processes, but more and more organizations are turning to support for knowledge workers who do work that is anything but routine. At the level of knowledge workers, the organization is not a machine. It behaves more like an adaptive system, and applying machine principles can actually harm the organization.

"The only sustainable competitive advantage is an organization's ability to learn faster than the competition."
Peter M. Senge

4. ADAPTIVE SYSTEMS CRAVE STRESS

Adaptive systems not only respond well to stress, they actually need stress. This seems surprising when stated that way, but we already know of many examples around us.

If you don't use muscles, they atrophy; they shrink and become weaker. A large muscle uses resources, and that is a waste if a large muscle is not necessary. Growing and *shrinking* muscles are the balancing adaptive forces that allow the body to optimize resource usage. Yet if muscle strength declines too far, it is possible to be injured by something that a normally healthy person would not be hurt by. So exercise is an important part of remaining healthy.

If a forest is protected from fires, the undergrowth grows up, and makes the forest more susceptible to fires, and if a fire breaks out it is likely to do far more damage. The policy of preventing all fires in a forest has had the disastrous consequence of indirectly causing far larger and more damaging fires that are harder to recover from. In a very real sense, protecting a forest from fire makes it grow

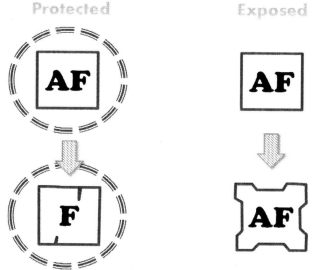

weaker. To maintain the strength of a forest, you need to have regular, modest sized forest fires.

Here is the surprising conclusion; adaptive systems need a certain amount of stress. *If they are protected from all stress they become fragile.*

The same is true with organizations. I mentioned earlier that fire drills are required to ensure that the employees are prepared for the case that an actual fire occurs. Suspending all fire drills will cause the organization to be less prepared for fire. Emergency response teams that do not drill themselves on different simulations and scenarios in advance, would find themselves ill-prepared to meet the next unexpected situation.

If a football team wants to win the tournament, it does so by practicing and playing many scrimmage games on the field. If it spent the time instead sitting still, resting, and conserving muscle movement, team members would be less likely to win the game. Unlike a machine, a team is an adaptive system, which gains from being exercised, and is actually harmed if it does not exercise.

Such exercise must include variations. Olympic swimmer Michael Phelps was forced by his coach to swim in unexpected circumstances: sometimes with the lights turned off, sometimes woken up in the middle of the night without warning. This intentional variation in training has been credited with his ability to win a gold medal in the Beijing Olympics even though his goggles cracked and filled with water.

Business teams crave this as well. Running simulations and scenarios as a business team is a well-known way to improve team performance. Doing things differently allows the team to understand how to coordinate on the fly. Then, if a situation comes along where the team has to do things differently, they are more prepared to meet this challenge.

5. THE BEST PRACTICE CONUNDRUM

It is ironic that the very purpose of most business process management initiatives is find the single best practice, and institute that best practice by forcing employees to follow it. Here we get to the central theme of this paper—if you remember nothing else—remember this; *enforcing a single best practice on an organization can make it **fragile***.

This can be hard to understand if you think of an organization as a machine. After all, a diesel truck will perform best (no matter how to define best) at a particular speed in a particular gear. A truck driver wants to find that speed and gear and use it whenever the situation is favorable. But organizations are more like muscles than trucks.

I mentioned Michael Phelps above. A coach searching for the single best practice might run a lot of tests, and find out that Phelps swims best at 2:00 in the afternoon, after sleeping to 10am and when the pool temperature is 72 degrees. He might then institute this best practice, asking Phelps to rise at 10am every day, swim and 2:00, and keep the pool at 72 degrees. But doing this would not prepare Phelps for many important aspects of actually competing in the Olympics. If the final swimming environment was not at 2:00pm, or he would not be able to sleep until 10am, then he would not be prepared.

The same thing happens in business teams. If a process is put into place that enforces that 'A' is done first, then 'B', and then 'C', the people working in the office come to expect it to always be this way. By acclimatizing to *always* having this pattern, the organization loses the ability to handle cases in any other order.

If you continually take antibiotics, your immune system gets weak possibly allowing you to die from a minor but novel infection. In a complex adaptive system constant stress is not to be mistaken as overreacting to noise but must be understood as environmental tuning information. We need to re-learn that in a complex world the notion of a single logical cause or a predictable outcome of an action is suspect. Constant, random stress is information that aligns the small anti-fragile system with the changes in its environment

The central point of Taleb's book was that antifragile systems crave stress, and if you withhold stress, they wither or become dangerously unstable. He went further to say: "Stability is a Time Bomb." While an adaptive system is able to readily accommodate modest perturbations, if you protect the system from those changes, attempting to provide a static environment, then the system becomes fragile and dangerous.

For the IT professionals reading this, let me make one thing clear: the system is the organization, not just the computer system. The computer system may or may not be adaptive on its own. Our goal is clearly to make the business run better, and that involved people as well as the computer system. Organizations are adaptive, and it is the role of IT systems to support that adaptiveness.

This is not really a new idea. Management guru Tom Peters' 1988 book "Thriving on Chaos" discusses organizations that thrive on the churn and turmoil around them. It is common to suggest that an organization need occasional "shaking up" to keep it healthy. Agile software methodology works on understanding that software development is complex and unpredictable, and does not try to define everything perfectly in advance.

6. PLANNING AS PART OF WORK

Part of the reason for attempting to identify and isolate the single best practice is to eliminate the need to spend time planning what to do. If there is a fully elaborated best practice, then there is no need to waste time planning. Planning is viewed as a waste, and if planning can be eliminated, then workers can spend all the time doing productive work.

That, at least, is the theory, but many leaders have expressed opposition to this point of view. For example, the following two quotes:

> "No plan survives contact with the enemy."
> Helmuth von Moltke the Elder

> "Planning is essential, plans are worthless."
> Dwight D. Eisenhower

The military is the place where you might expect to see the most rigorously defined and standardized modes of operation, but these respected leaders go out of their way to stress the importance of the planning activity itself. The importance is not just the end result–the plan–but the actual activity of planning itself is important.

Translated to modern terms, it is almost as if Eisenhower was saying that it is important to model your business processes, but when you are done you can throw the resulting models away. It is not the models that have value, but the activity of doing the modeling that provides the value.

From this we can conclude that planning itself should not be eliminated, but in fact should be done as part of work. A best practice should be enforced without question, but instead as a guideline that might, or might not, be followed. There should be a point where the team sits down and evaluates whether the best practice is going to work in this case, and if not, to come up with an alternative. Planning needs to remain part of what the knowledge worker does.

7. INFORMATION TECHNOLOGY TO SUPPORT THIS

We hire knowledge workers to think outside the box. A IT system dedicated to anticipating every move of a knowledge worker in advance will simply an elaborate box constraining on what the knowledge worker can do. If we want organizations that are strong in the face of varying market conditions, if we want them to be responsive to new situations, then instead of enforcing a single best practice, the IT system should allow for myriad different practices.

This is very surprising and quite disturbing. It flies in the face of everything we learned about finding and instituting the best practice. There are two approaches one might take to allow may varying paths, one I call the "radical" approach, and another I call the "innovator" approach.

The radical approach is to suggest that the information itself system should mix things up a bit. That is, it should randomly alter some parts of the business process in order to see what happens. This would exercise the workers in the same way that a vaccine exercises the immune system. Workers would certainly learn how to accommodate variations in the process, and they would certainly be able to accommodate future changes. In the long run the system might identify a novel, improved business process, however this approach is wasteful.

The less radical approach is the "innovator" approach in which knowledge workers are allowed to do the process differently if it seems necessary to them. This relies on the knowledge worker coming up with an idea about what might be a better way to do things. In my own personal experience many knowledge workers have plenty of ideas on how things might be done better. The innovator approach would allow them to try out their idea and see if it works.

This is not really a new idea either. Before the advent of BPM systems, managers would redesign their processes as needed when they thought they could do it better. Generally, if successful, they would be rewarded for "taking initiative." An IT system that enforces a particular best practice can actually stand in the way of these innovators, which is why we need specialized system that allow for these kinds of changes.

8. ADAPTIVE CASE MANAGEMENT

This is precisely the purpose of an adaptive case management (ACM) system to be a BPM system for intelligent workers. It does not constrain the workers to any given business pre-defined process. The process can be changed by any participant, and changing the process is a natural part of everyday activity.

A lot of systems talk about their ability to change, but in most cases they assume that a specially trained person will do the changes. Here, when we say that the process can be changed by any knowledge worker, it is necessarily understood that no special skills or knowledge must be necessary for making these changes. The users must be not only allowed, but also able to make those changes. This activity rules out most of the more formal ways of modeling processes which require specialized training. The process must be expressed in a way that a completely untrained knowledge worker can modify at will.

We don't think of this as process modeling, but instead planning. Knowledge workers don't work on pre-planned units of work, but instead planning itself is part of doing the job.

This approach is very hard to accept by those who view an organization as a machine that operates on a set of simple principles. It is contrary to the idea that there is a single best way to do something, and our goal is to find the one best way and make sure that everyone does it. Failure to accomplish goals in the organization is seen by these people as an inability to follow the best course.

> "The future is uncertain—but this uncertainty is at the very heart of human creativity"
> Ilya Prigogine

9. Summary

We started by defining a few concepts:

- **fragile**—the quality that when disturbed has a propensity to break. Kicking around a fragile object reduces or destroys its value.
- **robust**—the quality that when disturbed it remains the same. Kicking a robust object has no effect on it at all.
- **antifragile**—the quality that when disturbed it improves. Kicking an antifragile object actually makes it more valuable.

Antifragility is a quality that emerges from an adaptive system. While it sounds crazy, there are adaptive systems all around us, and a human organization is one of those.

Not only do adaptive systems respond well to stress, they actually degrade when all stress is removed. Like muscles that need exercise, an organization needs a certain amount of variation in order to remain healthy.

Adaptive case management is an approach to supporting knowledge workers that does not constrain the working patterns to a predefined best practice. Instead, it allows knowledge workers to evaluate what the options are in this case, and to plan a course of action that might be unique for this case. It then focuses on communications about the plan, and in support of the plan.

This approach is likely to be very uncomfortable to traditional scientific managers who view their organization as a machine that has a single best mode of operation. Experienced managers already know that knowledge workers are not simple gears in a clock, but instead are capable of far more than would be expected, if they can only be given the ability to experiment and try to do things better.

Adaptive Case Management for Railway Freight Operations

Helle Frisak Sem, Steinar Carlsen, Gunnar John Coll and Thomas Bech Pettersen, Computas AS, Norway

ABSTRACT

CargoNet AS is the primary Norwegian freight train operator, and GTS (Goods Transport System) is their system for logistics handling. GTS adaptively unifies contributions from knowledge workers across the organization, from marketing and sales to train configuration and composition, scheduling, real-time monitoring, handling of dangerous goods, truck operations and container quality assurance. It is an ACM system, multiplying as an ERP solution.

GTS is a mission-critical system used by most employees involved in the primary value chain, fully integrated with CargoNet's Internet customer portal. Since going online in 2002, GTS has been gradually enhanced in terms of end-user functionality.

GTS uses case folders with built-in task support—referred to as work folders in similar ACM solutions. Each work folder represents either a particular freight train "flight" or a freight train wagon / container booking. Work folders provide access to worklists, giving users active and dynamic task support while ensuring compliance with business rules and statutory regulations. Work folders are augmented with integrated tools for detailed scheduling and train composition, providing an elegant mixture of auto-generated and manual plans.

Showcasing a non-traditional application of case management technologies, the GTS architecture is information centric. A range of tasks and tools operate on a shared information platform. The integrated customer portal for placing orders contributes to the contents of work folders. A ruggedized mobile client is deployed in cargo handling trucks, used for container reception, placement and depot management. Another mobile client handles container damage assessment

BACKGROUND AND INTRODUCTION

An ACM system as arbitrator between recurrence and uniqueness

Any organization necessarily rests on roles and practices that follow more or less recurring overall patterns. Wherever stakeholders have complementary needs and mutual expectations, evolving slowly or not at all, it is possible to develop predictable ways of co-acting that stay relatively stable over time. Overall scenarios can be described, as default flows. A business scene example could be manufacturers, transporters, retailers and customers. Macro-patterns evolve and stay, although sometimes disrupted, to be replaced by new patterns. Mastery of current and emerging patterns makes the winners.

Whereas macro-patterns develop slowly, the rate of change can be much faster when penetrating into the lower levels of everyday business operation patterns. The same goes for a range of variation in how such patterns get instantiated and tweaked. At the lowermost level—the execution of real-time work cases—patterns will continually be challenged by unpredicted events and variations, and the ability to respond quickly and adaptively can be critical for success.

Knowledge work, as opposed to repetitive manufacturing, is based on ability to understand and cope with possibly myriads of variations at the execution level, to master complex business demands—beyond the reach of linear BPM process approaches. To respond effectively requires knowledge and experience, in order to challenge the default patterns and adapt to the uniqueness of every case. Offering leeway is just as important as providing structure—and vice versa.

Business context

CargoNet is Scandinavia's leading railway company for the transportation of containers, swap bodies and trailers. The company operates more than 190 trains carrying containers and trailers between the largest terminals and cities in Norway, in addition to a large number of "system trains" for major industrial companies. In 2011 CargoNet had a turnover of NOK 1.452 billion, with a staff of around 550. Road transportation is the main alternative to CargoNet; in 2012, CargoNet relieved Norwegian roads of more than 590 articulated lorries daily.

Below is a bird's eye view of the train freight process, showing how the beginning and the end of the process is handled from the order perspective, whereas the middle (rounded boxes) is handled from the train perspective.

Figure 1: Bird's eye view of the train freight process

Changes are the name of the game

Train freight operations are subjected to strict conditions. Important physical issues must be considered, such as brake limits, tractive power, weight, and length.

Most of the railway network in Norway is single track, and if a train is not on schedule, it will be downgraded. Hence, a five-minute delay at the starting point may grow to several hours delay at the destination. It is therefore important that trains depart from every station precisely on time. To operate as cost-effectively as possible, CargoNet needs a good real-time planning system supporting work right up to last minute checks before departure.

External events affecting transport occur all the time; containers do not arrive at the starting point on time, they are damaged, or they do not arrive at all. A wagon or a locomotive may be out of order. A train may have an accident, there may be too much snow on the line, the signal system does not function, or the power cable may have fallen down. An operating environment like this requires IT systems that can adapt—quickly and easily.

Before GTS, much effort went into handling train events or changes in plans due to containers not arriving at the terminals in time. Hence, much attention was paid to how to achieve good and efficient error handling. GTS as an adaptive system has shifted the focus from error handling to supporting change as part of the normal procedure.

Basic GTS concepts

GTS uses dynamic iBPM technologies in an innovative manner by handling trains and cargo orders as *cases*. Every such case has a corresponding case folder that provides access to a worklist with adaptive task support for the tasks pertaining to the relevant train or order.

The shared information platform has also enabled the inclusion of new mobile clients closing the gap between "field work" and "office work", enabling capture of valuable operational data at its source, with high data quality.

The adaptive alternative to linear BPM end-to-end process support is not "one-off" improvisation. Paradoxically, a strong implementation of pattern support can arguably create a context for enhanced adaptivity. In this paper, we are going to show how GTS accomplishes this, using:

- A task template library and an organization model as a maintainable vehicle for work pattern management.
- Flexible, non-monotonic task support.
- User-controlled case folders representing the main business entities (orders and trains), reflecting real-time case status.
- A data-centric architecture, enabling continuous event- and task-driven recombination of process snippets and tools.
- Tool support for planning across several cases, both order cases and train cases.
- Worklists, collections of tasks, enable easy collaboration offering alternative access to impending tasks.

The shared information platform enables each user group to concentrate on their relevant information and interleaved tasks. This information will always be up-to-date and integrated with the information relevant to other user groups, where all users are both producers and consumers of information.

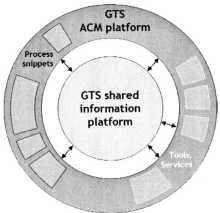

Figure 2: Information-centric architecture of GTS

USE OF ADAPTIVE CASE MANAGEMENT FOR FREIGHT TRAIN OPERATIONS

In this chapter, we provide an overview of how ACM-technologies on top of a shared information platform enable iBPM support for freight train operations.

Case folders for trains and booking orders

A "case" may be anything that needs to be managed and controlled throughout its lifecycle. The cases in GTS are not similar to cases in traditional "public sector" case management systems - they reflect trains and orders. Nevertheless, they do correspond to "the stuff that must be adaptively handled" as part of the daily work performance.

GTS supports two different case types—booking orders and trains. Each case type has its own set of task templates.

All freight items, be it containers, swap bodies or wagons, are handled through the placement of an order. Each placed order constitutes a case, and will handle the transportation of a set of containers or a set of wagons.

When planning how to transport the wagons and containers, the necessary capacity in the train will be checked, and if there is sufficient capacity, the reservation can be made. In case of wagons, the capacity checked is the overall train restrictions, like weight and length. In case of containers, the capacity is given by the booked capacity of the container wagons as well as the overall train restrictions.

At first, the reservation is registered as 'unconfirmed', later on in the process, it will be changed to 'confirmed'. Confirmed and unconfirmed capacity is displayed in the train composition tools and in the train folder, giving important information to the booking department as well as the train plan responsible and the train production crew.

Invoice information is automatically sent to the CargoNet invoice system, based on the information in the order case folder.

Figure 3: Order case folder with worklist and task support

Every train also constitutes a case. A train may have one or more distances, depending on the number of stops. Each distance must be planned with respect to train composition. The planning goes from less specific to fully specific, starting with restrictions for length and weight, via types of wagons and containers to specific wagons physically placed together where it is permissible to place specific containers. In all stages, the system applies complex rules to reason about brakes, weights, and which wagons can take what sort of load.

The train case folder is automatically created from the train timetable, with a worklist containing all those tasks that logically follow from the timetable. Moreover, the train case folder contains functionality to add new tasks in case of deviations from the original plan, such as adding an extra stop on the fly, and notifying customers of changes.

The two types of case folders interact closely, in a many-to-many relationship. Each order is fulfilled by transportation on one or more trains, whereas each train is made up from many orders.

Adaptive task support

Instead of trying to support linear and static "end-to-end" processes, GTS is based on supporting well-defined process snippets known as *task templates*. These are instantiated and recombined by events, rules and human judgment. Tasks operate on a shared data model of the particular case, and as a side effect they update and modify the data model and the documents of the case folder.

A task template consists of a set of steps as a general "recipe" for task performance. These steps are subject to several conditions, defined using predicates and rules, which make it possible to derive a contextualized task template as a unique recipe for a particular instance, always reflecting its state and data.

The use of active task support in the manner described here makes it possible to build support for the compliance aspect of work performance, i.e. the work support system can be designed to ensure that work is performed according to "business rules", be they government regulations or internal best practice requirements.

This contextualized task template is the basis for offering active task support to the user. The user selects and executes permitted steps, based on personal, professional judgment. Step conditions specify pre- and post-conditions in addition to repeat-conditions (step can be repeated), include-conditions (step is made available dependent on context) and mandatory-conditions (step must be performed); the interplay between these conditions result in a relevant offering of actions to the user. Each such step may utilize any functionality offered by the system, and may include a user interface component for operating on relevant case data.

GTS contains a task library, with a task template for each task type. The template consists of a set of steps with conditions as described above. The functionality needed to perform the step is brought to the user when invoking the step, as part of GTS-supported activities.

Most of the time, a task must have a context in order to make sense. In GTS, it is not possible to start a context-dependent task unless this context is given at the time of task startup. When such tasks are not part of an emergent flow with a set context, they may be started from the task library in the GTS workbench. Alternatively, specific task types are directly accessible from buttons in GUI components where the needed context is available, for instance in a case folder.

When a task is started from the task library and requires the creation of a new case folder, this information is available in the task library, and such an object will be created and connected to the task when the task is created.

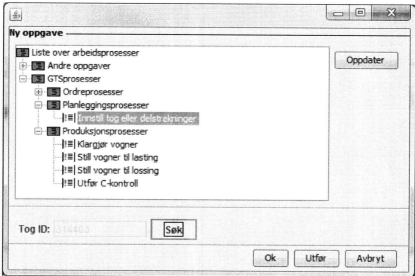

Figure 4: Task library with tasks for a train context

The task instance is equipped with the possibility to hold data, either simple data particular to the task or references to complex objects in the common database. Each data element may be global to the task, or local to one of the steps. The data particular to the task are mainly used for the calculation of the conditions connected to the steps, but they may also have consequences for the functionality connected to the steps. The references to objects in the database may be used as arguments in the methods used in the conditions and actions, and are in particular used as the data that the functionality in the steps are all about.

The interaction between task support and tool support

An order case folder starts by the placement of an order. It continues by the planning of which trains the containers or wagons are to travel with. This planning may take place in several rounds, and be subjected to change, either because of something under control of the customer, or of something under the control of CargoNet. This part of the process is handled through tasks with task templates in the context of the order case folder, obeying the capacity conditions for each train involved.

When the time of the train departure comes close, the actual build-up of the train must take place. This is an operation focusing on a train, involving many orders, both for the wagons and the containers involved. It is useful to be able to move quickly from train to train. Since this functionality has to be performed repeatedly, be available at any time, is needed across orders, and also more or less, across trains, this is performed by means of a tool rather than through tasks with task support. This functionality is logically single step, performed an unknown number of times, and there is no completion status other than the checkout and departure of the train.

Train production, checkout, check-in and unloading of containers, are operations performed by means of tasks in the context of the train. These operations are subject to severe compliance control, and must be performed according to specific fulfillment conditions for each train and station.

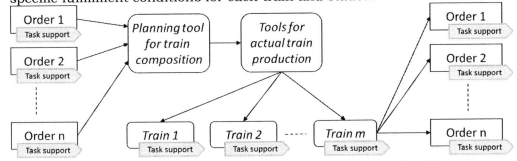

Figure 5 Case folders with task support and tools

EXAMPLE—HANDLING RECURRENT ORDERS IN GTS

In train transport, as in other areas, each day is not so different from the next day. Train number X of one day is quite similar to train number X on another day. Often exactly the same wagons go every day. Major customers may send a similar transport regularly, such as four containers of lemonade every Monday, Wednesday and Friday.

In GTS, it is possible to use an order as a pattern for many orders. When a recurring order is placed, an order case folder is created for each day the pattern specifies. If there are days without the necessary capacity, GTS informs about this, and these days must be handled separately.

On a particular day, the customer may want to send one container less, or even a container or two more than the regular pattern. Similarly, some other transport may have to be given higher priority, so that this transport must go on another train, or even on road. This is handled through a flexible order completion task, handling a plethora of possible changes.

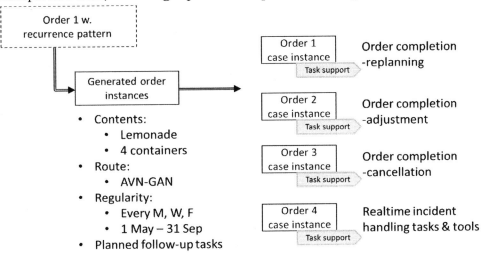

Figure 6: Recurrent order—dealing with the unpredictable

CargoNet employees must plan and produce the transportation. The first part of the planning takes place by means of task support connected to the order case, and involves planning which train(s) the container or wagon is to be part of. All the wagons or containers in the same case folder need not travel by the same train. If, later on, the planned transportation cannot be carried through, either in full or in parts, the case manager may create a task to change the plans. All parts of the plan may be changed, unless they have already been started.

Containers that are not fit to be transported on train are rejected at the gate. The app utilizes data from the order folders, and offer functionality to add pictures taken with the phone to the documentation registered in the app entry forms.

The planning of the making-up of the train takes place in a dedicated tool. This tool handles both wagons and containers, and functions both for unspecified and specified carriers. The output is only a plan, and does not yet contain information about where these carriers are physically at any point in time.

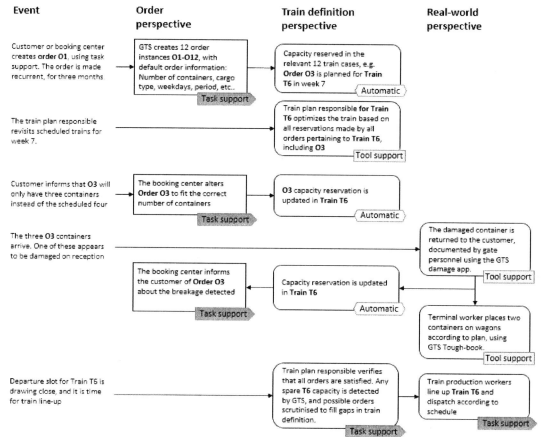

Figure 7: Interwoven streams of action in railway freight operations

The tools are mainly used to handle situations where carriers from many orders must be planned or produced simultaneously. GTS is used outside at the terminal with the carriers as they arrive and are placed in depot or on train.

The fact that GTS is present where the physical work takes place is favorable for user acceptance.

For the registration of the physical position of wagons, containers and the make-up of the train, there are both tough-book and main client tools as well as task support in the train case folder.

GTS AS A COLLABORATIVE ENVIRONMENT

Worklists for different perspectives

Case work folders, railway stations and users all have worklists.

Each case work folder maintains a continuously updated overview of all tasks pertaining to the case at hand—a train or an order. The user may set a desired time interval, to see which tasks are due inside that period. The same task may simultaneously sit in other worklists, enabling easy collaboration.

For the railway station, the worklist keeps track of the incoming trains and the tasks connected to handling the arrival of trains and, in case the station is an intermediate stop for the train, the following departure.

For a user, the worklist represents the personal inbox-component of their electronic workbench. A personal worklist contains the user's own planned and ongoing tasks.

Both the station worklists and the user worklists display information about which case folder the task is connected to. It is possible to navigate from the task directly to the case folder.

Organization model and railway station worklists

The ACM framework comprises an organization model with organization units, roles and permissions. Each organization unit, be it a person or a group unit, may have a worklist in the system. In GTS the stations are organization group units with worklists.

The organization model supports parallel organization structures, each structure built by a set of roles. The main organization is built by the roles 'employed in' and 'part of'. The organization model is maintained by means of an organization editor. Here, CargoNet may regulate which users have which roles, and which roles have which permissions, thus regulating who has access to what functionality, tools and tasks. It is also possible to regulate who has access to which worklists.

The train as an adaptive relay baton

The train case folder is initiated with a complete set of tasks for all operations necessary for the standard production of the train flight. As the train checkout task is executed, the train's tasks for the next station are added to the worklist of that station. Thus under normal conditions, the train functions as a relay baton of tasks.

In case of deviation due to external events or human decisions, it will be necessary to change the train plan accordingly. The GTS train folder supports the creation of the appropriate tasks. This includes tasks for introducing extra intermediate stops, changing the train configuration and alerting customers.

GTS utilizes a combination of task support, or adaptive process snippets, in combination with user oriented tools. The shared information platform of planning and production tools, order portal and tools used at the terminal enables each user group to concentrate on their relevant information. This information will always be up-to-date and integrated with the information relevant to other user groups. They are all both producers and consumers of information.

Adapting to mobile clients

Since GTS is based on one common information platform in a data centric architecture, adding more clients has been unproblematic. GTS' prime purpose is to record and manage a physical reality, and it is a great benefit if the recording can take place as close as possible to the physical events.

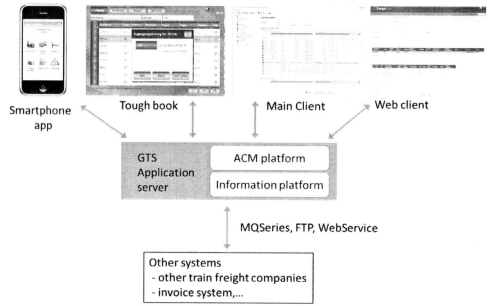

Figure 8: Overview of GTS with its different clients

GTS has a web portal for customers. This enables large customers to place their orders and specify information about dangerous goods and other details and to monitor the freight from start to delivery.

The information initiates an order case, ready made with all relevant information. This increases the efficiency both for the customer and for CargoNet. The customer can ensure the order is correctly placed, and receive information on progress.

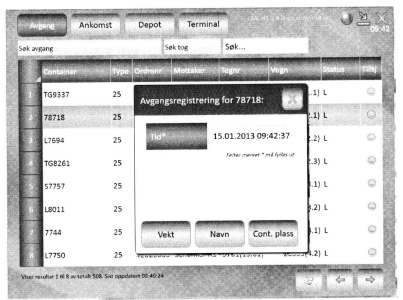

Figure 9: CargoNet ruggedized "tough-book" touch client

All containers coming from the road are received at a station gate terminal. Terminal trucks and lifts are equipped with a ruggedized mobile client with touch functionality, a "tough-book". The tough-book is used by terminal workers for directly registering the arrival, storage in container depot and placement on train. This ensures more accurate and continuously updated information in the system than before, when this information had to travel manually to the terminal office to be entered into the system.

A container will not be allowed beyond the gate unless it is in sufficiently good condition to be placed on a train. Even so, it may have minor damages that CargoNet needs to document, in order not to be held liable after delivery. The GTS mobile smartphone app records damage to a container in context of the transport order. It utilizes the information in the case folder, enables textual and photographic documentation of the damage, and a damage report may later be printed from the main GTS client.

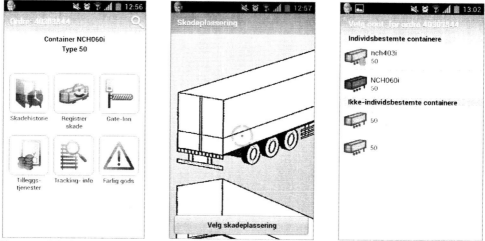

Figure 10 Screenshots - smartphone container damage assessment app

CONCLUSION

The innovative use of process support technologies in GTS has resulted in a very robust system with sufficient adaptability for actually dealing with a world where change is the name of the game. Instead of detecting and responding to "errors", GTS enables CargoNet to adapt to changes in its business environment in a flexible manner.

The inclusion of new mobile technologies bridges the gap between "office work" and "field work", and has resulted in much better work support for the cargo terminal workers. They are now able to capture data at the source in real-time, instead of having data entered back at the office. This also results in higher data quality. GTS uses dynamic iBPM technologies in an innovative manner by handling trains and cargo orders as *cases.*

GTS is an ACM system that is adaptive not only in the flexible support offered to knowledge workers; it is also adaptive in the sense that the application itself was conceived as a "built-to-change" solution. This business adaptability is partly due to the use of an ACM framework, and partly to the information-centric architecture. As an enterprise ACM, this adaptability has enabled responsiveness to new technologies. GTS has been operational for more than ten years, and all this time the system has been subject to continual improvement.

Adaptivity is along at least two orthogonal dimensions—end user flexibility in planning and performing work, but also organizational flexibility in adapting to business logic and environmental changes. Both are equally important. Enterprise ACMs built-to-change benefit from a data-centric architecture.

TECHNOLOGY AND SERVICE PROVIDERS

The task templates, worklists and task support functionality and engine, rule engine, work folders, xml terminologies and code- and relations framework were implemented using a complete ACM framework developed and used for process oriented business applications during the past 15 years. In GTS, this ACM framework was used in its Java Platform Enterprise Edition version.

Computas AS is an employee owned Norwegian IT consulting company with around 220 consultants, which provides services and solutions for business processes and co-work. Computas AS has delivered numerous work process support applications to the Norwegian public sector and private enterprises, based on the ACM framework FrameSolutions™.

FrameSolutions™ currently has more than 100 000 users, and handles an annual cash flow of around 50 billion NOK. IT solutions based on FrameSolutions ™ provide work process support and task support resulting in higher efficiency and quality in organizational processes. FrameSolutions™ is a framework for realizing bespoke process-centered case management solutions.

REFERENCES

(Sem 2012) Helle Frisak Sem, Steinar Carlsen and Gunnar Coll. Norwegian Food Safety Authority, Nominated by Computas AS, Norway. In Fischer, L. (ed): How Knowledge Workers Get Things Done - Real-world Adaptive Case Management, Future Strategies Inc, Florida, 2012

(Sem 2012) Helle Frisak Sem, Steinar Carlsen and Gunnar Coll. On Two Approaches to ACM. ACM 2012 1st International Workshop on Adaptive Case Management and other non-workflow approaches to BPM, Tallinn, Estonia, 2012

Creating an Integrated Platform for Enterprise-Wide Process Intelligence

Roy Altman, Peopleserv, Inc., USA

INTRODUCTION—WHAT IS YOUR STRATEGY?

When we talk about a company's strategy, what do we mean? How is it different than the operational objectives of maximizing income, reducing costs and risks? Each company must decide for itself what its strategy is, and what business outcomes to tie it to. The role of technology should be to assist a company in achieving that strategy.

Many companies confuse strategy with tactics. They think that stringing together tactics, although worthwhile objectives by themselves, will amount to a strategy. It will not. An example would be an HRIT department wanting to deploy learning management, talent management, talent acquisition and workforce management solutions as its strategy. Each of these solutions may be part of an overall strategy to attract, retain and develop talent for the organization, but these goals should be a stated objective that helps define the tactics for achieving those ends.

Earlier in the history of the information technology field, having state-of-the-art business technology was sufficient as competitive differentiator, because the field was new, technological standards were still in development, and techniques to effectively manage the deployment of technology were not mature. In 2003, Nicolas Carr published a famous paper in *Harvard Business Review* entitled: "Does IT Matter,"[1] in which he argued that technology had become commoditized. In his view, having superior technology did not truly deliver a competitive advantage. The best way to manage a commodity was to reduce costs while retaining reliability. This paper resulted in an uproar among the IT community (which had a vested interest in maintaining its status in the organization). Entire books were written to refute it, including Howard Smith and Peter Fingar's "IT Doesn't Matter, Business Processes Do."[2] Smith and Fingar's point was: it's not the technology per se that creates a competitive advantage; it's how you use it to solve problems consistent with the business outcomes you're trying to achieve.

Business Process Management focuses on the end-to-end business processes and attempts to optimize them using technology. Regardless, whether interacting software components or humans serve the processes, it's the end-to-end process that counts, not the snippet of the overall process.

MOVEMENT TO THE CLOUD

There is a trend in IT to move applications to the cloud. The advent of the World Wide Web meant that when application software had to be upgraded, it no longer needed to be distributed to each desktop. If the system ran in a browser, the update occurred at the server and it would automatically affect all users. However, web architectures existed in-house, behind the company's firewall. This was a holdover from the client-server days (actually much "web" based software was originally client-server retrofitted to the web once that technology became available) and reflected customers' purchasing preferences. However, with the advent of strong encryption technology, which became legal to export in the late 1990's, there was no technological need to house servers at the company's site and still maintain secure storage and transmission of information. As a matter of fact, business-to-consumer (B2C) applications had already been working that way for several years. The trend began with application providers "hosting" applications for clients in their own data centers. Therefore it was the responsibility of the application provider to maintain the hardware and software, and apply updates as they become available. The business model changed as well. Instead of purchasing a perpetual license and paying ongoing maintenance fees, companies would just pay a monthly fee for usage of the software. This trend became known as Software-as-a-Service (SaaS).

SaaS trend was at first met with resistance from companies that were reluctant to give up control over where their information is stored. Over time, though, companies have become increasingly accepting, as vendors have been able to demonstrate their (often superior) security measures, along with the many advantages of SaaS:

- Predictable costs
- Funding comes from the company's operational, not capital budget
- No need to maintain IT staff to maintain hardware needed to run the application
- No need to devote resources, time and budget to applying upgrades when available
- The vendor is responsible for keeping the software current for compliance purposes and is able to deliver accelerated innovation to the customer

Traditionally, companies would license software, and then customize it for their unique business processes. This practice made upgrading the software more difficult because the customizations needed to be reapplied to the new version, which could be problematic if architectural changes were required as part of the upgrade that conflicted with the design of the customization. There is an implementation of SaaS many call "pure SaaS" which means that all customers' information resides in the same, multi-tenant database, and all customers are executing the same version of the application. This means that the application can only be configured, not customized, to the business needs of each customer. This has the advantage to the vendor that the environment of all clients is the same so upgrades can be applied easier and thus more frequently.

The advantage to the customer is that it can receive updates several times a year, instead of once every few years, thereby enjoying software that is continuously innovated and improved. However, it means that the design of the application must be flexible enough to be configured for the business needs of every customer without having to be customized. Customers may inevitably have to make some compromises, but on balance it is worth the trade-off.

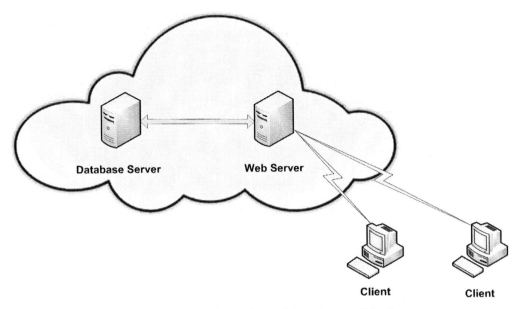

Fig. 1: Cloud-based architecture of today

CHANGING ROLE OF IT

With the acceptance of cloud-software in the organization, the role of IT is changing. IT is no longer responsible for maintaining computer hardware, internal networks, and software upgrades and tuning. So what should IT do? Was Nicolas Carr right; are IT's days of contributing strategic, competitive advantage over? IT can now focus of getting closer to the businesses they serve. It is IT's role to integrate the many systems, both in-house and cloud-based, to ensure that each software asset is available to all users who need them, and that software agents operate as an integrated whole, rather than silo'd horizontal towers. Thus IT should focus on facilitating end-to-end business processes for the user, leveraging any software agent that fulfills any part of the business process. IT's role, therefore, rather than being minimized, is being elevated to a more strategic function, if CIO's are savvy enough to take advantage of this opportunity.

INTEGRATIONS

Integrations have always been the bane and Holy Grail of IT. Since the dawn of the digital era, it has been recognized that systems were designed to do a specific thing and needed to interface with other systems to accomplish business processes. With the emergence of the World Wide Web (WWW) in the 1990s, the stakes became higher as business-to-business (B2B) e-commerce depended on disparate systems interacting with one another over a public network. Before the Web age businesses have made many attempts at integrations, although on private networks.

History

Flat file interfaces have always existed. The problem with them is that the sending system needs to know the format of the file that the receiving system expects. If the file format is at all different, the interface will break, revealing its fragility. A commonly used flat file format is comma-separated values (CSV), which is supported by Excel spreadsheets. It's shocking to note that this is still the most commonly used file format for interfaces between systems. Also, flat file interfaces must be run in batch mode, meaning that the interface cannot occur in real time, but on a pre-set schedule. Many processes would benefit from real-time interfaces.

Early attempts at automated interfaces yielded a standard called the Common Object Request Broker Architecture (CORBA) released in 1991. Designed by a committee of the Object Management Group (OMG), CORBA was considered by some complicated to implement and never reached widespread acceptance. Microsoft released its own standard, called Common Object Model (COM) in 1993, which suffered the same fate.

Companies involved in e-commerce needed a standard for computer-to-computer interchange to execute the transactions. To that end, Electronic Data Interchange (EDI) was released by the National Institute of Standards and Technology in 1996. A data standard was developed for each industry, thus it represented a tight coupling that lacked flexibility.

Current technology

Enter the age of the World Wide Web. In his 1999 book "Weaving the Web,"[3] original designer of the Web Tim Berners-Lee likened adoption to a bobsled, which starts slowly and is very soon hurtling at tremendous speed. The Web is based on Hyper-Text Markup Language (HTML), which is a standard markup language that describes how a document should *look*. The Web quickly became pervasive because HTML is a based on a single standard that is adhered to by everyone. This is in stark contrast to the previous generations, when industry "standards" became de-facto, perpetuated by the perceived market leader of the time.

Berners-Lee felt no one should own web standards, so he formed the World Wide Web Consortium (W3C) to determine universal web protocols.

In 1998, the W3C proposed a standard called Extensible Markup Language (XML) that describes what data should *mean*. An XML document has tags indicating what the data item is along with the value. This method of data transfer is not fragile as flat files are, because an XML parser can search for targeted data items regardless where they reside in the XML document. XML has become the standard method of data interchange between systems.

The Service-Oriented Architecture

This and other protocols based on universally accepted standards spawned a software design methodology called Service-Oriented Architectures (SOA). The premise is rather than access entire software applications, parts of the applications could be accessed individually as services. For instance, in an onboarding application, a service can be called to add the employee to an external vendor who processes benefits for the company. This is an example of loose-coupling, because the calling and called service don't need to know very much about each other, just the application programming interface (API) needed to retrieve the desired information. A set of related technologies emerged which collectively comprise what is called Web Services, which are the technical underpinnings of SOA.

With the emergence of standards-based protocols supporting SOA, one would think that the Holy Grail has finally been obtained. Unfortunately, that has not yet proven to be the case. The primary obstacles to widespread SOA adoption include:

- A lack of maturity in using SOA techniques in companies, even though the technologies are mature.
- While simpler than previous generations of integration technologies, SOA integrations are still difficult and require technical expertise.
- Functionality exposed as web services, upon which integrations with divergent software depend. This is counter to the marketing strategies of many software companies, which license more software by offering a wider breadth of functionality under their own brand names, rather than encourage integration.

It is incumbent on the customers to force vendors to expose their functions as web services, so they can be integrated. Many companies shy away from integrating because of the difficulty, and vendors aren't helping this cause. As a result, we have the silo'd applications mentioned in the first section. But with the changing role of IT, perhaps we'll see progress in this area.

Levels of integration

When one says "integrations" it means many things. There are several levels of integration, ranging from simple interfaces to true interoperability. Here is some explanation:

- **Data**—each system shares a common set of information so each knows whom the current user is. Key indicative data is transferred from the system of record to every other system. For example, if you're a manager working on an employee's performance review, then you want to review her salary history; when you transfer over to the compensation function it will take you directly to the information for that employee, because the system knows who the user is and which employee she's working on. The processes are attached by means of a "deep link," which means that the link will take the user directly to the function requested (in this case the salary history page) rather than returning to the landing page of the compensation module and forcing her to navigate to the salary history page. Implicit in this process is single-sign-on, which means that the user just authenticates once and those authentication credentials are passed to any other software agent she interacts with.
- **Process**—rather than deep links, which takes one to a particular page within a module, process integration invokes a service within the module, using web-services technology described earlier. An example would be the manager is doing a performance review of an employee, and the performance module fetches all interactions the employee had with others from the company's collaboration software.
- **People**—this layer of integration involves the system knowing the context of the function being performed, and being sensitive to the important relationships the employee has with others with regard to that function. For instance, in the performance review, the system is aware of all other team members the employee works with on various project teams in a matrix-management environment. In the compensation function, the system knows to whom to route transactions for approval in the case that the recommended salary increase exceeds guidelines based on the employee's position.

A deep integration involving all three layers can be said to be a *"functional"* integration because it has contextual sensitivity to the information, the processes and the relationships between the participants.

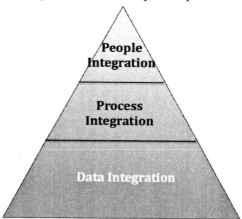

Fig. 2: Levels of integration

Today and Onward

BPM technology is effective for automating structured processes, where all of the possible execution paths are known in advance. The more recent concept of Adaptive Case Management (ACM), or Dynamic Case Management, is concerned with providing tools to empower the knowledge worker, operating in an unpredictable environment. As Paul Harmon noted in his keynote at the 2013 bpmNEXT conference[4], BPM technology evolved from early attempts at Artificial Intelligence and Expert Systems, which essentially consisted of business rules. Artificial Intelligence fell out of favor after early enthusiasm waned, but the technology has advanced and is now quite pervasive, as MS Word reminds me every time I write a sentence with an invalid structure.

All of the above technologies should be available to business users to construct an ecosystem of automated agents to assist with their work. Also at bpmNEXT, Dominic Greenwood said that BPM and ACM exist in a continuum, whereby tasks may start as structured, take an unpredictable turn, then resume a predictable path. The technologies to address each step should be readily available to invoke as needed.

The market for BPM suites and application-specific software are very competitive, with innovations frequently emerging. A customer should not be locked in to one product if another one that better suits its business needs is available. The cloud makes it (in some ways) easier and quicker to deploy applications. Users should be able to swap out software and replace it as needed.

Technology is advancing rapidly, with enhanced machine intelligence, miniaturization and new input devices. The platform should be agnostic to the point where it can integrate anything as long as it conforms to accepted standards.

THE INTELLIGENT BPM PLATFORM

At long last we are within reach of the "Holiest of Grails," a platform with true *functional* integration and interoperability. The idea behind the platform would be to "plug in" any application and have it be interoperable with any other application already connected to the platform. Whether it's a data or process integration depends on the degree to which the application exposes its processes as web services. However all applications will be "people" integrated by virtue of the centralized repository of rules, roles and relationships (see next section for more detail). Such a platform would have to possess the following characteristics:

- **Portal approach**—the platform should appear to the user as a portal, with all of the information and services aggregated on one, configurable page. The portal should know who the user is, what she is allowed to access, and what's she's likely to want to access.

- **Single sign-on**—it seems obvious, but an essential ingredient of a streamlined user experience is single sign-on. It's very annoying for a user to be challenged for login credentials each time she encounters a new system.

- **Configurable look and feel**—when switching between systems, it's best to have a consistent look and feel. To some degree this will be a compromise as the degree of configurability varies widely between software products. However, there should at least be consistent branding.

- **A centralized information hub**—see the next section for a more detailed explanation.

- **Fully web-services enabled**—should support all current accepted standards for integrations. Should be backward compatible to support several flat-file formats as well.

- **Centralized workflow**—all action items/approvals should appear on a single action list. See the next section for more detail.

- **Extended Relationship Management (xRM)**[5]—an essential component of this platform is the xRM application, which allows configuration and management of all roles and relationships in the extended enterprise.

- **Configurable by business users**—some degree of configuration should be available to business users, rather than technical folks.

- **Extensible**—the platform should not be confined to information only within the company. The value chain extends beyond the firewall, and the platform should have the ability to extend to the web for additional information.

- **True Platform-as-a-Service (PaaS)**—the platform should be a true Platform-as-a-Service. It should exist in the cloud, rather than on-premise, be a single code-base for all users, and have a multi-tenant database. Therefore, it should be highly configurable, but lack a facility for code customization (see the discussion below on extensibility, which will allow certain users to invoke business rules unique to them without infringing on the common code-base). This will allow the vendor to roll out upgrades on a frequent schedule and maintain a quick pace for new and more innovative features and functionalities, which also serves the customer.

- **Integrated analytics**—in that this is an information repository, a great deal of mission-critical information is at the user's fingertips. The platform should have an integrated analytics engine, which can provide a management dashboard of relevant metrics for the user.

- **Collaboration tools**—social media tools, such as wikis, blogs and discussion groups should be available to communities defined and maintained by the relationship management tool.

A Look Under the Hood

At the heart of the platform is the centralized information repository. It draws information from multiple systems of record, and indicates the source of each piece of information so it cannot be changed in the repository, unless it has been created there. The repository can also serve as a real-time Global Data Warehouse, and can provide analytics to the dashboard.

The Extended Relationship Management engine ensures that any time a data element changes, it's re-sent to the repository in real-time through web services. The information acts as meta-data, and can be used to construct business rules that drive groupings of workers. For instance, logical statements can be created using the meta-data (e.g.: DEPARTMENT = '26001'), which will enforce that all workers in that department will be grouped together.

Business rules can be used for any purpose, but are intended to group workers in the construction of organizational structures. These structures are the life-blood of the company, and can be mapped to any process in the company where sensitivity to organizational relationships are value enhancing. If one were to map all of the relationships that make a company work, it would be unfathomably complex. The Extended Relationship Management tool allows that complexity to be managed effectively; the meta-data driven business rules contribute to keeping the information current automatically.

Extensibility

The system is extensible in two respects: "virtual" data items and "virtual" business rules. Virtual data is information that isn't derived from internal systems through an application interface; they can exist anywhere on the web and be accessed through web services. For instance, if I want to group all stocks whose stock price is over 100, I can access the ever-changing stock prices on the web and dynamically maintain that group of stocks. This aspect of the architecture can be open source. Since the architecture has a published API, anyone can develop connectors to the information they want and make that connector available to anyone else who would like to use it.

The other aspect is "virtual" business rules. As a pure PaaS, any features designed into the product are available to all, and typically if a feature is not designed into the product it is unavailable. However, due to the published API, any user of the system can write her own business rules and host them elsewhere. The results of the business rules can be used within other business rules or to trigger behaviors within the system.

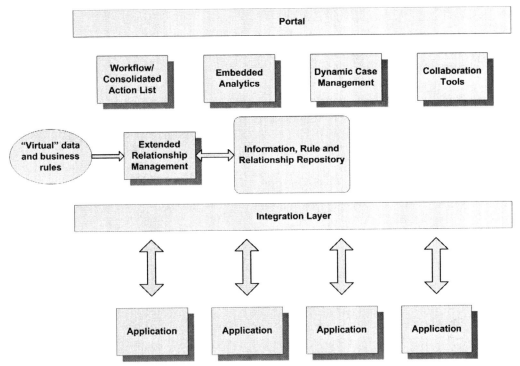

Fig. 3: Intelligent architecture diagram

Centralized Workflow

An important feature of this platform is a centralized workflow that can span processes, and present a single consolidated action list to the user. This is not easy to achieve. It requires deep integration with the workflow engine of each application; many software products don't expose components of their workflow as web services. Once an item is worked within the action list, it must be removed from the list, and synced with the action list in the target application.

Breaking down silos

A big issue in organizations is the silo'd structure, whereby people are only concerned with their own narrow area of focus. This emerged from the old hierarchical model of organizational management, and has persisted despite the emergence of interoperability tools based on open and accepted standards. Part of the reason it has persisted is that integration between software agents is contrary to the marketing goals of software vendors—many of whom seek to sell the widest breadth of functionality to alleviate the need to integrate. Another reason is the mindset fostered by the single hierarchy management structure—if you report to only one person it stands to reason that the priorities of that one person would take precedence over those of other reporting structures, or even the overall goals of the organization.

This platform is a tool to break down the silos by recognizing the connections between people in the organization across contexts. Processes concerned with management of tasks that cross boundaries can now be recognized and built into reward and feedback mechanisms.

Ownership

It is difficult to assign ownership of a platform whose goal is to break down silos, as assigning ownership is by nature a siloing process. There are many who suggest that this platform should be owned by IT, since (as stated earlier) it complements the changing role of IT. However I challenge IT to be forward thinking enough to want to deploy a platform that is configurable by business users, rather than IT. Just as responsibility should be distributed and shared, ownership of this platform should also be distributed. If there is to be any single ownership, it should be in the "C" suite, as this platform is instrumental in helping companies achieve their strategic objectives.

The Future

In 1965, Intel co-founder Gordon Moore observed that the number of transistors on integrated circuits double approximately every two years.[6] This has held remarkably consistently or increased since that time, and can be expected to continue. As a result, smart phones in our pockets have more processing power than supercomputers of yore. In the not-too-distant future, computers will be wearable. They will be on a shirt button or in an ear insert. Input devices will become more intuitive. Speech recognition has made great strides in recent decades and we can assume that this technology will continue to improve, obviating the need for a keyboard. Eventually, speech recognition will be semantic (rather than syntactic), as it will understand the meaning of what we say. Berners-Lee envisioned a Semantic Web, which the W3C defines as "...a common framework that allows data to be shared and reused across application, enterprise, and community boundaries."[7] This can result in machines that search the web to understand each concept that it encounters.

Futurist and inventor Ray Kurzweil predicts that the confluence of advances in processing speed and non-invasive brain scanning technology will result in "The Singularity"[8] whereby we can reverse-engineer the neural state of the brain on a typical computer within 20-30 years (maybe sooner if President Obama's brain mapping initiative[9] comes to pass). Between now and then, processing power will increase in a continuum, resulting in smaller and more intelligent devices, thus more value placed on uniquely human attributes. MIT's Frank Levy and Harvard's Richard Murnane argue that the automation of business processes has heightened the value of two categories of human skills: "expert thinking—solving new problems for which there are no routine solutions; and complex communication—persuading, explaining, and in other ways conveying a particular interpretation of information."[10]

In 1950, Alan Turing devised the "Turing Test"[11]—whether an observer could distinguish between a conversation with a machine or a real human. To date, no machine has passed the Turing test. How much longer will it be until one does?

The platform proposed here represents a bridge to that future—a place to integrate all of the automated agents at your disposal and replace them as new, more sophisticated technology becomes available.

CONCLUSION—YOUR STRATEGY

Bringing this discussion back to Earth, I began this paper with a discussion about strategy, and that's where it will conclude. What is your strategy? Is it operational in nature—create efficiencies and effectiveness; maximize profits and curtail waste? Is it broader—provide a valuable service for the customer;

be a positive force in the universe? In either case, one needs to manage the dynamic and rapidly changing paradigms. This requires an open-ended platform that is ultimately adaptive to changes in business and technological needs.

Epilogue

While out walking her dog Tasha, Jen received a call from Molly, her digital assistant. She touched the top button on her shirt to receive it. "Jen, James called and wants to meet with you at three. Apparently there's a glitch with the Kiplagat deal that he wants to talk through with you." Sometimes Jen forgets that Molly's not a real person. The personality designers did a good job with her.

"You're booked will Gil then to discuss staffing, but that's lower priority, so I can bump Gil to Friday at 2. I've accessed the documents concerning the hold-up with Kiplagat, and opened a sub-case. I can stream them to your retinal projector when you're ready. If the issue's resolved by tomorrow, we can still get sign-off on the deal on Thursday as planned, otherwise I've identified a couple of other windows next week." Jen rattled off a few instructions and ended the call.

Jen can't imagine what life would be like without Molly. It was just a few years ago that people would stagger around like zombies, thumbing at their "smart" phones, eyes downcast on the clumsy devices. It seems as though Molly has a deeper understanding of her motivations than her coarse brain scanning technology can achieve. And she's always agreeable (unlike real people)! Tasha did her business and they headed home. Now that all of the administrative details of her job are just taken care of, and everything she needs for the knowledge work is at her fingertips, she can live a balanced life and still produce more than enough value to justify her high income. Back home to her sometimes disagreeable, but definitely human, husband and daughter.

REFERENCES:

[1]: Carr, Nicholas, 'Does IT Matter? Information Technology and the Corrosion of Competitive Advantage', 2003, Harvard Business Review

[2]: Smith, Howard and Fingar, Peter, 'IT Doesn't Matter-Business Processes Do: A Critical Analysis of Nicholas Carr's I.T. Article in the Harvard Business Review', 2003, Meghan-Kiffer Press

[3]: Berners-Lee, Tim, 'Weaving the Web: The Original Design and Ultimate Destiny of the World Wide Web', 2000, HarperBusiness

[4]: Harmon, Paul, Keynote and Greenwood, Dominic, 'Goals in the Process Continuum: from BPM to ACM and Beyond', March 20th-21st, 2013, bpmNEXT Conference, Pacific Grove, California

[5]: Altman, Roy, 'People Relationship Management - Completing the BPM Value Proposition', '2009 BPM and Workflow Handbook', and Altman, Roy & Altman, Kenneth, 'Dynamic Clinical Pathways—Adaptive Case Management for Medical Professionals', 2011, 'Social BPM', Future Strategies Inc., FL.

[6]: Moore, Gordon E., 'Cramming More Components Into Integrated Circuits', 1965, Electronics Magazine

[7]: 'W3C Semantic Web Activity', World Wide Web Consortium (W3C), 2011

[8]: $100 million brain mapping initiative proposed by President Barack Obama, April 2, 2013,

http://www.whitehouse.gov/the-press-office/2013/04/02/fact-sheet-brain-initiative

[9]Kurzweil, Ray, 'The Singularity Is Near: When Humans Transcend Biology', 2006, Penguin Books

[10]: Levy, Frank and Murnane, Richard, 'The New Division of Labor: How Computers Are Creating the Next Job Market', 2004, Princeton University Press

[11]: Turing, Alan, 'Computing Machinery and Intelligence', 1950

Process of Everything

Setrag Khoshafian and Don Schuerman
Pegasystems Inc.

INTRODUCTION

One of the most important trends in the technology industry will be the *Internet of Everything* (Evans, 2011). The Internet of Everything (IoE) will involve billions of devices or "things" connected over the Internet: generating data, sensing, firing and consuming events, and being controlled remotely. These things will be intelligent, and increasingly, the IoE will extend beyond traditional electronic devices to include everything—any device or thing, from food products to cars to airplanes to utilities to medicines to appliances and the houses in which we live. In the next decade, digital-enabled things will generate more Internet traffic than people. They will be the main source of Big Data, characterized by enormous volume, velocity, and variety. Through embedded intelligence, these things will be semi-autonomous. The IoE will transform both individual lives and open new opportunities and challenges for businesses.

These connected devices will be generating billions of events every day. *Intelligent BPM (iBPM)* will provide the *context* to coordinate these events. iBPM will instantiate, complete, and resolve work created from the intelligent devices. iBPM will connect these devices to human and system participants. Through iBPM intelligent devices will execute business rules and decisions, drive processes, and instantiate dynamic cases. They can learn and adapt, while being "process"-connected to other devices or humans.

Figure 1: Process of Everything (PoE)

This is a natural evolution of BPM: human participants in iBPM solutions are already augmented with guided interactions, coaching hints, and next-best-action that leverages data analytics, including predictive and adaptive models. When associated with "things," the process automation extends from the confines of humans and computer-based automation to include intelligent devices participating in processes. Data from intelligent devices will be included in the analytics that drive process decisions. Billions of devices driving trillions of events will create incredible complexity, demanding the aggregation provided by Dynamic Case Management (which is a key iBPM capability). Welcome to the *Process of Everything (PoE)*.

THE EVOLUTION OF iBPM

Business Process Management has evolved from a number of disciplines and trends.

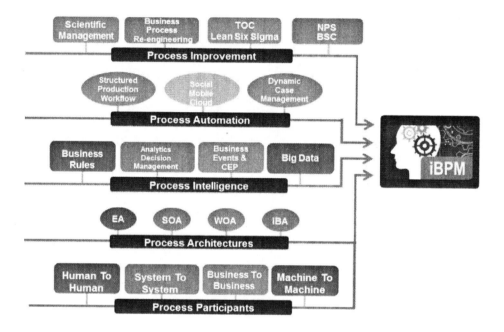

Figure 2: Evolution of iBPM

As in Figure 2, there are five key trends that have evolved into intelligent BPM.

- ***Process Improvement***: The evolution of "improvement" for process efficiency and productivity within organizations goes back to Taylorism, or Scientific Management. In the 1990s, business process re-engineering took a top-down approach on process improvement and re-organization. Due to the radical amount of change that was attempted, most re-engineering initiatives did not succeed. Process improvement methodologies such as Lean and Six Sigma attempt to eliminate waste in work processing, while increasing the efficiency as well as the effectiveness and quality of products or services. Theory of Constraints (Goldratt, 2012) and

Net Promoter Scores (NPS)[1] provide robust and complementary improvement frameworks. The key point is that, whether improving NPS or Critical To Quality measure for a Lean Six Sigma project, iBPM allows organizations to keep their critical to measure and control their customer experience and operational efficiency in *real-time* (Khoshafian, 2011) (Khoshafian, 2006).

- ***Process Automation:*** Automation has also evolved from structured production workflows to collaborative, unstructured, and dynamic cases. Production or structured "workflow" BPM focuses on predetermined, clerical or transactional work. Social and mobile technologies are expanding the scope of automation empowering connectivity as well as engagement of different categories of "workers"—especially knowledge workers and knowledge-assisted workers (Khoshafian, 2011). Dynamic cases are holistic: involving tasks organized in a case hierarchy, aggregating information and content from many sources. They can handle unstructured and collaborative work with social and mobile capabilities, as well as structured production workflow. Cases are dynamic, adding or changing any of their elements often during the course of work, driving towards a concrete business objective or goal. Cases respond to and generate events. The anatomy of a typical case is illustrated in Figure 1. The case will have a hierarchy. It will have subcases. Various tasks will be executed in the context of the parent case or one of its subcases. Dynamic cases can adapt when requirements, behaviors, circumstances, or events change.

- ***Process Intelligence:*** The "intelligence" in processes emanates from a number of core capabilities in the iBPM. These include a rich collection of business rule types, predictive analytics (Khoshafian, 2010), adaptive (learning) decisioning, event rules, and recommendations from Big Data[2]. Business rules—such as constraints, decision trees/tables, expressions, etc.—are an integral part of business process solutions. A business is a collection of policies (often implemented as business rules) and procedures (often implemented as process flows or cases). Often this process intelligence is harvested from knowledge workers. Other sources include policy manuals and legacy code. Increasingly, the intelligence is mined and harvested from data. The sources and types of data vary: process or case data, transactional data, data warehouses, data from social networks, and of course the increasingly popular "big data." Predictive and adaptive analytics mine these data sources to create actionable predictive models.

- ***Process Architecture:*** An Enterprise Architecture (EA) is the *blueprint* of the enterprise, capturing business, application, information, and infrastructure models and their relationships (Kappelman, 2010). EAs attempt to modernize legacy systems and govern change through complex organizations. Service Oriented Architectures (SOA) and Web Oriented Architectures (WOA) are important patterns that provide the ability to loosely couple applications, trading partners, and organizations via standards. The

---

[1] Net Promoter Score, Net Promoter and NPS are registered trademarks of Bain & Company, Satmetrix Systems and Fred Reichheld

[2] http://en.wikipedia.org/wiki/Big_data

next phase in the evolution of architectures is iBPM-enabled *intelligent Business Architectures (iBA)*. Increasingly, business applications are becoming iBPM applications—or at least modernized through an iBPM agility layer. With the emergence of the cloud, infrastructure is being outsourced as a service. Another trend is to combine data and process architecture—thus making the revamped iBA based on iBPM the core of the enterprise ecosystem.

- **Process Participants:** The last, but perhaps most important, trend is the evolution of the process participants. BPM has its roots in "Human Participant"-focused workflow systems. The coordination in this category is Human-to-Human. While some BPM technologies and methods are still purely workflow-focused, iBPM is much more than that. Other significant categories of software that have influenced the evolution of iBPM include Enterprise Application Integration (EAI) and Business-to-Business (B2B) integration, which enables System-to-System and Human-to-System BPM. With IoE, we now have a new category of Machine to Machine (M2M) integration. iBPM coordinates all these participants (Humans, Systems, Machines / Devices) in complex, dynamic processes and cases to achieve business objectives.

iBPM is a platform that helps organizations succeed through automating their policies and procedures. The culmination of the trends driving iBPM has opened the door for the "adaptive enterprise." An adaptive enterprise aligns its business objectives to operationalized policies and procedures with complete transparency, visibility, and control. More importantly, an adaptive enterprise is agile and proactive in responding to change. The only constant in business is change!

THE INTERNET OF EVERYTHING (IoE)

The previous section described the evolution of iBPM. This section expands upon the history of the Internet and the emergence of IoE as the most significant milestone of its maturity.

A Brief History of the Internet

With its roots in host-to-host communication on the ARPANET, the Internet, and especially the World Wide Web of interlinked "pages," was initially developed to provide hypertext and hypermedia connectivity between technical documents. This "academic Web" was based on a stack of enabling technologies—often referred to as "TCP/IP" in reference to the Transfer Connect Protocol (TCP) and the Internet Protocol (IP) that provide much of the core functionality. The TCP/IP stack remains the core of today's Internet and provides a means for sending data between devices, standardizing how data is formatted, addressed and routed. By design, TCP/IP is a "lightweight" protocol: most of the application intelligence lies at the endpoints of the network—i.e. the machines that are using it—not in the network itself. The HyperText Transfer Protocol (HTTP) is a part of the TCP/IP stack allowing applications to send and receive content, such as a web browser requesting an HTML document from a web server.

While the Internet was initially developed for the government and research institutions, individuals and organizations soon thereafter built their own web presences. Static pages built in basic HTML quickly evolved into powerful applications enabling "e-Commerce" and Web self-service. The internet standards originally developed for transmitting and linking between research documents were extended to form the backbone of Web Services. HTTP was now carrying a payload of rich XML (eXstensible Mark-up Language) and JSON (JavaScript Object Notation) documents, and triggering transactions and processes at the network endpoints. Businesses began to use the Services Oriented Architectures (SOA) enabled by Internet standards like HTTP and TCP/IP to build bridges between their applications and to communicate with applications outside of their firewalls.

Social networks, blogs and other sites led to an explosion of user-generated content and a more collaborative internet. The Internet itself was becoming a key platform for applications. Many of the applications in this "Web 2.0" (O'Reilly, 2005) were part of the growing trend of cloud-based applications: applications that run on hosted environments and can be accessed from anywhere with a browser. We now manage our email, our calendars, even our finances on the cloud, and organizations are increasingly using the cloud to run their own applications, reducing operating costs and speeding time to market. With the emergence of mobile devices—now close to a quarter of all internet traffic, and growing rapidly (WalkerSands, 2013)—we are all part of an always-connected, always-online world.

The Internet of Everything

In 2012, an estimated 2.45 billion people were connected to the Internet via PCs, smart phones, tables and other devices[3]. Increasingly, however, people are not the primary inhabitants of the Internet. In 2003, about 500 million devices (PCs, servers, etc.) were connected to the Internet, or about .08 devices per person. By 2010, there were 12.5 billion devices on the Internet, or about 1.8 devices per person (Evans, 2011). Considering that only about 2.45 billion of the world's nearly seven million people are on the Internet, devices now outnumber people by over five to one. This is the Internet of Things, and increasingly, it is becoming the Internet of *Everything*.

Some of this growth in connected devices is being driven by smart phones and tablets. Especially in the developing world, mobile devices have become the primary means for people to access the Internet, but that fact reveals their link to past. Like personal computers and laptops, mobile devices are in the business of connecting people to the net. The real explosion of the IoE will come from devices that aren't connecting people at all. It will come from "Things."

This category of Things will be different from the systems and devices that already populate the internet. These Things will ultimately be more like a semi-autonomous robot than a simple service responding to requests. The Thing can be intelligent and potentially learn. While they will span the range from microscopic to enormous, from machine to organic, these Things will share many key characteristics:

- *They are "things": In other words they are real objects in the real world—a light bulb, a package of food, even a human or an animal. Typically, especially for live objects such as humans or animals, there are sensors associated with the Thing: for example a wrist band that continuously monitors the health of the subject or an electronic tag that identifies livestock.*

---

[3] http://www.internetworldstats.com/stats.htm

- *They have "IDs": Things have unique identifiers. These "IDs" are independent of the status and location of the Thing. They are like the "DNA" of the Thing—and always associated with it.*
- *They are Event-Driven: Things participate in an event-driven architecture: they generate and respond to events. Things can perform complex event processing and event correlation. This means, the intelligent Thing can readily take action based on the correlation of events. The events could be temporal, based on state changes, or communication with other devices.*
- *They connect to the Internet: This means they can communicate with and be controlled over the Internet. Some Things can be accessed directly using standard API protocols such as REST. Most Things will communicate with other Things (M2M), as well as with other systems and humans. Intelligent Things also continuously and pro-actively generate event data that can then be mined to discover and operationalize predictive models.*

You can walk into your local mall today and purchase any number of these Internet-connected Things:

- Thermostats that let you monitor and control your home's temperature via the web;
- Speakers to which you wirelessly stream music;
- Baby monitors that use the web to stream video footage of a sleeping child;
- Refrigerators that let you access an electronic shopping list wherever you are;
- Scales that record your weight and publish it online;
- Electronic pedometers that track your daily activity;
- Set-top boxes that you can program via your smartphone when you are running late and need to record your favorite show;
- LED light bulbs that you can turn on and off via a smartphone.

These are consumer devices that you can buy today. Businesses are already exploiting the IoE.

- Trains, buses, trucks and planes broadcast their location via sensors, enabling improved scheduling and logistics;
- Medical devices that let doctors monitor patients remotely;
- Smart shipping containers that can be inventoried and tracked electronically;
- Animal tags that help farmers and ranchers manage herds and regulators respond to disease outbreaks.

These examples are real. They are happening today. And the size and the impact of the IoE will only explode over time. Later on, we'll look at how iBPM will be essential for managing this world of connected things. But first, let's take a deeper look at what the IoE will look like.

Enabling Internet of Everything

In many ways, the IoE represents an extension of the technologies and standards that have made the Internet as we know it possible. But the IoE will also exploit and demand new technologies. We'll focus on key three concepts: Machine to Machine communication (M2M), Radio Frequency Identification (RFID), and the impact of Cloud computing. In this section we focus on M2M and RFID. The cloud is now ubiquitous and we'll refer to it on the next section on iBPM for the Process of Everything. First, however, let's take a look at exactly how all these Things will start connecting to the internet.

In the Internet of computers (including things like smartphones and tablets and even printers), each computer that is online is given an IP address: a numerical address that allows the network to find it, and route traffic to it. But the IoE goes beyond that.

Imagine a home of smart devices connected to the IoE. That includes everything from light switches to thermostats to appliances to security systems. It also includes the bulbs in the lighting, the clothes in the closets, even the food in the refrigerator. Some of these devices may be directly connected to Internet, but most of them connect through other managers and readers. You can think of the "home of the future" as a collection of networks of smaller devices: controllers managing a floor of "smart" LED light bulbs, the refrigerator managing all of the food inside, etc. The IoE is the ever expanding network of these mini-networks. But how do your light bulbs talk to their switches? And how does the refrigerator know what's inside?

M2M: Machines talking to Machines

Machine to Machine (M2M) networks have been around since computing began, but the growth of cellular and explosion of "smart" devices have greatly expanded the range of M2M communications. Once relegated to large, industrial operations, M2M has moved inside our houses as new classes of devices allow us to build Home Area Networks (HAN). Many of the expanding areas of M2M communication use low-power wireless networks to communicate between devices. Commercial standards and components such as ZigBee and zWave have been the basis of DIY developer's kits which are now being OEM'ed into commercial products. Devices can use ZigBee or zWave componentry to talk to local "hubs" which either manage the device or relay that data to the Internet (Frenzel, 2012).

RFID: Tracking Everything

Perhaps the greatest explosion in the size of the IoE will come from Radio Frequency Identification or RFID. RFID are small devices—often as tiny as a grain of rice—that allow the object they are attached to transmit data about itself to "RFID Readers." RFID chips can be self-powered with small batteries but can also be passive, generating the power supply needed from the magnetic field created by the reader. Some RFID technology is designed to work only when in close proximity to other devices: this Near Field Communication (or NFC) forms the basis of many "smart" credit cards. RFID is already pervasive: for example, Walmart for several years has been using it to track inventory (Bastillo, 2010); ranchers and farmers use RFID chips to track livestock; casinos use RFID to monitor and validate high-value poker chips. You can even have a small RFID chip implanted in your pet. Someday, your refrigerator will be able to read the RFID chip on your eggs and tell you when it's time to purchase new ones.

Intelligent Agents

When your refrigerator discovers that your eggs are past their "sell by" date and texts you to remind you to pick up eggs, it is acting as an *Intelligent Agent*. Traditional software agents are defined by being autonomous, reactive and able to communicate. "Intelligent Agents" combine this with being able to set goals, make decisions and learn (Fingar, 2012). The analog thermostats in most homes are basic agents: they sense the current temperature, and toggle the heating and cooling system on or off to achieve the goal of their set temperature. Now imagine a thermostat that doesn't just sense the temperature nearby, but communicates with other thermostats in your house to know the temperature in other rooms. From the internet, it knows the current and historical weather trend. It has activity sensors that can detect if you have left the house. It learns that you turn the temperature down every night at 10PM, so it begins to do it for you. This is a Thing acting as an intelligent agent. You can walk into Best Buy and get this thermostat, called the Nest®, today.

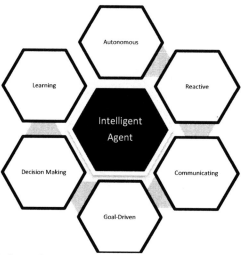

Figure 3: Intelligent Agents

The IoE will be full of intelligent agents like this. Some of the Things will be agents in and of themselves. Others, like the RFID-tagged food in your fridge, will provide data and events that allow other intelligent agents to act. These Things will act as intelligent agents: they will communicate with each other and other inhabitants of the Internet take actions necessary to achieve goals they set, and—most importantly—they will learn.

Events, Big Data and Analytics for Internet of Everything

The Intelligent Agents that make up the IoE will learn through Big Data. As every object we touch becomes "smart," able to share its information with the world around it, the IoE will generate massive amounts of data. "Big Data" is the growing suite of technologies and platforms that allow organizations to analyze massive, rapidly-changing data sets of a mix of data and media types. Most importantly, Big Data allows organization to draw new conclusions—to learn—from the data. Algorithms like "Map Reduce," that split large data sets into smaller chunks for processing across a network of computers, have allowed systems to process larger and larger sets of data. As the number of events, messages and data packets crossing the internet grows exponentially, Big Data will provide the tools for extracting actionable intelligence.

Of course, massive systems of connected devices and ground-breaking analytics mean nothing if there is no way to drive processes and goals across the IoE. In the next section, we'll look at how iBPM, especially with Dynamic Case Management, will provide the foundation for linking the IoE into intelligent, powerful and dynamic processes: the Process of Everything (PoE).

iBPM FOR PROCESS OF EVERYTHING (PoE)

The previous sections discussed the evolution of business process management to iBPM as well as the evolution of the Internet to the IoE. This section combines these two significant trends to illustrate how iBPM will launch a new era in automation and productivity through the *Process of Everything.*

The New Process Participant Category

In any workflow or BPM solution you have *activities* that are assigned to *participants*. The process flow is an essential building block and it basically consists of activity steps organized in flow charts. There are typically three categories of activity task assignments:

- Human participants: this involves specific workflow performers, groups, roles, or users with specific skills.
- System participants: this could be back-end systems of records, typically with service interfaces.
- Trading partner participants: process *choreographies* can involve B2B trading partners exchanging messages with specific structure and order of exchange.

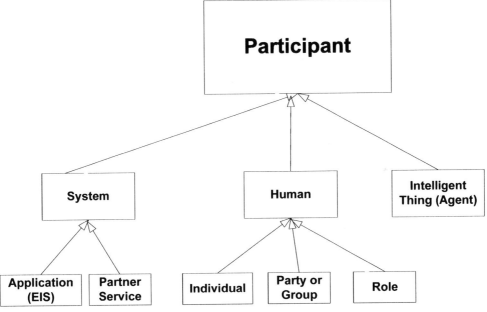

Figure 4: Participants in iBPM

Figure 6 provides a high-level illustration of the categories of participants in iBPM—including Intelligent Things. With the IoE there is a new category that is added to this mix:

The intelligent Internet Thing

One could argue that this Thing category is no different than System or even trading partner category. But, as discussed in the previous section, a Thing is different from a traditional system or trading partner: it is or is tied to a physical object, it has an ID and it is event-driven. The Thing can be "intelligent" and potentially learn.

Dynamic Case Management

Figure 7 illustrates the anatomy of a case. Unlike pre-determined and process flow-centric models, dynamic cases manage multiple processes organized in a case hierarchy. The parent case and its subcases execute one or more processes and assign tasks to participants, as described above. The coordination of the tasks is organized in a case hierarchy (subcases). Some of the tasks will be planned in predetermined process flows, others will be ad-hoc. The case will also have a business objective: e.g. resolve a customer claim within 24 hours. There will be collaboration between various case participants to resolve the case. While processing these tasks, a case will have content, often from multiple enterprise information or content management repositories. Cases generate and respond to business events. Different types of policies and business rules, such as decision-ing rules, expressions, decision tables, and constraints, are associated with the case and drive the automated and dynamic cases. Cases also have data properties pertaining to the parent case or subcases, and multiple process fragments executing in the context of the case hierarchy. Cases are dynamic, often adding or changing any of their elements in response to events.

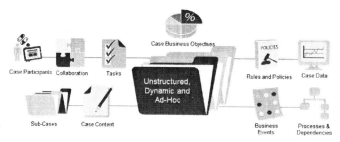

Figure 5: Anatomy of a Dynamic Case

Social, Mobile, and Cloud:

- *Social iBPM: Social iBPM (Khoshafian et al. 2011) is bringing the successful paradigms of social networking to the enterprise, and this is providing increased connectivity, transparency, communication, and collaboration with customers, as well as within the organization. Social collaboration can be synchronous (same time) or asynchronous (different times). Increasingly, BPM solutions are leveraging social tools, providers and metaphors in all the phases of BPM solution lifecycles. Most importantly, BPM is providing the context for social networking and collaboration.*

- *Mobile iBPM: Mobile devices are also intelligent devices that are connected on the Internet. iBPM will allow organizations to seamlessly initiate and complete automated case work, end-to-end via mobile devices. This work will pertain to dynamic cases involving various categories of participants all interacting via mobile devices. The instant accessibility of case status, case work, and case collaboration via mobile means empowerment of a whole new category of mobile workers. Not only are they looking to merely stay connected, but they are actually completing transactions and work via smart devices.*

- *Cloud iBPM: Software, platforms, and infrastructures on "the Cloud" (which means accessed via the public Internet through a browser or mobile device) are fast becoming the preferred mode of provisioning enterprise software. With the cloud you can have enterprise applications that are built securely with the iBPM platform on the cloud: iBPM for PaaS. Once the iBPM solution is built and deployed, it can also execute or run on the cloud: iBPM SaaS. Due to regulatory or security constraints, a key requirement for next generation iBPM on the cloud is the flexibility in building / deploying either on the cloud or on premise and easily moving between the two options, with secure "tunnel" access of on-premise enterprise data, when applicable.*

Business Rules and Events:

Business Rules implement business decisioning logic and business policies. Rules drive iBPM solutions. There are many categories and types of business rules such as decision trees, decision tables, constraints, and expressions. The focus on business rules is on externalizing the business logic, as close to the business as possible, without worrying about execution time, execution method, or execution order. Business Rules are declarative. As noted in (Khoshafian, 2010), there are many sources of such policies that end up in business rules, including policy manuals, the "heads" of experts or knowledge workers, and legacy applications. Rules can also be discovered from data: be that transactional, event data, or data-warehouses. Predictive modeling techniques can be used to detect business patterns and then invoke or operationalize the discovered rules in the context of iBPM solutions.

An important category of business logic that is especially important with intelligent things is event rules. The ability to respond to events, subscribe to event or state changes, and handle the events by any category of participants is an essential building block in iBPM. Temporal rules include service levels at either the dynamic case or task granule. Complex events can be correlated within temporal windows.

Analytics and Adaptive iBPM

One of the most important trends in the industry is the emergence of data engineering and especially Big Data analytics. This is delivering tangible benefits to organizations by unlocking the insights hidden in vast amounts of digital information. iBPM, through both predictive and adaptive analytics, enables the insight that is discovered to become actionable. The sources and types of data are heterogeneous and span social networks, transactional data, data warehouses and even stores of media. iBPM solutions leverage predictive and adaptive models to provide the next best action in various dynamic case interactions. iBPM solutions are adaptive: they can continuously learn and adapt from external events or the behavior of its constituents and participants. Leveraging the business rules and achieving this continuous real-time analysis for actionable decisions provides tremendous business value: the faster decisions are made the more the business vale. "Adaptive iBPM[4]" provides the platform, solutions, best practices, methodologies and governance for adaptive enterprises

This brings us to the crux of our paper:

The Process of Everything (PoE): As noted above, the PoE involves Things as active participants in dynamic cases. This means:

---

[4] http://www.pega.com/resources/adaptive-bpm

- **Tasks are assigned and completed by Things**: This is similar to human work queues and task assignments. Things could belong to specific classes or categories. Hence tasks could be assigned to a queue for the semi-automated or fully automated intelligent agents to execute and perform. Tasks assigned to things could be scheduled and executed periodically, either through explicit settings or rules-driven constraints.

- **Adaptive**: Intelligent things are part of adaptive iBPM solutions. As noted above, one of key aspects of this adaptability is to learn and accordingly adjust the behavior of the intelligent Things' actions (as participants in iBPM) based on history or behavior over temporal windows. Adaptability also spans to the behavior and control of the dynamic case. For instance the "path" across processes and subcases could adapt based what the intelligent thing learns from previous instantiations.

- **Pro-Active:** Things are proactive. They constantly generate event data and can also monitor data (or leverage services that monitor data intelligently). For any participant or iBPM solution category, you take action based on detection, event correlations, or adaptive predictive analytics, the greater its business value. Thus the data / event analytics as well as the core capability of iBPM in powerful decisioning as well as event rules are leveraged to support pro-active interactions by intelligent Things.

- ***Long Duration Cases with Intelligent Things***: In conventional BPM, we are used to relatively short duration processes such as approving an expense. There are also processes that are of medium duration—a few days to a few weeks—such as onboarding an employee or processing a warranty claim. But dynamic cases can also be long duration—spanning weeks to even several months, such as cleaning up after a hurricane or managing a long-term health care plan. An extreme case (no pun intended) is a dynamic case associated with the lifetime of the entity: human or thing. This could be years or decades. Thus the ability for dynamic case status to persist long durations is a key enabler in process of everything.

- ***Assisting Humans:*** The majority of workers in iBPM solutions are "knowledge assisted workers." Knowledge assisted workers need to apply policies and procedures in the work that they are trying to complete, and sometimes make on the spot decisions in particular situations. They need to be instructed in the application of the business rules; however, they are not coming up with the rules. Customer service representatives are a good example of knowledge assisted workers. They are usually trained so that when they interact with a customer, they know what to do. There are several sources of "assistance" to the worker:

    o ***Guided and Intent-Driven Interactions:*** Providing the needed and meaningful screens, hints, coaching, or interactions for particular tasks, even proactively.

    o ***Knowledge and Insight from Data & Events:*** Advanced analytics capabilities, such as predictive and adaptive analytics, can take the guesswork out of many categories of tasks to offer a prioritized list of next best actions for the worker.

- Now both of these could be through Intelligent Things. That is, the device associated with the human can provide the assistance—within the context of goals and objectives of cases that involve the human either as a case subject or a case participant (or both).

- **_Collaborating Intelligent Things:_** Intelligent Things have M2M communication. They can communicate. They can also collaborate to accomplish tasks. For example, on any type of "grid"—networks, sensors on infrastructure, distributed software, etc.—the distributed and federated Things could be aware of the overall performance of the grid. With collaborating Things, the overall _performance_ as well as _resilience_ of the grid is strengthened. The former is due to the divide and conquer of the tasks: very much in the same vein as work queues. Things can pick up tasks assigned to the collaborative unit, as soon as they become available. Resilience is achieved through operational picking up tasks, where other things fail.

EXAMPLES OF PROCESS OF EVERYTHING

The PoE will be everywhere. We'll see it in our homes, in our cars, and at our offices. Businesses across industries will use the PoE to improve the way they service their customers while optimizing the efficiency of their operation. By applying iBPM to the IoE, businesses will be able to coordinate humans, intelligent things, and their enterprise applications in ways that achieve optimized business goals.

This section describes a few of those use cases in key industries. Some of these are descriptions of potential solutions that are on the horizon. But many of these are happening right now, evidence of the powerful impact the PoE is already having on our world.

Insurance: P & C and Life

Many insurance companies are offering their customers an innovative new way to control their premiums. The company gives you a smart device that is installed in your car.[5] It tracks your driving habits (distances, average speed, locations, etc.) and sends that data back to your insurer. The insurer now has more accurate data with which to underwrite your policy. Treating the policy as a case allows it to receive events from the tracking device, and automatically adjust your premiums on the fly. If you drive less during a particular month, your insurance premium drops for that month. The device can also detect if you've been in accident and automatically start a claim process, noting the speed you were going, the strength of the impact, and the location.

Finance

With mobile payments and smart cards, people can now pay for their purchases with a smart device. Mobile payments not only offer security and convenience, they offer the opportunity for the business to interact directly with the customer at the point of sale: not only does the device have the ability to carry the customer's payment information, it can hold their purchase history, their location information, and other data that can be used to deliver tailored offers and rewards to the customer immediately at the point of purchase.

Healthcare

Effectively managing patient health is key to lowering healthcare cost and delivering a better quality of life. A healthcare management provider uses iBPM as the core of their next generation care management platform, driving dynamic cases and processes to direct plan participants, doctors, health coaches, and clinicians

---

[5] http://progressive.com/snapshot

toward the best possible health outcome.[6] The application is able to receive real time data from a variety of smart devices, including blood pressure monitors, scales, glucometers and INR meters. These devices provide valuable data that may, for example, trigger an automated outreach to the patient if a blood pressure spike or a weight trend is detected. Being able to wrap process and case management around the events allows the healthcare management provider to coordinate the smart device data with the patients core medical records and history and drive the right responses at any point during care.

Agriculture

Since 2004, the governments have asked farmers to use RFID tags for tracking cattle. Using electronic tracking enables farmers and regulators to track an animal's entire lifecycle from birth, through each transition between owners, up until slaughter. Combining this electronic tracking with process and case management, health agencies, such as the Animal Health Agency of the UK, have been able to respond more effectively to outbreaks of disease or health risks, managing a growing range of regulations and an increasing animal population with a smaller number of staff.[7] The process and case management pulls together electronic ID data, with case data collected from field researchers, and ensures that appropriate processes for case resolution and escalation are followed.

Transportation

Coordinating airport traffic is a complicated logistics problem. In order to ensure a plane lands, is quickly unloaded, refueled, cleaned, catered, reloaded and pushes back to take off on time, hundreds of automated and manual systems must be coordinated. Many of these systems, including the plane itself, the fuel lines, and gates and ticketing systems, comprise smart devices that can generate messages and events. Heathrow Airport in London uses an iBPM solution to manage the overall turn-around process.[8] In this solution, a case is created for each arriving flight and linked via process to a case for the corresponding departing flight. The case receives and correlates events from the airlines, the ground crews, the control tower even the airport security screeners in order to manage the overall airport operation.

This solution automatically creates and dynamically coordinates every element of the operations required for flight turnaround in the shortest time possible, such as the exact minute the aircraft will land, which gate will be used, how much baggage must be offloaded, how long refueling will take, when the next crew will be onboard, the time required to load passengers for the next flight and the minute the flight should push back from the gate. Following implementation, on-time departures increased from 60 percent to 85 percent.

CONCLUSIONS

The IoE is changing entire ecosystems: from cities, to innovative businesses, to intelligent buildings, to farmlands and residences. Every day new intelligent things are joining the IoE. The trend is starting to generate considerable amount of data. As more and more intelligent Things join this ecosystem, opportunities for

---

[6] http://www.pega.com/resources/hc-summit-2012-video-pegapanel-optimizing-consumer-engagement-to-improve-customer

[7] http://www.pega.com/resources/top-animal-health-agency-improves-crisis-response

[8] http://www.youtube.com/watch?v=sgZ8F6XqoKc

innovation increase. Intelligent Things augment humans with increased automation and efficiencies—which improve life.

iBPM provides the *context* as well as the *container* for intelligent Things to collaborate to achieve objectives. Key iBPM capabilities such as business rules, event correlation, analytics, and especially dynamic case management are ideal for this spectrum of participants collaborating for continuous improvement and optimization of objectives.

Over the next few years the majority of Internet traffic will be sourced for Things. Things can be small. They can be RFID augmented small devices. They can be sensors that we can wear. Things can also be large. In the next couple of decades, semi or even fully automated human robots and avatars will become increasingly pervasive. iBPM is about automation involving different categories of participants, including *intelligent things* in dynamic cases, with Things collaborating with humans and systems to complete tasks and drive business outcomes. Additionally, intelligent Things or software agents can also *assist* human workers in iBPM solutions. In fact, automated processing and the processing of dynamic cases—all through the iBPM platform—provide the best milieu to leverage and demonstrate the potential of this new generation of intelligent workers. As this trend matures, increasingly humans will be focusing on innovation and cognitive work, delegating the routine and even the knowledge assistant work to automated Things. So a new era in process automation is on the Internet horizon. This is The Process of Everything (PoE).

REFERENCES

Bastillo, M. (2010). Wal-Mart Radio Tags to Track Clothing. *Wall Street Journal*. Retrieved from http://online.wsj.com/article/SB100014240527487044213045753832130 61198090.html

Evans, D. (2011). The Internet of Things. Retrieved from http://www.cisco.com/web/about/ac79/docs/innov/IoT_IBSG_0411FINAL.pdf

Fingar, P. (2012). Agent-Oriented BPM (aoBPM)—and a Confession. *BPTrends*. Retrieved from http://bptrends.com/publicationfiles/12-04-2012-COL-ExtComp-AgentOrientedBPM-Fingar%20%28SHLSeR5LQnSrTYYzb3R78w%29.pdf

Frenzel, L. (2012). What's the Difference Between ZigBee and Z-Wave? *Electronic Design*. Retrieved from http://electronicdesign.com/communications/what-s-difference-between-zigbee-and-z-wave

Godratt, E. M. (2012). *The Goal: A Process of Ongoing Improvement, Third Edition*. Great Barrington, Massachusetts: North River Press.

Kappelman, L. (2010). *The SIM Guide to Enterprise Architecture: Creating the Information Age Enterprise*. New York City, New York: CRC Press, Taylor and Francis Group.

Khoshafian, S. (2006). Business Process Management for Six Sigma Projects. *2006 Workflow Handbook*. Lighthouse Point, Florida: Future Strategies, Inc., Book Division.

Khoshafian, S. (2006). Real-Time Six Sigma with BPM Suites. *BPTrends*. Retrieved from http://www.bptrends.com/deliver_file.cfm?fileType=publication&fileName=10%2D06%2DART%2DReal%2DTimeSixSigma%2DKhosafian1%2Epdf

Khoshafian, S. (2010). Predictive BPM. *2010 BPM and Workflow Handbook.* Lighthouse Point, Florida: Future Strategies, Inc., Book Division.

Khoshafian, S., Tripp, P., Kraus, S. (et al 2011). Voice of the Network through Social BPM. *Social BPM: Work, Planning and Collaboration under the Impact of Social Technology, 2011 BPM and Workflow Handbook.* Lighthouse Point, Florida: Future Strategies, Inc., Book Division.

Khoshafian, S. (2008). MyBPM: Social Networking for Business Process Management. *2008 BPM and Workflow Handbook.* Lighthouse Point, Florida: Future Strategies, Inc.

Khoshafian, S. (2011). *BPM: The Next Wave for Business Applications.* Cambridge, Massachusetts: Pegasystems Inc.
http://www.pega.com/products/bpm/setrag-khoshafian-bpm-the-next-wave-book

The iBPM Ecosystem:
More Human than System

Gianpiero Bongallino, Openwork, Italy

INTRODUCTION

Man is the most evolved organism on Earth. The characteristic that distinguishes men from other living creatures is the ability to detect stimuli from the external environment, then to process, contextualize, and react to them. The difference that made the human race the dominant one on planet Earth is the ability to learn, to adapt dynamically to the environment, to store and reuse the knowledge by means of logic and similarities through some mechanisms such as abstraction, correlation, deduction and reasoning. To define intelligence [1] it is necessary to take into account these characteristics, but how can a system like BPM, based on barely flexible and structured predefined rules, be intelligent?

The intelligent Business Process Management system is able to:
- Manage structured and unstructured processes.
- Adapt to the environment that can depend on different data sources, such as events resulting from external systems or social interactions.
- Process events through rules, and to react to them asking for services.
- Produce intermediate events that are the result of the processing of several events.

The more the human nervous system is analyzed in its functional details, the more it is possible to find similarities with the iBPM technologies in an Event Driven Architecture.

The human nervous system and the iBPM Ecosystem

As in most animals, the nervous system in the human being allows the transmission of stimuli among the different parts of the body and consequently their processing. The human nervous system consists of two main parts:
- The central nervous system (CNS), that processes the information received and coordinates the activities of all the parts of the body.
- The peripheral nervous system (PNS) that connects the CNS to limbs and organs.

The iBPM is composed of different systems, which communicate with each other and interact via events, messages and service invocations.

Some of them determine its behavior, through business rules, business processes and CEP rules, and some others allow human interaction, visualization (smartphones, tablets, web form), as well as data and events transmission, such as the Event Channel.

The peripheral nervous system, the Event Channel and the SOA

The peripheral nervous system receives impulses from the receptors and transmits them through the nerve ganglia and nerves located outside of the encephalon and the spinal cord.

It is divided into two categories:
- The sensory system, that receives information from external (sight, hearing) or internal systems (balance, kinaesthetic sense).

- The motor system that is divided into autonomic and somatic.

The autonomic system manages involuntary actions, such as the heart rate, the digestion and the respiratory rate.

The somatic system allows reaction to stimuli that must have an immediate reaction, such as reflexes.

It is curious when, during the knee jerk reflex test, we have an immediate and not voluntary reaction, but at the same time we perceive consciously the impact with the hammer.

The Event Channel has the same capacity of the peripheral nervous system to transmit information. It is able to receive impulses from external or internal sources, to transmit them to different parts of the system, be it CEP, BPM, BAM or user interfaces, or to invoke directly adapters that answer, as in the case of reflexes, immediately to the received stimulus. If we think that an event can also be generated by a timer, even the heartbeat or the breathing can be considered, in this comparison, reactions to internal stimuli. In fact, a reaction to a nerve stimulation corresponds to a muscular action inside or outside the body. The actions of a system of EDA or BPM are invocations for services, internal or external to the system, and they allow to change the state of the ecosystem and to receive a response from them.

The central nervous system - CEP, BPM, Rule Engines, ACM and Analysis Systems

The central nervous system is divided into:
- **The spinal cord** that transmits motor and sensory information and coordinates some reflexes.
- **The encephalon** that allows both the control and the coordination of complex actions, and the reaction to stimuli generated by other parts of the body.

The encephalon, which receives the raw signals from the spinal cord and the peripheral system, processes them according to the memory, the context and the human needs and generates a response that maximizes the human wellbeing.

At the microscopic level, the encephalon is made of processing units called neurons, interconnected as a dense network via the synapses. Based on this structure, some computational models have been developed, called neural networks.

Neural networks are one of the machine-learning techniques, which are still being investigated and are showing interesting evolutions and combinations with other techniques of Artificial Intelligence.

The network model is also used by some implementations of the Complex Event Processing (CEP), but in this case the networks are computational models that represent flows and rules that can be set up and recognized by a human.

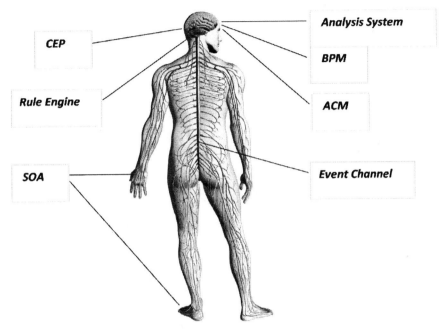

Figure 1: Human Nervous "iBPM" System

TECHNOLOGICAL OVERVIEW

CEP

The Complex Event Processing is a set of theories and technologies that allows to process event streams from different sources, to correlate them with each other, in order to achieve both higher-level events and a derivation of them.

The CEP is a superset of the ESP (Event Stream Processing), because it allows to define patterns of events, and it is able to correlate in real time different event streams and data stored in the hard-disk (or cached).

Event Patterns are conditions expressed by logic rules mixed with temporal and frequency rules applied to events or events fields such as "If event A occurs .. and.. or .. n times.. and not.. before.. with event.property $< m$... in n hours.. then..".

Some CEP producers represents the processing through networks, called event processing networks (EPN), composed by the following entities:
- Event generating nodes (or event sink): all that is able to produce an event;
- Processing nodes, or Event Processing Agents (EPA), that receive events from different sources and produce other derivative events;
- Connections among nodes, representing the streams of events.

The EPA allow to perform computations on single events (filtering, transformation, completion with existing data) or on sets and partitions of multiple events, grouped on event characteristics or temporal and spatial partitions.

The output of the EPN is composed of one or more events that can be intercepted in order to execute an action (to call a service, a BPM process or a data analysis system).

BPM and Adaptive Case Management

Events coming from the Event Channel, generated by different sources (including external or internal systems, business processes or EPN) can trigger one or more business processes. These processes can be described as a "flow chart", whose constituent elements are activities (human or automatic ones), resources, gateways and events. We could compare business processes to the mental processes that coordinate the actions of our organs, where the resources are the memory, the other organs, and other generated stimuli, able to recall sub-processes that allow, in combination with others, to achieve the goal of the main process.

The BPM has certainly been enriched of adaptive capacities by the Dynamic (or Adaptive) Case Management. As a matter of fact, unlike strict rules, the ACM allows to take advantage of the typical innate human abilities of problem solving and reasoning. Using the ACM, business processes can be composed at run-time, based on the context, the events, the situations, the reasoning and experience that only a skilled human can have. Moreover, the social media tools help to provide a distributed, emerging and therefore more objective knowledge, useful to achieve company goals.

Rule engine

During the process modeling it is possible to set process or activity variables that represent the data in the execution context. These data are then collected, processed and assigned to the activities that form business processes. The assignment is done by means of the Rule Engine, which during the run-time phase, is responsible to assign the values of the variables to the involved activities. The Rule Engine can also be used in other phases, such as validations and assignments of each constituent of the whole system as, for example, in human interaction and in the CEP.

Analysis systems

There can be multiple analysis systems in the iBPM. They can either concern the modeling phase (simulation of business processes or of EPN) or the run-time one (Business Activity Monitoring, Recommender System, run-time analytic tools) and not only they allow system users to monitor the current state of the system or of the processes, but also to make predictions.

The goal of the implementation of these tools is to support both managers and end-users in the decision making, through the automatic extraction of knowledge from data.

Comparative functional analysis

The functional analysis proved that the iBPM ecosystem is intelligent.

Through the evolution of our species in time, nature gave us amazing adaptation tools, one example for all being the nervous system.

Similarly, the iBPM is able to adapt to different business needs through communication, monitoring, forecasting and human interaction tools.

The functional aspects of the two systems can be compared in the following table:

iBPM Ecosystem	Features	Human Nervous System / Body
BPM	Coordinates activities	Encephalon
CEP	Correlates events and data for real-time processing	Encephalon, spinal cord
Data and Activity Analysis System (BAM, Recommender System, Process mining)	Analyses data, in order to optimize resources and activities. Knowledge extraction from data	Encephalon
Sensors, human interfaces, social interaction tools	Receive and generate inputs and signals from internal and external systems	Sense organs and/or organs connected to the peripheral nervous system
Event Channel	Rapidly transmits signals, data and events to different consumers	Peripheral nervous system ,spinal cord, encephalon
SOA	Allows to invoke services for the interaction with internal and external systems	Muscles connected via the nervous system
ACM	Allows to execute processes not completely linked to determined fluxes, but able to adapt to the context	Encephalon
Rule engine	Executes rules on context elements	Spinal cord, encephalon
Simulation tools	Simulate fluxes to optimize processes	Encephalon

HEALTHCARE GOALS

Also in the clinical management exist peripheral systems that must be able to respond effectively to the specific needs of the hospital in different departments.

There are cases in which it is necessary:

- To react promptly, as in first aid or emergency cases.
- To apply strict procedures to understand the disease by the patient symptoms.
- The doctors and nurses interaction and experience to resolve a situation or diagnose a disease or a problem in patients.

Even a hospital or a healthcare organization can be considered a living organism, where it is necessary to communicate from the peripheral to the central system and vice versa, composed by internal and external events, procedures and rules, sensors and actions, analysis, cooperation and coordination. There are management needs, like in Resource Management such as personnel, equipment, facilities, patients, supplies. Management must be able to optimize time, resources and costs but also maximize the satisfaction of patients and staff.

Therefore the goals that must be reached are:
- reducing unnecessary costs to patient care,
- reducing the waiting time of the patient, and
- enhancing service, satisfaction and skills of the patient and medical staff.

These objectives are common to all health institutions in the world, but are different in priorities and methods, based on social, economic, cultural and political environment.

Some issues that we will analyze are already solved in some countries but in other ones are currently a source of great discomfort.

For example, fraud and corruption at all levels of the structure lead to a deterioration of the health services. The reduction of economic resources brings to a lack of personnel, tools, supplies, creating a problems chain that has effects on the patient health and on the healthcare personnel performances.

Creating the conditions for a real economic development, it is possible optimize resources management through mechanisms that include:
- Data retrieval in a paperless environment.
- Medical and administrative staff decision-making support.
- Procedures automation.
- Permanent patients monitoring.

BPM and ACM for the Clinical Intelligence

These issues have already been largely faced and resolved through BPM suites in the past. In fact, in the article "Workflow Opportunities and Challenges in Healthcare" [2], it is clear that the combination of Workflow Engine, Rule Engine and Healthcare Information System not only can meet the needs for time and procedures optimization, but also provides a clinical decision support. In that article, however, was highlighted the need for flexibility in the procedures, which was later resolved by ACM technologies.

The ACM in Healthcare, besides allowing to collect different patient data, allows:
- A direct or asynchronous interaction between doctors, nurses, physiotherapists and laboratory technicians.
- To add or receive elements in a dynamic environment, such as events, chat, attachments, resources, audio / video stream or other social tools for communication.
- To subdivide the case into sub-cases or folder, to be able to navigate easily between the information relating to the case.
- To start sub-procedures based on the choices of the physician (or fragments of processes) required for collecting additional data, such as laboratory tests and x-rays.

The results of these tests may be notified immediately to the physician in order to be able to make a diagnosis in a timely manner to save a life or reduce the time of treatment of a patient.

The ACM, in combination with data analysis classic tools, allows us to realize the "Clinical Intelligence" theories. Clinical Intelligence is the derived knowledge when data of the clinical process is queried, analyzed and understood specifically to the asked question.

The queries can be different and are useful to support both the medical and administrative staff:

- Optimized management of internal processes and care flows.
- Personnel motion and hygiene control, security.
- Food supplies, medicines and equipment control.
- Patients' vital sign check.
- Queue control.
- Risk management (lack of resource, disaster recovery).
- Organization management.
- Procedures management.
- Budget and cost management.

The current focus is on new technologies introduced with iBPM and EDA, on possibilities that technological innovations offer and on some decision-making support techniques related to Machine Learning.

HEALTHCARE PROCESS ANALYSIS AND DECISION-MAKING SUPPORT

The precondition to be able to reduce costs and improve the performance of an entire healthcare enterprise is the data retrieval. In order to perform the analysis, report fraud, monitor the status and give suggestions it is necessary to collect data from structured sources (Databases, systems) or unstructured ones (Log files) and be able to track or detect at run-time the tools and resources movement and the use. For example, by using appropriate sensors, it is possible both to generate events during the objects or persons interaction and to send the patient vital signs to the central system.

The current NFC technology, now also available on mobile devices, allows patient remote monitoring thereby reducing the time and cost. A blood testing microchip, implanted under the skin can be used to give an early warning of an heart attack, or monitor cancer patients having chemotherapy.

The NFC also allows us to trace the drugs used in the treatment [3], replacing in some cases the bar-codes. This type of technology can be used both in health care facilities and in domestic environments, eliminating the problems related to hospital overcrowding.

Mobile technologies also allow a two-way interaction in which the patient can be followed by a physician or trained automatically on self-care. These data can be used for simple elaborations, such as reminder activation in the patient's home care (schedule alert to take a pill, do physical activities etc.) but also complex elaborations, such as CEP based rules that allow to detect at real time huge risks for the health of patients.

The CEP, for example, can avoid false alarms because it is able to consider different sensors signals and context elements in a time window. So, only if different conditions are satisfied in a time interval, an alarm will be sent to the sanitary personnel.

Process Mining and CEP in the Care flow Management

The process mining allows us to recognize the most common processes in a hospital in a highly complex environment from the data logs. Indeed, depending on the patient and the diagnosis, there are different clinical pathways involving different departments and equipment. Usually the mined process instances are used to obtain the process models that can be executed on demand.

In the paper "Clinical Intelligence, Complex Event Processing and Process Mining in Process-Aware EMR / EHR BPM Systems" [4] it is possible to observe how the BPM EHR systems through the CEP and the process mining can be used to:

- model and understand the workflow,
- coordinate the steps in the activities of patient care,
- monitor task execution at real time, and
- improve systematically the clinical workflow and results.

The need to have the most dynamic systems in the healthcare environment is quite well described [5] and is applied in solutions that allow to have typical workflow control, but with the flexibility needed for a dynamic environment. This paper highlighted that one workflow scenario should consider the spatial, temporal context, and the resources required to achieve a goal, using process mining to get the rapidly changing processes.

The idea, that is carried forward in this paper, allows to "compose" the workflow in a supervised manner when they need for, led by a domain expert (in this case is a physician or a health director), that can manage dynamically exceptions.

This "Human Expert Centric" vision is consistent with ACM, and the knowledge workers are at the center of decisions, and have all the tools to understand the patient status, his anamnesis, the healthcare setting status, the events that are triggered at run-time, that can affect their choices and reactions.

The reactions to these choices not only allow to call to a simple service, but can start different processes, in a decoupled way, usually generating an event. The interaction between these systems makes the system at the same time dynamic but structured, flexible but controlled, agile but manageable, efficient and effective.

Moreover, the iBPM technologies, not only allow to support the health personnel decisions, assisting in the phases of care of a patient, but also to monitor and report faults in the patient treatment phase and personnel and supplies movements sequences. The real-time analysis is able to provide a tool to monitor the overall status at run-time for health directors and to manage both the normal flow and exceptions, disasters, risks.

Then we will show how flexible tools that take into account the context are useful for decision-making support.

Diagnosis and Clinical Pathway Recommender System

The Rule Engine limitations for decision-making support about the diagnosis are:

- They are based on preset rules that may change over time based on new scientific discoveries or technologies and treatment techniques.
- Do not consider the previous context.
- They are not very flexible if there is lack of data.

There are different techniques able to support the decisions based on data, on past experience, on the context. Among these techniques are very effective the Case Based Recommender Systems that allow us to suggest the clinical case more similar to that examined according to the context values.

These values can be the test results, vital signs detected by sensors, the patient personal data, his anamnesis and the treatment performed. All these context data, collected in an ACM case folder, can be compared automatically with the previous cases, selecting the more similar ones. According to an objective function that consider different parameters (hospitalization duration minimization, results of patient recovery maximizing, costs minimization, etc..), it is possible to sort this case list positioning the better cases on his top.

Usually Recommender Systems do not consider, however, the semantics of descriptive fields that, in this case, are the descriptions inserted by the health personnel after the medical examinations or tests. This problem was solved using the semantic similarity computational techniques applied to text fields combined with the calculation of similarity between cases.

A recommendation system of this type, allows to recommend a diagnosis based not only on the current data, but also based on the step of the clinical pathway that is performing, comparing the data with the other procedures, suggesting the variations that lead to the best results.

HEALTHCARE FRAUD AND RISK MANAGEMENT

In the previous section we dealt with supporting healthcare professionals in choices, optimizing and automating processes, thus reducing costs. Now we are dealing with another kind of waste, that is due to fraud or lack in risk management. Fraud can be carried out in all stages of the patient's care, from the prescription to the discharge.

Frauds reported are:
- A supplies refund higher than the real one, due to the falsification of identification codes and forged prescriptions.
- False analysis and unnecessary surgery.
- Passing patients on another hospital for personal profit.
- Absenteeism.

In the past studies were carried out for fraud detection using techniques related to the statistical and Artificial Intelligence [6].

The traceability of all resources (human or not), the traceability of patients and their care, is a necessary step to detect problems or fraud.

For instance, using a smart card with a digital identity chip (in the future a chip implanted under the skin), it's easy to identify medical personnel, paramedics and patients. Through an RFID or NFC antenna is possible to trace all movements of any resource, through bar-code is also possible to identify equipment, medicines or any other object.

A unified identification, a centralized management of the supplies and iBPM technologies, can cut down the risk of fraud and provide a better service for patients and for the healthcare personnel.

The events generated by these systems constitute a part of the event cloud that we are able to intercept, monitor, then make inferences and react. Instead, another part of the events is generated by the internal systems, by devices such as tablets or mobile phones which also constitute the supports able to receive the output of the possible processing. These processors are CEP and BPM that may be also generate events reinserted in the event cloud for further treatment.

The CEP Engine in collaboration with BPM Engine through Event Channel allows us to recognize the risks and frauds and then react in timely manner. In order to create a solution is necessary to:
- make interview or research in order to analyze the scenario and needs,
- understand what are the available technological and informative resources,

- hypothesize conditions or rules that allow fraud and risk detection,
- hypothesize reaction to the previous condition

But what kind of CEP rules or conditions could we express in healthcare scenarios?

It depends on goals and available data, but some examples could be:

1. Detection of fraud or waste through a statistical calculation of the excesses of the treatments compared with diagnosis. If the count of specific treatments exceeds a threshold then the medical director is alerted by the system.
2. If the number of supplies (medicines, equipment) is higher than what is used, then there is a theft risk.
3. If the number of supplies is higher than the average compared to the average beds plus a certain threshold, then there is a theft risk,
4. If the staff which is in service does not provide a frequency of detections higher than a certain threshold, then there exists an absenteeism risk.
5. If after more than a certain time the heart signal is not received, then an alarm alerts for the risk of cardiac arrest.
6. If the number of emergency room receptions with high priority is higher than a certain number, then the ambulance must be redirected to another hospital.
7. If the number of vacation requests in a certain period in the same department is above a certain threshold, then it is necessary to replace the staff or reorganizing the department.
8. If the cycle of sterilization of equipment is not complete or are not carried out some phases detected by proximity sensors, then the tool can be infected [7].
9. If a doctor prescribes a kind of medication to a patient and the nurse makes a mistake when she brings the medicine to the proximity sensor, then the error will be reported to the nurse.
10. If a patient is allergic to certain substances and the nurse gets the drug containing one of the dangerous substances close to the proximity sensor, the nurse is warned.
11. If the doctor prescribes medicines of the same brand more than the average, then it is possible that they are prescribed to the detriment of public health (or insurance) to get benefits (amounts in cash, trips, etc.) by a pharmaceutical company.

CONCLUSIONS

The BPM Suites are evolving by incorporating techniques and technologies taken from other fields or areas, as it happens for the sciences. The interaction between these technologies can satisfy the needs of an organization through the optimization, forecasting, automation also in very complex or dynamic scenarios. Nanotechnology allows us to produce and exchange information at an acceptable cost, while the ability to process huge data volumes and automatically extract knowledge at run-time allows us to find experiences, solutions and useful information to make the right decision.

REFERENCES

[1] Intelligence definition, http://en.wikipedia.org/wiki/Intelligence

[2] Jonathan Emanuele and Lura Koetter, Siemens Medical Solutions USA, "Workflow Opportunities and Challenges in Healthcare", 2007 BPM and Workflow Handbook, Edited by Layna Fischer, Future Strategies Inc., Lighthouse Point, FL, USA

[3] Rian Boden, "Harvard Medical School develops NFC medication tracking system", NFC word, http://www.nfcworld.com/2013/04/04/323325/harvard-medical-school-develops-nfc-medication-tracking-system/

[4] Charlie Webster MD, "Clinical Intelligence, Complex Event Processing and Process Mining in Process-Aware EMR / EHR BPM Systems", http://chuck-webster.com/2011/07/clinical-intelligence/clinical-intelligence-complex-event-processing-process-mining-process-aware-emr-ehr-bpm-systems

[5] H. Dominic Covvey, Donald D. Cowan, Paulo Alencar, William Malyk, Joel So, David Henriques and Shirley L. Fenton, "The Representation of Dynamic, Context-Informed Workflow", 2008 BPM & Workflow Handbook, Edited by Layna Fischer, Future Strategies Inc., Lighthouse Point, FL, USA

[6] Jing Li & Kuei-Ying Huang & Jionghua Jin & Jianjun Shi," A survey on statistical methods for health care fraud detection", Springer Science + Business Media, LLC 2007, http://www.public.asu.edu/~jli09/publications/HCMS2008_survey.pdf

[7] Mo Liu, Medhabi Ray, Dazhi Zhang, Elke A. Rundensteiner, Daniel J. Dougherty, "Realtime Healthcare Services Via Nested Complex Event Processing Technology", Worcester Polytechnic Institute, Worcester, MA 01609, USA

http://www.edbt.org/Proceedings/2012-Berlin/papers/edbt/a62-ray.pdf

Marketing Intelligent BPM to Healthcare Intelligently

Charles Webster, MD, MSIE, MSIS

ABSTRACT

Health information technology (HIT) professionals who learn about business process management (BPM) technology are usually impressed. Nonetheless, BPM has been slow to diffuse into healthcare. HIT has technologies corresponding to some BPM suite core components. But process orchestration engines remain rare. Fortunately, there are signs that the HIT market is entering a period of greater need and appreciation for BPM ideas, products, and services. I describe the current state of affairs within the health IT industry and suggest how BPM vendors can engage, educate, and communicate, about BPM's unique value to healthcare and health IT.

INTRODUCTION

Health information technology (HIT) professionals who learn about business process management (BPM) systems and suites (BPMS) and related process-aware technologies are usually impressed with their potential to manage and improve healthcare processes. Business process management and process-aware information systems, including offshoots such as adaptive case management and process mining, are relevant to central issues of healthcare reform: identification of best practices, coordination of care, consistency across processes, and efficient use of resources.

Nonetheless, BPM has been slow to diffuse into healthcare. HIT has technologies corresponding to some BPMS core components, but engines executing executable process models remain rare. Fortunately, the HIT market is entering a period of greater need for, and receptivity to, BPM-related concepts and software. Making a successful pitch to healthcare, for applying BPM tech around and at the point of care, requires an educational approach that addresses healthcare workflow's unique pain points.

The following is an exercise in "meta-marketing." If marketing is communicating value of BPM to healthcare, then meta-marketing is about communicating to you how to do so successfully. In this essay I recount what I say about BPM to interested healthcare audiences and consider how we can improve marketing from BPM into healthcare. I'll talk about the health IT "wall"; opportunities and obstacles for BPM in healthcare; how to hone the "intelligent" BPM message; and a program to educate, highlight, and recruit health IT and BPM stakeholders.

HEALTHCARE NEEDS BUSINESS PROCESS MANAGEMENT

When addressing a healthcare audience, I may start out this way:

> "Mobile, social, cloud, big data, etc. move over: PAIS.
>
> Process-aware information systems (PAIS) ideas and technology — workflow management, business process management (BPM), and adaptive case management systems — are diffusing into healthcare from other industries. A Process-Aware Information System is 'a software system that manages and executes operational processes involving people, applications,

and/or information sources on the basis of process models.' The best known PAIS is a business process management system or suite.

[...BPM 101 and healthcare specific use cases...]

Takeaways include a powerful new idea (the executable process model), examples of successful applications of PAISs in healthcare, and a positive but skeptical attitude useful for further investigation. The next big idea in healthcare IT is the process-aware information system."

Healthcare is like a very large country that has been closed off to the rest of the IT world for decades. It's been so large, so well-funded, so lacking in market-competitive forces that it's not had to invest in workflow technology. While healthcare automated workflows, it didn't use true (that is, process-aware) workflow automation.

We (I'm now speaking as a longtime health IT professional) have no way to represent (and edit and improve) healthcare workflow so it can be designed and executed without requiring computer programmers to hardcode it. Today, "workflow" is spread throughout the implementation code of every electronic health record (EHR) and HIT application involved in this workflow. EHR and HIT-mediated interactions, inside hospitals and clinics and outside with patients and payers, are fragile, prone to ambiguity, don't cross organizational boundaries well, and scale badly. In fact, the more we automate healthcare workflows with workflow-oblivious software, the more static healthcare workflows become and the harder it is to propagate change and new players into these workflows.

Current health IT workflow-oblivious EHRs and health IT systems are hitting a wall. Tens of billions of dollars of subsidies are being paid to hospitals and physicians to convince them to "adopt" (with an unintended, but ironically accurate connotation that these systems would "orphans" otherwise) health IT systems that slow them down, whose workflow can't be changed or improved, and are losing their users money.

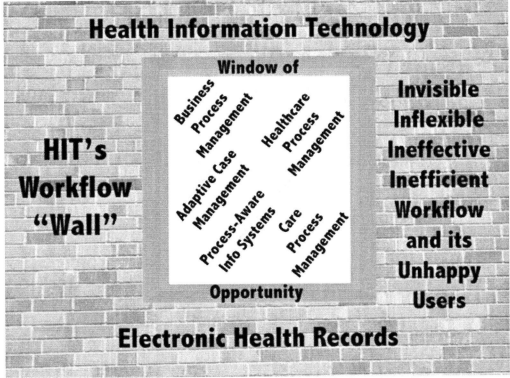

Health Information Technology

Window of

Business Process Management

Healthcare Process Management

Adaptive Case Management

Process-Aware Info Systems

Care Process Management

HIT's Workflow "Wall"

Invisible Inflexible Ineffective Inefficient Workflow and its Unhappy Users

Opportunity

Electronic Health Records

Health IT's Workflow Wall and BPM's Opportunity

The health IT "wall" has a window of opportunity in it for proponents of BPM (including adaptive case management and process mining). Health IT is increasingly arguing with itself about "What went wrong?"

"What went wrong" was that health IT prematurely settled on, and then locked into, workflow-oblivious structured-document management information systems, instead of modern process-aware workflow management.

Health IT focuses on representing data and manipulating data, leading to emphasis on meta-data, data about data. This is fine, as far as it goes. It's just that it doesn't go far enough and it is not sufficient to address healthcare's thorny problems of (lack of) productivity, inflexible workflows, and unhappy users. The only way to systemically improve workflow is to represent workflow, and then think hard about steps to improve workflow. Just as data about data is meta-data and thinking about thinking is meta-cognition, workflow of workflow is meta-workflow. And thinking about meta-workflow in healthcare, health IT and medical informatics is sorely deficient.

Attempts to educate healthcare and health IT about the workflow of workflow will fail unless education is wrapped around healthcare and clinical use cases. This is why it is so important to find and highlight use cases at the border between healthcare and BPM. One source is examples where BPM vendor supplied technology has been applied to an area of interest within healthcare. In some cases, business process management is rebranded as healthcare or care process management. However, there is also another source. While healthcare is literally decades behind other industries when it comes to applying workflow technology, it's also large and varied. There are some homegrown health information workflow management systems and products. But they are infrequent, unknown, and under-appreciated.

There's a potential common cause among health IT vendors who have self-developed workflow engine, process model-oriented platforms one hand and BPM vendors who have provided or adapted their workflow platform to healthcare purposes on the other. Why? The importance of achieving a critical mass of pro-BPM voices and the importance of clinical and healthcare-specific content and workflow. Healthcare data and workflow is idiosyncratic and confusing. It can take years of try-and-try again before a traditional health IT solution can be deemed successful and achieve market traction (regardless of whether it "gets" workflow or not).

Healthcare IT buyers don't want "empty" BPM software, just as they did not want "empty" EHRs in the early years of that industry. EHRs (then called EMRs) lacked lists of drugs and diagnoses, forcing early adopters to have to enter this content for themselves. Most current BPM software does not come with already created and road-tested clinical and healthcare workflow. This is why we are seeing BPM used first in healthcare in those areas that most resemble content in other industries, such as human resources, insurance and other routine "paper work". As these back-of-the-house systems are implemented, their implementers, familiar with other, more clinically and healthcare specific domains, are recognizing the potential for applying process-aware information systems closer and closer to the point of care.

Meanwhile, some (though not many, mind you) indigenous health IT vendors, have also implemented workflow engines and represented workflows (workflows represented as structured data in a database where it can be inspected, executed, and improved). While these workflow management systems may not have all of the bells and whistles of a pure-play BPM suite, they do have one advantage: healthcare and, in some cases, clinically-specific content.

By common cause between health IT and BPM I don't necessarily mean partnerships between specific EHR or HIT vendors and BPM vendors, though this is beginning to happen. I do mean that a rising tide of interest and understanding of process-aware technology, such as BPM, benefits both "native" health IT workflow vendors and BPM vendors.

THE TOP TEN REASONS BPM HAS BEEN SLOW TO DIFFUSE INTO HEALTHCARE

The issue we have right now is how to get that figurative light bulb to start going off over health IT heads. If we are to successfully connect and combine two different universes of discourse (as the linguists say) we really do need to drill down into the nitty-gritty of what has been retarding diffusion of BPM into healthcare. I've already alluded to some of these following. But it's worth to more formally and explicitly layout the conditions of the terrain we attempt to traverse.

1. *Workflow Complexity*: Complicated data and simple workflow is complicated. Simple data and complicated workflow is complicated. Healthcare's complicated data and complicated workflow is hyper-complicated.

2. *No Cost Competition*: In other industries, companies are forced to adopt technology to optimize workflow to minimize cost while maximizing flexibility.

3. *Regulatory Environment*: EHR and HIT vendors are stretched thin addressing Meaningful Use requirements.

4. *Screens vs. Workflow*: It's easier to appreciate EHR screens (layout of data and controls over space) than workflow functionality (sequences of events over time).

5. *Threat to Revenue Streams*: Switching to new platforms is risky and threatens current revenue streams.

6. *Billing Over Clinical Emphasis*: As long as the right codes are generated to maximize revenue, nothing else matters.

7. *Skeuomorphism*: Misguided attempts to model EHR user interfaces on paper medical record forms.

8. *Workflow Stereotypes*: Workflow management systems and business process management once emphasized automating human users out of processes. Not true now!

9. *Not Invented Here-ism*: Medical informatics (for which I designed the first undergraduate curriculum) is, in it's own way, as insular relative to informatics research outside of healthcare, as health IT is to the larger IT world.

10. *Paradigm Shifts*: You stick with a paradigm unless you're forced to change. Health IT picked a document-based, instead of workflow-based, paradigm.

One of these top ten reasons is worth discussing further.

6. *Billing Over Clinical Emphasis*: As long as the right codes are generated to maximize revenue, nothing else matters.

So many healthcare and health IT stakeholders invested so much, and convinced so many others to invest so much, in current health IT models, that there is considerable resistance of admitting that current structured document management systems, with human users having to simulate workflow engines, have failed. So the argument is made that it's not health IT's fault. It's incentives. While I agree that incentives play an important role, they are not the only cause of health IT's current predicament.

The following is adapted from my blog post titled *Fixing Our Health IT Mess: Are Business Models or Technology Models to Blame?*

[begin blog post extract]

You may not agree with me that Health IT is a mess. Check out my sentiment analysis of Twitter's reaction to the New York Times coverage of the recent RAND report. You'll at least agree that many people do agree with me.

That said, reasons offered for the mess are all over the map. You can read my summary. I'll focus on one defense of Health IT: It's the business model, not the technology. Sometimes it's put differently, as in: It's the incentive model, not the technology. But business models are all about incentives: to create a business, to sustain a business, to do business with a business.

So, to those who say it's the business model, not the technology, I say the opposite: It is, in fact, the technology model, not the business model.

I'm a fan of business and models. I understand the importance of financial incentives to mold behavior. I have degrees in accountancy and industrial engineering, the spiritual homes of cost, revenue, and profit engineering and performance-based incentive systems.

But, no matter how much you persuade, pay, or punish frozen workflows, they won't change. You have to unfreeze the workflows, change them, and then refreeze them. Most current EHR and health IT systems have relatively frozen workflows. They don't have the necessary innards: workflow engines, process definitions, graphical editors, or similar means to achieve similar ends. Process-aware systems include workflow management systems, business process management and adaptive case management. Executable and malleable workflow is what these systems do. It's the opposite state of affairs in the EHR and health IT world.

The problems of Meaningful Use [a Federal subsidy program for EHRs] are entirely predictable through the lens of the infamous Iron Triangle anti-pattern of software development. Attempting to bring too many features to market too soon usually results in unstable, less usable, and hard to maintain software.

Wait, you say. Why can't we add resources? You can. Up to a point. At the beginning of a software project, adding the right programmer or two can be helpful. The problem is, as the number of personnel grows, you run into Fred Brooks' most enduring law: "Adding manpower to a late software project makes it later."

There is no way out of the Iron Triangle. You can only make it bigger. It should be renamed the Carbon Nanotube Triangle (strongest, lightest material known). You can change the triangle's shape by shifting emphases among features, schedule, and resources. And you can change its size through technological innovation. So far we've been trying to do the former, mostly via stakeholders asking, begging, demanding that we slow down. Some innovators nibble at the problem, creating workarounds and crafting end-runs: EHR-lite, EHR-extenders, mEHR etc.

The only way to increase the size of the Iron Triangle (to deliver more and better features sooner) is to change what economists call the "factors of production". In this case the factors are the software technologies we use to attempt to meet the requirements of Meaningful Use.

Most EHRs and many HIT systems are based on structured documents represented in relational databases. What do users of Meaningful Use certified EHRs complain about? Workflow! It's the wrong workflow. It's laborious workflow. The workflow doesn't fit their specialty or special needs. The workflow can't be changed. The workflow slows them down.

Well? If the problem is workflow and we aren't using workflow technology, maybe we *should* use workflow technology? This seems so obvious that one must ask: Why hasn't it already happened? I cover that in Top Ten Reasons EHR-BPM Tech Is Not (Yet) Widely Deployed in Healthcare.

To expand the Iron Triangle we need to move from structured document management systems to structured workflow management systems. Workflow management systems have been used in other industries since the mid-nineties. With improvements and complementary technology (business activity monitoring, process mining, simulation, graphical editors, adaptive and adaptable workflows) workflow management became business process management and adaptive case management.

I agree that even malleable systems won't change and improve unless they are caused to do so by outside forces. Business and incentive models play a role here. But frozen systems won't change even in the face of those outside forces. Our current workflows can't change because they aren't modeled, reasoned about, executed, tracked and improved. EHR workflows are frozen. We need to unfreeze these workflows to, if not escape from Iron Triangle, at least expand it to accommodate our goals and needs.

To those who say it's the business model, not the technology, I say the opposite: It's the technology model, not the business model.

[end blog post extract]

Cloud, mobile, social, and data technologies, which health IT looks toward importing into healthcare, often rely on process-aware technologies. For example, when innovators look to cloud and mobile for EHR alternatives, workarounds, and wrappers, they also get the process-aware technology that makes cloud and mobile workable. Secure, flexible, scalable, context- and process-aware cloud-based backends will be key to secure, flexible, scalable, context- and process-aware front-end mobile apps used by patients and healthcare providers. BPM vendors are further along than HIT vendors in use of cloud, mobile, and social technology. So: cloud, mobile, and social will be important "vectors" for transport of BPM's process-aware ideas and technologies into healthcare.

INTELLIGENT BPM VS. INTELLIGENT HEALTHCARE BPM

What about that "intelligent" in front of BPMS in the title of this chapter? (Well, then, what about the "intelligently" at the end, too?) I've been holding off addressing this adjective, as there is some debate within the BPM industry about what is "intelligent BPM." When I present BPM ideas to a healthcare audience I usually use a list similar to this:

1. Executable process models
2. Codeless development
3. Content management
4. Groupware-based collaboration
5. Connectivity
6. Event-driven processes
7. Process intelligence and monitoring
8. Simulation and optimization
9. Business rule management
10. Process component archives

Some of the components of this depiction of intelligent BPM systems correspond to rudimentary systems and subsystems already familiar to EHR and health IT professionals. Many EHRs have built-in document management systems (3) or use third-party software. Many EHRs manage clinical rules (9) as part of their clinical decision support functionality (some mandated). Interoperability (5) among EHRs and HIT systems is generally recognized and increasingly achieved. Business intelligence (7) and componentized architectures (10) are increasingly popular talk about. However, BPM's core technology innovation, a process execution and statement management engine (that is, a workflow engine executing process definitions) and "end-to-end" business intelligence made possible by process mining, have not yet had impact, let alone achieved significant mindshare.

In summary, some BPM-related technologies have counterparts in healthcare IT. Others are just beginning to appear. Regardless of maturity of individual technology, perhaps the BPM suite's greatest value is as a model for how all of these technologies can fit together.

But I'd really like to take discussion of "intelligent" healthcare BPM in a slightly different direction. So as to not compete in current debates about "intelligent" BPM,

I'll use the more colloquial "smart." And I'll telegraph my punch with a rhetorical question and answer.

Question: Do We Need Smarter Users or Smarter User Interfaces?

Answer: Smarter User Interfaces.

Consider the distinction between intuitable EHRs and HIT systems (systems "figure-outable" by their users) versus truly intuitive EHRs and HIT systems (systems that figure out their users and do something useful with that insight). Intuitable usability corresponds to what I call shallow usability. It's the "surface" or skin of an EMR.

In contrast, intuitive usability (used "correctly") corresponds to what I call deep usability. It is about how all the components and processes deep down behind the user interface actively work together, to perceive user context and intentions, reason and problem solve, and then proactively anticipate user needs and wants. Deep usability is like having the hyper-competent operating room nurse handing you the right data review or order entry screen, with the right data and options, at the right moment in your workflow.

To perceive, reason, and act (let alone learn) EHRs and HIT systems need at least a rudimentary "brain." When many folks think of medical artificial intelligence, they think of medical expert systems or natural language processing systems (rule-based, connectionist, or statistical). However, the most practical candidate "brain" today, with which to improve usability by improving workflow, is the modern process-aware (and context-aware) business process management (BPM) engine (AKA workflow or process engine).

Intuitive EHRs and HIT systems need to represent user goals and tasks and execute a loop of event perception, reasoning, and helpful action. BPM process definitions represent goals and tasks. During definition execution, goal and task states are tracked (available to start, started, completed, postponed, cancelled, referred, executed, etc.) and used to coordinate system-to-system, user-to-system, system-to-user, and user-to-user activity.

BPM engines "perceive" by reacting to not just user-initiated events, but potentially other environmental events as well, an example of complex event processing. For example, a patient entering or leaving a patient class or category, going on or off a clinical protocol or regime, moving into or out of compliance, measuring or needing to measure a clinical value, or a clinical value becoming controlled or not controlled, are all complex events that can and often should trigger automated workflow.

Smart EHRs and HIT systems are adaptive, responsive, proactive, and capable of autonomous action.

- "Adaptive systems: these learn their user's preferences and adjust accordingly....
- Responsive systems: these anticipate the user's needs in a changing environment.
- Proactive systems: these are goal-oriented, capable of taking the initiative, rather than just reacting to the environment.
- Autonomous systems: these can act independently, without human intervention."[1]

Learn, anticipate, goal-oriented, initiative, independent...none of these describe the behavior of today's typical EHR or HIT system towards its users. As a consequence

---

[1] http://ubiquity.acm.org/article.cfm?id=764011

physicians must compensate with a torrent of clicks (so-called "clickorrhea") to push and pull these EHR and HIT systems through what should be simple interactions.

What "drives" this smart behavior? An executable process model. In older terminology, a workflow, or process, engine, executes a collection of workflow, or process, definitions, relying on user input and context (the who, what, why, when, where, and how) to select and control definition execution. If the engine encounters inputs for which there is no model, then fall back on general purpose adaptive case management techniques for tracking goals and tasks, making them visible and actionable by physician users. Traditional BPM technology automates the predictably routine. More recent adaptive case management supports dealing with unpredictable exceptions—the high value-added knowledge work that diagnoses and treats the complicated cases.

Usability can't be "added" to today's EHRs and HIT systems. It has to inform and influence the very first design decisions. And there are no more fundamental early design decisions than what paradigm to adopt and platform to use. No matter how "intuitable," EMRs and HIT systems without executable process models become, they cannot become fully active and helpful members of the patient care team. Wrong paradigm. Wrong platform.

A truly smart EHR or HIT systems, on the other hand, has a brain, variously called a BPM, workflow, or process engine. This is the necessary platform for delivering context-aware intelligent user interfaces and user experience to the point of care. Right paradigm. Right platform.

HOW CAN WE ACCELERATE DIFFUSION OF BPM IN HEALTHCARE?

I recently gave a webinar (viewable on YouTube[2]) called The Power of Process: Workflow, BPM, and Healthcare. Here's the outline:
- The need for workflow/BPM in healthcare
- How other verticals are using these technologies to their benefit
- Use cases in the clinical space
- Use cases concerning supporting/operational processes
- First steps to implementing workflow/BPM

I won't rehash my webinar here, as it's basically BPM 101 (but you may be interested in its clinical and healthcare scenarios). What I will include here, though, are a couple slides and the questions provoked from webinar attendees.

---

[2] http://ehr.bz/chuckyoutube

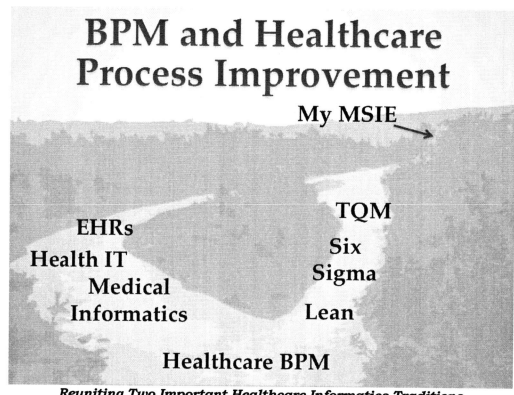

BPM and Healthcare Process Improvement

My MSIE

EHRs
Health IT
Medical
Informatics

TQM
Six
Sigma
Lean

Healthcare BPM

Reuniting Two Important Healthcare Informatics Traditions

Here's what I say:

"Now, I imagine we may have some healthcare process improvement folks out there, so what is the relationship between BPM and the healthcare process improvement? Back when I got my masters in industrial engineering (around the bend of that river), management engineers worked in hospitals and elsewhere, and they were involved in both sides of an equation. They measured and improved workflow, and created and implemented information systems. I worked in a hospital information systems department where the payroll system had been developed and implemented and managed by a management engineer, an industrial engineer.

Then what happened is a bunch of folks went off and started developing electronic health records, and other health IT systems, and you've got this research behind it, which is medical informatics. I don't think they spent enough energy and time thinking about workflow problems and workflow theories and creating workflow tools.

Meanwhile, over on the other side, we've got the Total Quality Management folks, Six Sigma and Lean. They're finding the causes of errors. They're finding the sources of variation and eliminating it. They're figuring how to do the same amount of work but with less waste. Well, more-and-more work is actually done in a kind of a mind-meld with the software. We really need to knit together these two traditions and I think that the healthcare business process management hybrid is a way to do that."

And here's what I say about the following slide:

"One more thing, I love hearing workflow success stories regardless of whether they involved workflow engines or not. I've created a directory on my Twitter account—@wareFLO—website at EHRworkflow.com. POW!HIT! stands for People and Organizations improving Workflow with Health Information Technology."

What's Your Story?

http://ehrworkflow.com/powhit

People and Organizations Improving Workflow with Health Information Technology

I hope you can see what I am doing. I'm appealing to two important constituencies, health IT and healthcare process improvement. And I'm asking for stories about healthcare workflow. Stories can move people. That "exploding" POW!HIT! is actually a badge, of different sizes, you can download if I've featured you as a POW!HIT! Profile.

I answered webinar questions, to the best of my ability, extemporaneously. I won't include those answers here. What's important are the questions themselves, and your answer to them, if you are a BPM vendor looking to market and sell into healthcare.

1. Who needs to be the champion of workflow? Is it the physician, the nurse, administration, IT, what's your thought?

2. Are there specific examples of high value, low complexity workflows that you can think of as low-hanging fruits?

3. How would you manage the 'But we're special,' pushback," most BPM theory gets from clinical care teams?

4. Could you comment on the similarities and differences at BPM within organizations versus across organizations?

5. How do we use this in inpatient flow management when the applications like ER systems, bed management systems and utilization management systems are all un-integrated?

6. Is Lean as a good first pass for healthcare entities looking to explore BPM?

If you are a business process management vendor, or a dynamic/adaptive case management vendor, or both, and you are interested in marketing to the healthcare and health IT market, a good answer to any of these questions might be a great place to start. That is, once you get past BPM 101. You may be able to think of even better questions. If so, fantastic!

To sum up BPM's excellent opportunity in healthcare:

- Business process management (BPM) and adaptive case management (ACM) vendors are eager to partner with healthcare organizations and vendors. Many already do substantial healthcare business, though usually not at the point-of-care (yet).
- EHR users are restive, increasingly critical of the workflow-challenged systems they feel forced or bribed to use. Their professional organizations ask whether too much has been attempted too soon and with inadequate technology.
- Some EHR and HIT vendors have more customizable workflows than others. They may not think of themselves as EHR or HIT workflow management systems or EHR/HIT BPM systems, but in effect they are becoming so.

Therefore, the next steps to intelligently market intelligent business process management into healthcare are:

- Leverage existing BPM and adaptive case management vendor products and services. Especially emphasize healthcare BPM case studies.
- Educate EHR users and HIT buyers so they can recognize systems with the more customizable workflows. Use social media and complementary methods to get process-aware ideas and technology noticed, discussed, absorbed, and acted upon.
- Find and highlight EHR and HIT vendors with the right stuff: workflow engines, process definitions, graphical editors, plus other valuable BPM-like and -compatible products and services.

As I wrote in the beginning to this piece, business process management and process-aware information systems, including offshoots such as adaptive case management and process mining, are relevant to central issues of healthcare reform: identification of best practices, coordination of care, consistency across processes, and efficient use of resources. BPM has a convincing story to tell healthcare, about designing, implementing, executing, monitoring, and optimizing healthcare processes. We just need to educate healthcare, and address its unique workflow pain points, more forcefully and with ever more compelling examples of healthcare BPM.

How to Make Mobile BPM Robust and Intelligent

Dirk Draheim, University of Innsbruck, Austria
Theodorich Kopetzky, SCCH GmbH, Austria
Josef Küng, FAW GmbH, Austria

ABSTRACT

In many of today's companies mobile computing has become a success factor. Those that work in the field need support by enterprise IT services, i.e., access to enterprise data and appropriate IT applications. Network availability is crucial and the quality of network access determines which IT support can be offered by detached devices. What if some Internet and Email access plus some office automation is not enough for our mobile work forces? What if we want to fully exploit important chunks of our process-based enterprise applications in the field? There is still no single BPM suite available that systematically handles the problem of disconnecting and reconnecting clients in a smart way. As we now from many discussions in CIO cycles, in practice only ad-hoc solutions, e.g., based on ECM systems or public mail folders, are used to deal at least with the data facet of the described problem. However, with these ad-hoc solutions a smart treatment of distributed workflow state is nigh on impossible.

In this paper we show a possible way out of the dilemma. We have realized a workflow enactment service as part of a concrete ERP (enterprise resource planning) system project that creates a sweet spot between the robustness of IT centralization and the flexibility of IT distribution. The crucial requirement and trigger of this technology simply was that traveling business agents can continue to work with their supporting enterprise applications even if they are disconnected from the enterprise IT infrastructure. Key characteristics of the solution are mobile and intelligent data and workflow state synchronization mechanisms. Beyond the possible smart realization of mobile BPM, we are particularly interested in the business value facet, i.e., the total economic impact of mobile BPM in this paper.

INTRODUCTION

Mobile computing has become a mission-critical success factor in many of today's companies. This is so for conventional mobile work forces like salesmen and the work forces in all the service-based industries. It becomes more and more important as work organization changes in modern enterprises towards decentralization and flexibility – telework, telecommuting, workplace sharing or the knowledge worker and even BYOD (bring your own device) are all buzz words with respect to this. Those that work in the field need support by enterprise IT services, i.e., access to enterprise data and appropriate IT applications, to get their tasks done. In the simplest case the employee needs some master data that he can easily hold on his laptop and maintain from time to time plus some appropriate office automation tools. But what if an employee wants to exploit the process-based enterprise applications in the field? Network availability is crucial and the quality of network access determines which IT support can be offered by detached devices. If network access were ubiquitous (Weiser 1991), we had no problem. Unfortunately, it is not – despite the ever increasing bandwidths, pervasion and stability of available wide area networks. Actually, the question of whether we need innovative architectures for enabling smart offline work or whether it is rendered obsolete boils down to the question of network ubiquity. However, at each point in time network ubiquity in the sense of our discussion is only given if the quality of service of the available wide area network keeps pace with the quality of service of the exploited enterprise networks. Only future will tell.

In this paper we discuss a concrete distributed workflow management system architecture that balances robustness of centralized services vs. the flexibility of distributed intelligent clients. The system has been designed in a concrete ERP (enterprise resource planning) project in the insurance domain. The concrete problem was that traveling business agents needed to work with the workflows of the central ERP system during their business trips even if they are disconnected from the enterprise IT infrastructure.

The realized workflow enactment service deals with both the data and workflow state facet of the described problem. It has intelligent data and workflow state synchronization mechanisms as key characteristics. It is realized as a module of a single, concrete ERP system. This means that it is currently about a neat overall design pattern or architectural pattern for process-intensive IT applications. However, conceptually, it is important that it can easily be turned into a generalized architecture for BPM suites if combined with features for code distribution resp. client-side software package management. This is the story told in the second part of this paper. Furthermore, an overall aim of this paper is to shed some light onto the business value of mobile BPM which has to be discussed against the background of the ever increasing importance of BPM in future organizations in general (Draheim 2010, Rivkin 2009). But first, let us delve into a succinct description of the PreVolution system.

THE PREVOLUTION WORKFLOW MANAGEMENT ARCHITECTURE

The PreVolution system (Auer et.al 2013) was built in a project at the AUVA (Austrian Social Insurance Company for Occupational Risks) which is a major Austrian insurance company serving a total of more than 4 million customers. One of AUVA's core missions is the prevention of occupational risks. Therefore, AUVA supports their corporate customers with occupational health and safety consulting as well as surveillance services. It is the task of AUVA experts to visit customer companies where they asses working conditions and workplace safety in order to recommend or, if necessary, even require improvements.

The PreVolution application is the central ERP system for maintaining corporate customers and supporting the prevention experts in planning and executing their consulting and surveillance activities. The point is that the expert is supported by complex workflows that he also wants to use at the customer's site. In particular, there are specialized workflows that consist of some tasks that must be fulfilled at the company, e.g., planning of a business trip with preparing all the necessary meetings and assessments, and other tasks that need to be fulfilled at the customer's site.

The Service Request Broker

The overall PreVolution system architecture is shown in Fig. 1. The complete code basis of the ERP application encompassing the graphical user interface, the workflow control and business logic is installed at each client, both transportable laptops and stationary PCs. Also, each client holds a local working copy of data in an Oracle Lite database (Oracle 2007). The workflow control and business logic is redundantly installed at the server side. Whenever a client is connected to the enterprise network, the application server and the master database at the data center is used. This way the overall application gains the full robustness of the data-center based IT services with all its redundancy and data backup facilities.

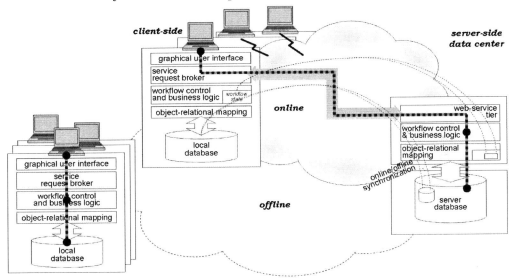

Figure 1: The PreVolution Approach to Mobile and Robust BPM

The idea is that each client is connected to the enterprise as often and as long as possible, i.e., most of the time. However, whenever a client is disconnected due to lack of network connectivity the user is not interrupted. The client redundantly holds copies of each application tier and also holds relevant data. The necessary mechanism is implemented by the interplay of a service request broker tier at the client and a web service tier at the application server. Whenever the client is disconnected, the service request broker switches request from the GUI tier to the local installation of the application.

Intelligent Online/Offline Synchronization

To enable the work with IT-based processes in online/offline scenarios to be experienced as seamless as possible particularly intelligent synchronization mechanisms are required. In the online mode the local database is continuously updated so that relevant data is available in offline mode. The local database cannot be a complete copy of the server data, which is simply too large to be held on a client device. Yet, a brute-force caching approach would not be appropriate. A solution is required that at each point in time forecasts data that might become necessary. The trick is that the work list of the embedded workflow management system is analyzed for this purpose. All data that is necessary to get the tasks in the work list done is predicted as accurate as possible and loaded to the local database.

Whenever a client reconnects to the enterprise IT data synchronization is triggered behind the scenes, this time in the direction from the client to the server database. The so-called context-oriented synchronization (Draheim and Natschläger 2008) that we have implemented in the system is characterized by the following design principles and features:

- *Guided, interactive synchronization.*
- *Synchronization of complex objects.*
- *Dialogue-sensitive synchronization.*

In case of synchronization conflicts the user is requested to resolve it. He is guided in these efforts by the system. Conflicts are presented to him based on the principles of synchronization of complex objects and dialogue-sensitive synchronization as described in due course. User decisions are not necessarily enforced after each short interruption of network connectivity, however, on a regular basis and at least after an expert has finished a business trip. With respect to this the system can exploit that it is aware of business trips and the tasks that belong to a business trip. With this approach continuous data cleansing is enforced by the system; the data does not deviate from very high quality – even in the long run.

Via the object-relational mapping tier it is possible to annotate groups of classes as forming complex object structures, i.e., aggregates or composites in terms of object-oriented modeling languages like the UML (Unified Modeling Language) (OMG 2011). Henceforth, a change of two or more different users to a whole object net of such complex structure is considered a conflict. This feature pays tribute to the real-world modeling approach. Without such feature, conflicts would only be detected at the granularity of single classes resp. single database tables and many domain-related conflicts would actually be undetected. An example from the insurance domain is the object net of an employee and its role of being a contact person for a company, where a single employee can be contact person for many companies.

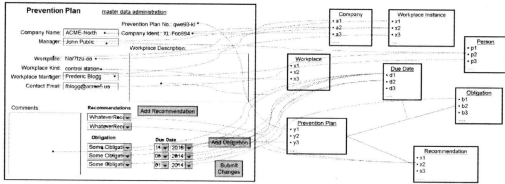

Figure 2: Dialogue-Sensitive Synchronization

Dialogue-sensitive synchronization is a further tool in guided, interactive synchronization. It is about presenting the user the dialogue context in which he made a change to data. Data might be structured in the system, i.e., in the database or the data model, completely different from the way it is presented to the user in a typical workflow step – see Fig. 2 for a fictive example (disclaimer: the figure shows no real cutout from the business logic of the discussed system). The data model emerged as the result of following conceptual principles like real-world modeling and design goals like maintainability and reusability. However the concrete dialog window needs to support the business logic of the current task. Therefore, the dialog window compiles snippets of data from many different database tables. The dialog window can be considered an updatable view, i.e., the user is able to change parts of the data via the dialog window. In our system the state of the dialog window is logged whenever a user makes a change to data. Then, later, if a user decision is needed with respect to synchronization, this context can be presented to him. This kind of information is a crucial support for the user to remember or re-understand why he changed what and therefore eases the decision to finally commit or reject a change.

Distribution and Synchronization of Workflow State

It is crucial that the solution does not only keep business data in synch between server and clients but also all workflow-related data (Hollingsworth 1995). Only this way the distributed workflow engines can guarantee a seamless work experience in online/offline scenarios.

ON THE BPM SWEET SPOT BETWEEN ROBUSTNESS AND MOBILITY

In this section we discuss the most important technological platforms that are available today to support distributed enterprise computing and compare them to the PreVolution approach. We will have a look at mainstream ERP infrastructure, standard web applications and mainstream cloud computing including the specialized client hypervisor technology. For a comparative summary of the discussed approaches see also Table 1 in the last section of this paper.

Mainstream ERP Infrastructure

We start with the rather proprietary classic SAP architecture for realizing ERP systems, i.e., the architecture of SAP R/3. We are not interested in technological or design-related details of this architecture but want to grasp its essence – see Fig. 3. The architecture has become and staid very wide spread in the past and it is worth to analyze why and how.

The SAP architecture is a holistic concept that grasped, at one point in time, all the aspects of and challenges to ERP-based enterprise computing and offered a solution for them. We call architectures that address whole bundles of components and their interplay deep standards, though they might be not standards in the true sense of the word but rather proprietary. Other examples for such deep standards as compared to the many shallow IT standards for languages and protocols are, e.g., the IBM AS/400 (called System i nowadays) architecture – holistically defining hardware, operating system, database, hypervisor and programming interface – in the midrange computer domain or the OSI standard in the networking domain. We assume that the SAP approach has been so successful, because it fixes and balances concepts for software development and testing, code transportation, distributed software deployment and system monitoring on the basis of a clearly defined ERP infrastructure.

In the classic SAP architecture all tiers are server-based. At the client a software stub is installed. This stub contains a sandbox, called SAPGUI, that interprets GUI code, which it requests from the server, and this way renders the user interface. This way scalability is explicitly addressed. There is no need for the roll-out of new software version to the distributed clients – a perfect software distribution mechanism. The client stub contains more value adding services, in particular, for overall system monitoring. However, the approach does not offer any support for offline phases which is the central difference to the PreVolution architecture that we have depicted once more in Fig. 3.

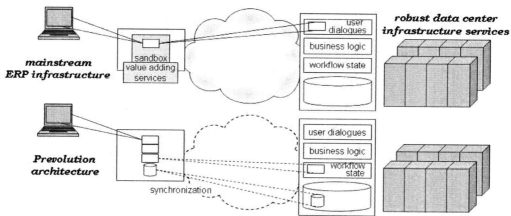

Figure 3: Mainstream ERP and PreVolution Compared

The PreVolution architecture is prepared for offline phases but does neither address scalability and nor offer value adding services at the client side. The assets of the SAP architecture and the PreVolution architecture do not contradict each other. We believe that a combination of the assets of both architectures into an open business process management suite is a candidate for future process-based IT infrastructure. It would bring together the robustness of data centers with mobility.

Cloud Computing

Web application architecture is the current mainstream, in particular, also for enterprise computing as far as we are not concerned with today's office automation tools and other GUI-heavy or GUI-proprietary applications. The architecture is currently the scalable architecture per se. The web browser is the most successful ultra-thin software client ever. However, it does not offer any added value beyond that, in particular, it does not address online/offline mobility.

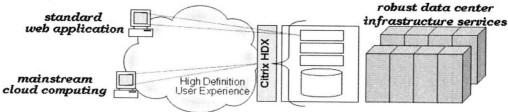

Figure 4: Standard Web Applications and Cloud Computing

Cloud computing (Mell and Grance 2009) is the emerging mainstream for enterprise computing. It has the potential to make the old middleware metaphor (Bernstein 1996) of turning computing into a facility like the power grid true, and actually completely true beyond the frontiers of the single organization. Technologically, cloud computing is mature; it is not at all a vision any more, but working. With current cloud transmission protocols like Citrix HDX (High Definition Experience) it is possible to run virtually all the applications that we are used to today in enterprises over the network as a service. For the purpose of this paper and without loss of generality, we loosely identify cloud computing with desktop virtualization here – see Fig. 4. Unfortunately, desktop virtualization does not address the mobile computing challenge of possible network interruption. Take a LAN- or MAN-based private cloud as an obvious example. If the network is down, in the age before cloud computing, employees could at least continue working with their locally installed office automation tools. A private cloud computing initiative puts notable pressure onto the IT networking group.

Client Hypervisor Technology

Remember that the cloud actually is nothing but the network – the cloud metaphor stems from the cloud as being the black box symbol in the network diagrams drawn by electrical engineers. Standard cloud computing is only as reliable as the cloud. Here is where client hypervisor technology like Citrix XenClient enters the scene. Client hypervisor technology is not mainstream and it is currently not clear whether it will take off. A client-side hypervisor enables the maintenance and operation of several images at the client. With respect to scalability and means of software deployment and management it is equal to usual desktop virtualization. In contrast to usual cloud computing it enables offline work, however, only for PC applications like office automation tools, however, not for the process-based applications we are interested in. Furthermore, the mobility realized by client hypervisor technology again comes at the prize of weakened robustness.

On the Total Economic Impact of Mobile BPM

Business process technology is here to stay. Process-based applications are a proven effective and efficient way to define and enforce business processes in an organization. Business process technology is a center pillar of well-organized modern enterprises. Currently, more agile kinds of applications are in the limelight, conceptually, social software and, technologically, mobile applications. But as these technologies gain ground in enterprises we observe that business process applications become ever more established and pervasive at the same time. Many large companies have their own software development department with often dozens, sometimes even hundreds of software engineers, merely to program enterprise applications and information system. In many organizations, it seems not to be possible to satisfy the hunger for ever new features and modules in process-based applications. How comes?

The Impact of Social Software

An increased usage of social software does not necessarily mean that the business culture is transformed. In organizations, strands of strictly organized work co-exist with strands of ad-hoc, rather unstructured work. Both kinds of work add value (Draheim 2012). And similarly, we always had enterprise content management systems in companies, a class of applications that ship today under the label of social software. Those activities or chunks of work that are highly repetitive and well-understood are amenable for process definition and workflow IT support. Other activities, e.g., from the realm of project management or knowledge work might be better supported by social software. What we observe is that social software becomes more and more important in those areas where we have to deal with unstructured data, turning them into semi-structured data. It is the field of office automation products where the usage of social software immediately helps.

The Impact of Mobile Applications

Now let us turn to mobile computing. How do we perceive the current infrastructure and the current mobile devices, i.e., our laptops and the like, or, let us say it better, the way we use our current mobile devices in our current networks? The community seems somehow to focus on the usage of PC applications like office automation tools and proprietary apps. However, the reality of mobile computing is actually also about the usage of process-based applications. Actually, we can use major chunks of our process-based applications mobile. The network is widespread and definitely performant enough for most of our purposes. Many of us use at least the basic server-based administrative tools of our companies at home, e.g., time tracking, requesting for leaves, business trip planning and so on. Managers usually use the whole range of ERP modules when they are on a business trip. Who really cares if a workflow is interrupted due to some network failure? In the worst case some changes to the current dialog window are lost. Of course, we need to wait for the network before we can continue, but usually there is enough work to do with some other locally installed PC applications. So, mobile business processes are a matter fact.

The special robustness required for a system as described in this paper is not the everyday challenge. Nevertheless, we believe in the importance of the discussed architecture.

RELATED WORK

The approach that we have presented in this paper is a distributed workflow management architecture. Distributed and often also mobile business processes are taken for granted in today's organizations. Thus the need for distributed workflow execution and management taking mobility aspects into account is inherent. Activities within one workflow instance are often processed by different people or use different automated services. The location should not be a constraint, neither for the people nor for the services. Schuster defines four basic algorithms for distributed workflow execution (Schuster 2005):

- *Remote access.* A centralized workflow server holds all users' work lists. Users access the server by their remote clients.
- *Migration of workflow instances.* Top-level workflow instances are migrated from the server to a client, which could be another workflow engine as well. This algorithm is reasonable to reduce the communication between client and server if they are not in the same place or nearby.
- *Partitioning of workflows.* The workflow is divided into disjoint sets of sub workflows for participants within the physical neighborhood. Data is not divided and can thus be accessed by different sub workflows.
- *Sub workflow distribution.* Sub workflows are distributed and act like ordinary workflows, i.e. each one is scheduled separately. Only in special cases, like competing sub processes, the nested sub processes synchronize with their father workflow.

The implementation of the offline-robust solution presented in this paper implements three out of these four algorithms partly adapted to the concrete requirements, i.e., remote access, migration of workflow instances and sub workflow distribution. Here, remote access plays a particularly important role in the application, because many user groups typically access their work lists on the server.

As opposed to the usual distributed workflow approaches our approach is asymmetric. It is not a peer-to-peer architecture but a master/slave architecture that distinguishes between the robust server-based installation of the workflow management system and the several detached installations that mirror the central system. Symmetric approaches like D-OSyRIS (Frincu 2011) can be considered as a kind of workflow-based EDI mechanism (Emmelhainz 1993). Robustness is achieved only by making each distributed computing node robust, i.e., a data center.

CONCLUSION

The presented PreVolution system proofs that with intelligent online/offline synchronization principles it is possible to realize an asymmetric distributed business process management application that balances between the robustness of data center based IT and the flexibility of mobile clients. The concrete application architecture can be turned into a general platform for mobile processes, a mobile business process management suite so to speak, if combined with best principles of ERP platforms. We have discussed the architecture against the background of the current IT architecture landscape – see Table 1. Whether intelligent extra-support for mobile processes as described in this paper add a selling point to business process management suites depends on network ubiquity, i.e., at each point in time, on the level of network availability and quality as compared to the local enterprise network.

	Mobility	*Scalability*	*Comments*
Mainstream ERP	—	explicitly addressed	client-side value adding services
Prevolution Architecture	• explicitly addressed • workflow stable	—	—
Web Application Architecture	—	per se	current mainstream
Mainstream Cloud Computing	—	per se	future mainstream
Client Hypervisor	• expliclity addressed • no workflow mechanism	per se	currently no mainstream

Table 1: Main Characteristics of Discussed Platforms

REFERENCES

(Auer et.al 2013) Dagmar Auer, Dirk Draheim, Verena Geist, Theodorich Kopetzky, Josef Küng, Christine Natschläger. Towards a Framework and Platform for Mobile, Distributed Workflow Enactment Services – On a Possible Future of ERP Infrastructure. In: Proc. of ERP Future 2012 - the 1st Intl. Conf. on Trends in Enterprise Resource Planning Systems. Lecture Notes in Information Systems and Organisation 4, Springer, 2013.

(Bernstein 1996) Philip A. Bernstein. Middleware – a Model for Distributed System Services. Communications of the ACM, vol. 39, no. 2, 1996.

(Draheim 2012) Dirk Draheim. Smart Business Process Management. In (Layna Fischer, Editor): Social BPM – 2011 BPM and Workflow Handbook, Digital Edition. Future Strategies, Workflow Management Coalition, 2012.

(Draheim 2010) Dirk Draheim. Business Process Technology – A Unified View on Business Processes, Workflows and Enterprise Applications. Springer, 2010.

(Draheim and Natschläger 2008) Dirk Draheim, Christine Natschläger. A Context-Oriented Synchronization Approach. Electronic Proceedings of PersDB 2008 – the 2nd Intl. VLDB Workshop in Personalized Access, Profile Management, and Context Awareness: Databases, 2008.

(Emmelhainz 1993) Margaret A. Emmelhainz. EDI – A Total Management Guide. Van Nostrand Reinhold, 1993.

(Frincu 2011) Marc Frincu. D-OSyRIS – a Self-Healing Distributed Workflow Engine. In: Proceedings of ISPDC'2011 – the 10th International Symposium on Parallel and Distributed Computing. IEEE Press, 2011.

(Hollingsworth 1995) David Hollingsworth. The Workflow Reference Model. Technical Report TC00-1003, Workflow Management Coalition, Lighthouse Point, Florida, USA, 1995.

(Mell and Grance 2009) Peter Mell and Tim Grance. The NIST Definition of Cloud Computing – version 15. National Institute of Standards and Technology, Information Technology Laboratory, 2009.

(OMG 2011) Object Management Group. OMG Unified Modeling Language – Infrastructure, version 2.4.1. OMG, August 2011.

(Oracle 2007) Oracle. Adding Mobile Capability to an Enterprise Application with Oracle Database Lite. White Paper, Oracle Corporation, June 2007.

(Rivkin 2009) Wolf Rivkin. BPM SaaS as the Foundation of a Cloud-based Post-IT Enterprise. In (Layna Fischer, Editor): Spotlight on Government – 2009 BPM and Workflow Handbook, Digital Edition. Future Strategies, Workflow Management Coalition, 2009.

(Schuster 2005) Hans Schuster. Pros and Cons of Distributed Workflow Execution Algorithms. In: Data Management in a Connected World, LNCS 3551, Springer, 2005.

(Weiser 1991) Mark Weiser. The Computer for the 21st Century. Scientific American, no. 265, September 1991.

Decision Support for Intelligent BPM

Pieter van Schalkwyk, XMPro, USA

INTRODUCTION

This paper covers the introduction of decision support for BPM to create Intelligent BPM. Decision support in information systems is not a new subject but advances in technology opens up new opportunities to provide better decision support that is more contextual and based on near real-time information. Newer, smarter business process management tools or iBPMS (Intelligent Business Process Management Suites) facilitate more intelligent BPM.

Intelligent BPM is not the next iteration of artificial intelligence but rather has a knowledge worker at the center of an operational process. Intelligent BPM is not only about efficiency gains but places higher importance on improving effectiveness. Intelligent BPM is about achieving operational, business and performance goals and relies on people's knowledge, experience and intuition. In order for intelligent BPM to succeed it needs better decisions to be made faster and this, in turn, requires better decision support for those people that are part of these smarter processes.

Decision support can take many forms. It can be based on analytics where information is made available to processes in real time to create Operational Intelligence (and it is in contrast with more strategic BI). It can be in the form of external data that help guide process decisions, like weather web-services that support logistics routing processes. It can be algorithmic decision trees that help guide the decision process.

Intelligent BPM without in-built decision support doesn't aid knowledge workers to drive process outcomes to KPIs or goals. Decision support is the GPS of Intelligent BPM.

The remainder of this chapter of the book is dedicated to examples of better decision support and how it makes BPM smarter or more intelligent for improved competitive advantage, lower costs, higher yields and higher customer satisfaction.

WHY DECISION SUPPORT IN IBPM?

"Almost everything that a human being does involves decisions," says Sven Ove Hansson [Hansson 2005] in a paper on Decision Theory at the Stockholm-based Royal Institute of Technology. Decisions and decision theory has long been a subject studied by philosophers and human sciences.

We are a result of the decisions we make. It is true of our personal lives and it is true of the work that we individually or collectively do. It is increasingly true for business processes that we are involved in. Modern business relies more and more on the knowledge, experience and intuition of workers to make critical decisions that will change the outcomes of the processes and ultimately business performance.

People understand context and have processing skills far superior to any machine. For that reason some decisions can only be made by people.

However, there are also a number of challenges with the decisions people make. Many decisions are made with limited information; it is based on previous experiences of the individual; and there is limited or no learning from similar decisions made by others in similar circumstances.

Decision makers are faced with vast amounts of data and information that cannot be processed as fast and consistently as analytical tools and emotional characteristics often influence decisions. Intelligent BPM not only acknowledges the role of experience and knowledge but also acknowledges that people can make better decisions if data is turned into information and that, in turn, is turned into intelligence.

This chapter addresses four types of process-based decision support to help process users to achieve better process outcomes.

FOUR TYPES OF DECISION SUPPORT FOR iBPMS

Figure 1 shows the response to a snap survey that the author posted on LinkedIn to the "Intelligent Business Operations" group with more than 1600 members.

The survey was designed to capture each of the four main types of decision support mechanisms.

Support Type	Scope of Support	High Level Survey Question
Prescriptive	What must happen?	Business rules make process decisions
Predictive	What is likely to happen or what should happen?	Predictive Analytics suggest options
Descriptive	What is happening?	Simple BI-style dashboards in the process
Collaborative	What do others think will or should happen?	Access to peers to ask process related questions

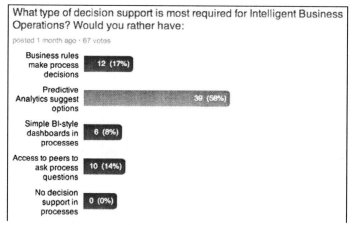

(http://www.linkedin.com/groups/Intelligent-Business-Operations-4278392)

Figure 1 - Decision Support Survey

The objective of the survey was to get a qualitative rather than a quantitative view of the sentiment for a target audience that has an interest in Intelligent BPM.

There were 67 respondents to the survey from the "Intelligent Business Operations" LinkedIn group.

The results show that 60% of respondents prefer a predictive decision support approach where process options are suggested based on analytical methods that use historical and/or real-time business data.

The survey results for the other three decision support styles are all statistically very similar, with "access to peers" rating the highest of the three. The interesting result from this is that all respondents indicated that Intelligent BPM should have some form of decision support.

Traditionally BPM and BPM technology solutions incorporated only prescriptive decision support through business rules. Where processes were not supported by BPMS or workflow solutions, rules were contained in Standard Operating Procedures (SOPs), Work Instructions and most often in policy and procedures manuals or documentation.

The quest for increased competitive advantage is fueling the drive to gather more and more data about customers, business operations, suppliers, employees and the environment we operate in.

The growth in the Business Intelligence and Analytics market support the fact that business is looking to use this "big data" to increase competitive advantage.

It is important to note that the 4 types of decision support share characteristics with the Analytics Maturity Model and the Gartner Analytic Ascendancy Model that depicts the maturity evolution of analytics using the following stages:

- Entity Analytics: How many widgets do we have?
- Descriptive Analytics: What happened?
- Diagnostic Analytics: Why did it happen?
- Predictive Analytics: What will happen?
- Prescription Analytics: How can we make it happen?

The analytics model is a linear progression, as businesses get more sophisticated in their application of analytics or BI, whereas the decision support model is merely various types of possible support for business users. Using predictive decision support will, however, require an organization to have the analytical maturity associated with predictive and possibly prescription analytics.

The results from the survey shows that Intelligent Business Operations is looking to predictive and prescriptive analytics to provide process decision support that will help knowledge workers make better process decisions faster. It hopes to learn from the past and optimize decision support to provide increasingly better business results.

The following sections describe the four decision support approaches in more detail with some use case and examples that show how these approaches puts the intelligence in Intelligent BPM.

PRESCRIPTIVE DECISION SUPPORT

The first approach is familiar to most BPM users and analysts. It is the basis of most traditional process analysis, trying to define and direct business processes to comply with policies and rules.

It is primarily concerned with *"What should happen?"*

Prescriptive decision support for Intelligent BPM can be "absolute" through fact-based business rules or more "directive" through best practice process guides. Both prescribe the next process action, but business rules enforce the action while guides use rule logic to suggest a next action.

Business Rules

Business rules are the most common and well-understood decision support system for BPM. For that reason, it is also well documented in the context of process management and the following section is just a short introduction to business rules and Intelligent BPM.

All businesses and organizations have business rules, whether they are formally documented or not.

"Rules are a first-class citizen of the requirements world. Rules build on facts, and facts build on concepts as expressed by terms," according to the Business Rules Group (BRG) (http://www.businessrulesgroup.org/home-brg.shtml)

The BRG's manifesto (http://www.businessrulesgroup.org/brmanifesto.htm) provides a detailed definition of business rules but the following summary captures the essence of business rules for the purpose of this chapter. Business rules are:

- Primary Requirements, Not Secondary.
- Separate From Processes, Not Contained In Them.
- Deliberate Knowledge, Not A By-Product.
- Declarative, Not Procedural.
- Well-Formed Expression, Not Ad Hoc.
- For the Sake of the Business, Not Technology.
- Of, By and For Business People, Not IT People.
- Managing Business Logic, Not Hardware/Software Platforms.

Most business processes are subjected to business rules at some point in time. These rules are often contained in Business Rules Management Systems (BRMS) and the rules are maintained separately from the process flows. Prescriptive business rules can either influence the process decision flow or information contained in the process itself.

A business rule for dispensing a certain restricted antibiotic may, for example, require an additional approval step by a senior pathologist whereas general antibiotics can be issued without the approval step. In this case the business rule will impact the flow, but the type of antibiotics that require approval can be managed external to the process.

In the Excel-based example in figure 2, the business rule influences the business information itself. In this instance the rule will determine what type of antibiotic <u>will</u> be prescribed based on the age and the allergy condition of the patient when they have acute sinusitis. (Example from OpenRules http://openrules.com/examples.htm)

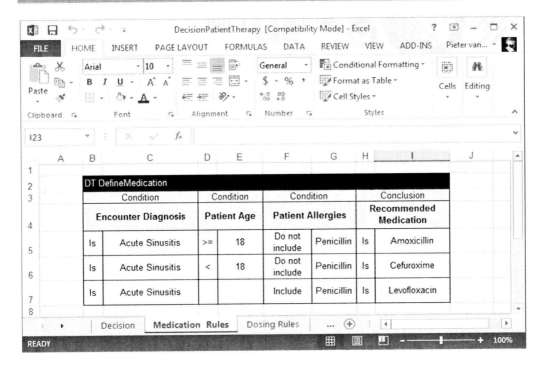

Figure 2 - Business Rules for decision support

The latter is a simple example but it describes the role of business rules in decision support for process management. Intelligent BPM relies heavily on business rules for both process flow and process information. For this reason it is highly recommended to manage business rules externally from the processes and to guard against scripting or coding business rules into process management tools. Most of the advanced Business Process Management Suites (BPMS) have a business rules module to define and maintain rules externally to processes. It, however, easily integrate those rules into business processes. These BPMSs will automatically execute business rules when faced with a process routing decision (for example approval limit for a purchase order) or process transaction information, such as prescribing the correct antibiotic based on process variables in the example above.

Business rules are not only applicable to structured (workflow-style) processes but also to unstructured (case-style) processes. Unstructured processes often use business rules for compliance "guardrails" that allow some flexibility around process routing but it ensures that it stays within the boundaries of the rules. It influences the process information for both structured and unstructured processes in a similar way.

The challenge with business rules is that all the conditions that may occur need to be defined upfront. We often find new scenarios or conditions where the rules are not defined yet. Or we find scenarios where we don't have enough data to execute a rule, but we find a process decision. The remainder of the chapter will focus on decision support where people make process decisions when we don't have all the facts that a business rule requires.

Best Practice Process Guides

Best practice process guides are based on business rules or decision logic and even though the guides are prescriptive, the rules are not enforced, as is the case with Business Rules decision support.

Process guides are typically structured as a series of questions to lead a process participant through a logical decision-making process. The person may have contextual knowledge that is not captured or known to the process management system and for that reason, may still choose a different option to what the process guide suggests.

The example in figure 3 demonstrates a typical best practice process guide as a "Best Next Action" as part of an "Office of Foreign Assets Control" (OFAC) compliance check during supplier on-boarding. In the example there was a partial information match to a "Specially Designated Nationals (SDN) list and a business rule routed the process to a manager for adjudication and a decision.

Figure 3 - Best Practice Guides for decision support

This process requires human intervention and decision-making as SDN lists are unreliable and often result in "false-positives" where a positive match most often turns out to be a false situation. If a "*business rules only*" approach was used it would result in a large number of incorrect decisions, as the "facts" are not reliable. It requires the cognitive skills of humans combined with the due diligence of following a repeatable set of best practice questions to ensure the best outcome.

In this example, the manager is taken through a series of questions based on best practice advice from OFAC. As the manager answers each question it will suggest a course of action. The decision is still left to the manager as he or she may have other contextual information that is not captured in the process.

Process guides are particularly helpful in the following circumstances:

- Where new employees are unsure of the next step in a case-style process.
- Where compliance decisions are based on a combination of experience of senior managers and governance rules, policies or legislation.
- Where best practices can be documented and presented back as a sequence of logical questions and answers.

Best practice process guides are particularly well suited to processes structured processes with a few routing options, or unstructured processes with multiple routing options. It is better suited to prescriptive decision support around process flow rather than process information when compared to business rules.

DESCRIPTIVE DECISION SUPPORT

The second category of decision support for Intelligent BPM is descriptive by nature. It describes the current context and performance of a process. It is primarily concerned with **"What is happening?"**

Prescriptive decision support (business rules & process guides) requires full knowledge of all the possible conditions prior to designing and implementing the rules. Descriptive decision support merely provides information on the current status and makes no attempt to prescribe a course of action. It differs from predictive decision support in the sense that it is not based on an algorithm or model that attempts to predict a "right" decision.

Descriptive decision support is the simplest of all the categories to add to existing processes to make it more "Intelligent". For the purpose of this chapter we will look at three examples of descriptive decision support for Intelligent BPM.

Dashboards

The simplest form of descriptive decision-support is data visualization through information dashboards, similar to those often found in business intelligence solutions. These dashboards are often referred to as "Embedded Analytics or BI" and can be presented to process users at relevant steps along the way. It provides operational intelligence at the point where operational process decisions are made. It is also known as Descriptive Analytics in analytics maturity models. The application of analytics for descriptive process decision support is somewhat different to that of conventional BI.

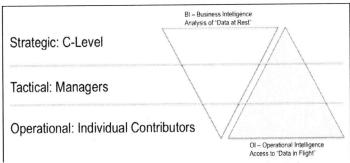

Figure 4 - BI and OI usage by role and decision types

Conventional business intelligence is strategic in nature and is typically based on analysis of historical information to determine strategies going forward. Operational intelligence on the other hand provides real-time or near real-time visualization of operational data to help process participants make better decisions faster.

A March 2013 Aberdeen Research Report "*Embedded Analytics: Enhancing Decisions with In-process Intelligence*" (Lock 2013) explains that Best-in-class companies gain significant advantage from "Embedded BI" compared to industry average and laggard businesses. Research shows the connection between analytical activity and enhanced business performance and business processes benefit most from "Embedded BI".

Embedded dashboards make it easy for process users to see the current status of critical process information. A simple example is to embed a bar chart graph on a procurement approval form that shows expenditure for the past 12 months, budget values and current commitments against the specific type of expenditure.

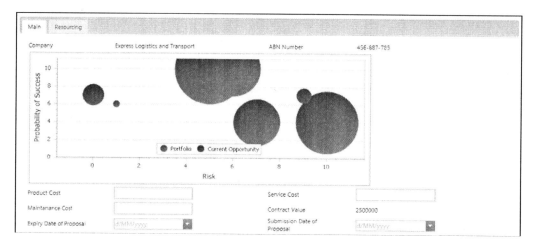

Figure 5 - Embedded Dashboards for Operational Intelligence

The example above provides descriptive decision support in the form of a snapshot bubble graph that shows a current sales opportunity in relation to other opportunities. It provides the decision-maker with a quick view of the current process context.

With all the "big data" that organizations have to their disposal the benefits of supporting decisions with operational intelligence dashboards are quick to realize. It is relatively easy to add "Embedded BI" to most existing BPMS forms and the benefits are immediate. Many of the Operational Intelligence dashboards can be derived from existing BI dashboards and analyzing those that will provide the right level of decision support for operational excellence.

These dashboards make no attempt at advising process options but merely present existing data to business users as decision support. Analytics with predictive capabilities are covered later under Predictive Decision Support.

Simple Data Sources

Simple data sources provide contextual information from internal or external data sources or a combination of both.

Internal data sources include ERP and CRM systems, Laboratory Information Management Systems (LIMS), Industrial Control Systems (ICS) such as SCADA (supervisory control and data acquisition) systems, and other business information systems.

There is a broad range of external data sources available today and many vendors package information that can be consumed as decision support for intelligent processes. The best example is web-service based data sources such as stock market information, credit scores and weather services. It is a rapidly expanding market and promises to add significant value to decision support for Intelligent BPM.

Internal data sources assist with descriptive decision support that is internally influenced.

Typical examples include:
- Current expenditure for a specific GL account line from the ERP for a manager that needs to approve a purchase order;
- Customer purchase history from the CRM system for a sales manager to support a credit limit change request;
- Pump pressure data on gas well water filtration units from a SCADA system for a maintenance engineer that needs to decide on increasing inventory on critical spare parts; and
- Experimental analysis data from a LIMS system for a pharmaceutical researcher to decide on a clinical trial plan for a new pharmaceutical product.

External data sources, in contrast, assist with decisions that are influenced by factors external to the organization.

Examples for external data sources include:
- The weather conditions over Eastern Europe and South East Asia from a subscription-based web-service for a procurement manager that needs to expedite critical orders from a supplier in China;
- The customer's credit score and history from a subscription-based web-service for the credit controller who is processing the credit limit change request;
- Geological profile data and maps from public web-mapping services for a geologist deciding on pilot drilling for oil or gas exploration; and
- Drug efficacy data published by healthcare payers and service providers for a pharmaceutical product manager to decide on pricing and marketing plans.

These simple data sources may be complex by nature but simple in its application for Intelligent BPM. It purely presents data from internal and external sources and makes no attempt to interpret it or use it for predictive purposes. It is descriptive and answers to the *"What is happening?"* question that knowledge workers have.

Simple Process Goals

Simple process goals are similar to dashboards and simple data sources in the sense that it describes a goal or metric as a quantitative value. There is, once again, no attempt to interpret the information or make recommendations.

It is often a graphical representation of a Key Performance Indicator (KPI) performance scorecard and shows actual performance versus planned performance. The advantage of providing this style of decision support to BPM is that better decision are made faster as the Intelligent BPM will aggregate the data and present current performance against planned goals. Managers don't have to search for the information. It is presented to them in the context of the work that they are busy with.

The example in figure 6 shows Tim, the sales manager, the sales performance KPI in context of a specific product line. It is a predefined process goal, sourcing data from internal and/or external data sources and it is based on a defined calculation.

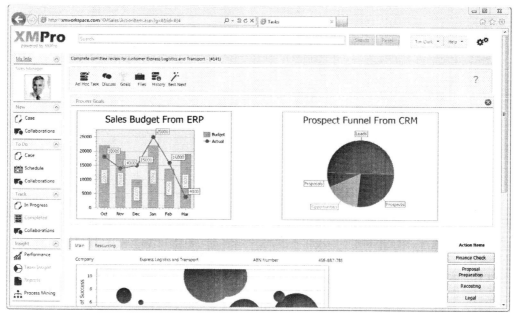

Figure 6 - Simple Process Goals

Simple process goals describe the current performance status and it is often a key decision support mechanism for managers making tactical decisions.

Descriptive decision support is very effective for Intelligent BPM and relatively easy to embed in BPMS solutions. There is no "intelligence" in the decision support itself but it helps people make better process decisions faster.

COLLABORATIVE DECISION SUPPORT

Often, we don't have data sources to give us the information that we need for the descriptive decision support. Often we have to ask others for advice, information, clarification or interpretation of certain information. We often collaborate and make decisions based on insights gained from the collaboration.

Collaborative decision support addresses the question **"What do others think should happen?"**

This type of decision support adds immense value to Intelligent BPM. It brings the knowledge, experience and intuition of others into process outcomes. The challenge has always been to incorporate it into processes in an orderly and controlled way. Traditional BPMS tools focus on discrete, pre-defined process steps and collaboration mostly happens externally through emails or phone calls.

There is a misconception that collaborative decision support is the same as socialization in the enterprise. Socialization that is based on social networking concepts inherited from social networking sites such as Facebook, LinkedIn, Yammer etc., is very different from collaborative decision support.

The need to participate and respond in a Social Network tends not to be mandated but rather voluntary. This aspect questions the reliability of Social Networks within the 'work' side of collaboration. Socialization tools support the concept of subscribing to news feeds from other users, similar to consumer networking tools. This is effective for keeping a finger on the pulse, but it doesn't fulfill the requirements of collaborative decision support that is often transactional based and in the context of a specific process.

Asking someone a specific question on a specific transaction is mostly still done in email. People don't want everyone to know that they are struggling with a customer account, have an issue with a specific purchase order approval or are questioning someone's reasoning for delaying critical clinical trials. You also don't want to subscribe to your boss' Social News to see if he/she is posting notices for you.

Collaborative decision support for Intelligent BPM is based on discussions and questions that are *directed* at specific users or groups of users.

Discussions

Discussions and conversations are key decision support mechanisms for knowledge work. How often do we email someone to ask them a question, copy a few other in the CC line and hope to get better information or context around a specific process, issue or transaction? How often do we build up an "email trail" that has the entire context for the decision that we made?

For this reason Intelligent BPM makes discussions part of the activity stream for a transaction as it provides context to decisions that are made. The decision support is in the form of questions answered, advice given and explanations provided.

The example in figure 7 shows Keith and John collaborating on a credit check for a new customer. It speeds up the customer acquisition time and improves the customer experience, as John doesn't decline it outright, but first checks with Keith on the reasons for the new credit check. It provides John with the decision support to make a better decision faster. In this instance it improves the customer satisfaction and speeds up customer acquisition.

Tim, the manager, has full visibility into the context of process and can make a more informed decision and in this instance decided to action an "ad hoc" task to address a concern for this unique case. The collaborative discussion provided decision support for both John and Tim.

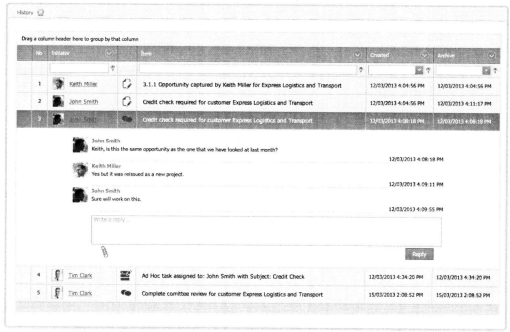

Figure 7 - Discussions as part of the visible audit trail

Knowledge of Crowds

Harnessing the "knowledge of crowds" has gained popularity with social problem solving sites such as InnoCentive.com and CrowdFlower.com and many other specialist sites.

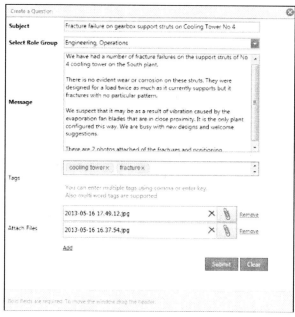

Figure 8 - Crowd Question

The best decision support for a new problem or situation is to tap into the collective knowledge of people across the enterprise. We ask peers and colleagues for advice and their opinions. It is normal work. Collaborative questions allow organizations to tap into this valuable resource right from within "normal" work.

How would this work? Let's say the R&D department at a large engineering enterprise is looking to improve the design of a component that often breaks during operations. During the course of the re-design (normal knowledge work) the engineer posts a question to a select a group that can include some PhDs in mechanical engineering as well as artisans who have 40 years' experience in operating these machines. The collective wisdom of the crowds is a powerful collaboration opportunity, but it is still just normal work.

PREDICTIVE DECISION SUPPORT

The survey in figure 1 shows overwhelming support for predictive decision support. People want more certainty that they are making the right decisions but they will only know the outcome in the "future." The best way to know what the possible "future" may look like is to predict it based on historical information.

Predictive decision support can either be static "Best Next Actions" or more dynamic goal seeking.

Basic predictive decision support is primarily concerned with **"What is likely to happen?"** while advanced decision support focuses on **"What should happen."** It is looking at how to influence the outcome and steer it towards a goal.

Predictive decision support leverages predictive analytics and prescription analytics to, firstly, assess what is likely to happen and then, secondly, how to influence the likely outcome to a more desired outcome.

"Best Next Actions" is an example where predictive decisions support turns basic processes into intelligent BPM.

Predictive Best Next Actions

Predictive decision support aims to predict future conditions and state by mining historical data, finding patterns, and creating predictive models based on the analysis.

Most of the examples of predictive decision support today are based on predictive analytics rather than on prescription analytics. Prescription analytics is a new frontier for most organizations and the analytics maturity models requires mastering predictive analytics before attempting prescription analytics. The "Best Next Action" predictive decision support currently focuses more on the use of predictive analytics than prescription analytics.

Wikipedia provides a simple description of predictive analytics:

> The core of predictive analytics relies on capturing relationships between explanatory variables and the predicted variables from past occurrences, and exploiting them to predict the unknown outcome. (Wikipedia)

Predictive analytics has strong support in sales and marketing where it has long been used to study the predicted behavior or consumers to best match products with customer, determine sensitivity to pricing and many other sales applications. It is also used extensively in credit card fraud detection and insurance underwriting.

For the purposes of this chapter we will look at 2 use cases of predictive analytics Best Next Actions.

The first scenario is based on mining process information internal from the BPMS to look for patterns of work, predict the outcome of the process and suggest process steps that will guide actions towards desired outcomes.

Process mining essentially analyzes process event logs to determine the real "paths" that processes follow.

> Process mining techniques allow for extracting information from event logs. For example, the audit trails of a workflow management system or the transaction logs of an enterprise resource planning system can be used to discover models describing processes, organizations, and products. (http://www.processmining.org/research/start)

The example in figure 9 shows a customer onboarding process with 23 potential actions or steps. Applying process-mining principles on the activity logs discovered 80 different patterns across 200 process iterations. Each of these process patterns are reviewed by a process or improvement analyst with various filters to identify patterns with the highest yield, shortest time, lowest cost or any other performance metric.

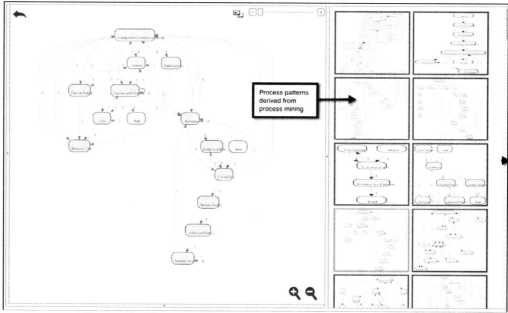

Figure 9 - Process discovery through process mining

In this case processes are optimized for revenue and "Best Next Actions" process steps are suggested as the process develops. In this instance the optimization is set to achieve the highest revenue and the "Best Next Action" analysis is done after every new process action.

It is important to note that the Best Next Action provides the suggested action to the process user, but does not automate the decision. It is still up to the process user to decide on the course of action. This form of decision support still relies on the knowledge, experience and intuition of a process user, but it is capable of analyzing vast amounts of data in split seconds and provides the process user with options that they may not have considered. It does not interfere with the process, but runs external to the process to provide decision support.

The second scenario is based on more general data mining, pattern detection and "Best Next Action" models that direct the desired actions to be taken.

An example of external data mining that helps with "Best Next Actions" is managing preventative maintenance schedules for offshore submersible oil pumps that pump oil from the bottom of the ocean to the rigs. These machines operate under extreme conditions and the cost of failures, downtime and potential environmental catastrophes has a great impact on maintenance schedules.

In a joint effort to manage the risk and cost of failure, competitors set up a joint database that contains information on more than 104,000 of these electric submersible pumps or ESP's. The data is made available to member organizations and can be used to predict failure for pumps that work under similar conditions. (http://jip.esprifts.com/project-background)

Using the data from the database in conjunction with process data for a specific oilrig to predict pump failures, provides a smart way for operations and engineering to schedule pump maintenance. It still relies on the experience of the engineering personnel as they may have contextual information about the environment or other conditions and they will still decide on the timing of the maintenance actions.

Predictive decision support in healthcare processes will not only lead to more affordable healthcare but also more effective care for patients. Consider the example of a healthcare payer organization that has access to efficacy of certain procedures under certain medical conditions. An analysis of historical case data for certain orthopedic procedures shows that in 20 percent of the cases the procedure proved not to be effective. Best Next Actions based on predictive analytics can identify those cases with a high likelihood of failure and suggest a review or alternative procedures.

Healthcare payers can review those cases with the patient and the specialist to determine a course of action with a higher predicted success. However, the decision on the actual course of action remains with the experts and the specialist. The billions of dollars saved in preventing ineffective procedures are secondary to the increased patient recovery rate, but it will lead to more affordable healthcare.

Predictive decision support enables intelligent BPM and allows business to make smarter decisions faster.

CONCLUSIONS

Intelligent BPM harnesses the experience, knowledge and intuition of knowledge workers and combine it with business rules, data visualization, collaboration and predictive analytics to create competitive advantage for those organizations that embrace it.

Decision support for these knowledge workers will give them the business intelligence to make better decisions faster.

Organizations need to match decision support for intelligent BPM with their own information architecture and maturity. Collaborative or predictive decision support, for example, will only be successful if the underlying maturity of the analytics or social platforms support it. Consider BPM tools that will provide the right decision support to make your processes more intelligent.

REFERENCES

(Hansson 2005) Sven O. Hansson. Decision Theory: A Brief Introduction. Stockholm: Royal Institute of Technology (August 23, 2005).

(Lock 2009) Michael Lock. "Embedded Analytics: Enhancing Decisions with In-process Intelligence." Aberdeen Group (March 2013).
http://www.aberdeen.com/Aberdeen-Library/8344/RA-embedded-business-analytics.aspx.

Emerging Standards in Decision Modeling—an Introduction to Decision Model & Notation

James Taylor, Decision Management Solutions; Alan Fish, FICO; Jan Vanthienen, KU Leuven; Paul Vincent, TIBCO

1. INTRODUCTION

The BPM market has expanded and matured in recent years, driven in part by the growing acceptance and broad use of process standards and common modeling notations. As companies transition to intelligent BPM, however, there is a need to focus on decision-making as well as process execution and workflow. Decision-making is important in intelligent processes, making them simpler and more agile as well as increasing the rate of straight through processing. However existing standards and notations do not readily support the modeling and specification of decision making. To address this need a new standard is being developed at the OMG, the *Decision Model and Notation* (DMN) standard.

The primary goal of DMN is to provide a common notation that is readily understandable by all business users, from the business analysts needing to create initial decision requirements and then more detailed decision models, to the technical developers responsible for automating the decisions in processes, and finally, to the business people who will manage and monitor those decisions. DMN creates a standardized bridge for the gap between the business decision design and decision implementation. As many analysts designing and building business process models are also referring to or designing decisions, DMN notation is designed to be useable alongside the standard BPMN business process notation.

In this paper four members of the submission team describe the importance and scope of decisions in intelligent BPM, introduce the basics of decision requirements modeling, discuss modeling decision logic in Decision Tables and provide an overall context for decisions in BPM more generally.

2. THE IMPORTANCE OF DECISIONS IN INTELLIGENT BPM

A focus on decisions delivers on three critical elements of intelligent BPM—increased agility and capacity for business-led change; dramatic increases in Straight Through Processing / numbers of totally automated processes; and the ability to extract and operationalize value from Big Data analytics.

Increased Business Agility

Simpler and Therefore More Agile Processes

Making decisions explicit and managing them in concert with processes ensures an effective separation of concerns and a more streamlined design. Specifically, combining process management and decisioning decreases process complexity.

Most, if not all, business processes involve decisions: claims must be approved or rejected, cross-sell offers must be selected, and product discounts must be calculated. Especially when a process must handle multiple scenarios, modeling the decision-making as a process using branches and steps can become very complex. Replacing such a nest of branches and steps with a single, explicit and reusable decision point clarifies the behavior of the process, makes it easier to see when the process or decision needs to change, and allows updates to the decision-making to be independent from process change. Rather than handling all of the different subtypes of a particular transaction with branches and exception handling, a process can decide on the appropriate scenario or process state and essentially "assemble" the best process from predefined process tasks resulting in a much simpler, yet more flexible process design.

Once decision-making is removed from the process model it can be modeled separately as described below. With the decision-making modeled in an explicit decision requirements model it can be expressed more clearly than when process modeling is distorted to handle decision-making. Simpler processes that can be more readily changed and updated, more agile processes, are the result.

Increased Business Agility through Decoupled Lifecycles

Organizations cannot change more quickly than their business processes—when business processes become difficult to change organizations cannot then react quickly or effectively to new opportunities, new regulations or new challenges. To be responsive to change, organizations need to keep their key business parameters visible, understandable and changeable. Flexible processes cannot maintain these critical parameters when buried in software code or company manuals where the business has zero visibility into their behavior. By explicitly identifying decisions and describing the logic behind them, this business logic can be parameterized and managed separately from the process itself, dramatically increasing the business agility of an organization.

Business users like Business Process Management software because it allows them to change their workflow easily—it increases the agility of the process. Separating the decisions from the process further increases this capability as business changes often involve updates to business decisions: to pricing, eligibility or risk assessment decisions, for example. Such decisions are often the most dynamic part of a process, the part that changes most often. For instance, a company's pricing rules are likely to change far more often that its order-to-cash process. If business users can only change the process, then they will not be able to respond to the far more numerous pricing changes without changing the process, an unnecessary step. Separately modeling decisions allows business users to control processes **and** the critical decisions within them. This increases the capacity for change built into a process and allows for a stable process even when decision-making is constantly changing and evolving.

Improved Business / IT Alignment

Different groups care about a process itself and the decision-making in a process. Organizations like risk management groups or compliance groups often care about specific decisions within a process, less so about the process itself. For instance, a credit risk group will care about the way credit is assigned, how the decision to grant credit is made. It is less likely to care about the process that wraps around this decision. By separately modeling and managing this decision an organization can focus each group on the piece of the puzzle that matters to them and so improve alignment.

Furthermore, business owners must be able to effectively collaborate with their IT department to define and manage the behavior of their business processes. Separately modeled decisions and processes are simpler and easier for business owners to understand and manage. Modeling the business process **and** the decision using a graphical notation allows the widest possible business audience to effectively participate, further improving alignment.

Increased Straight Through Processing

One of the key use cases for decision modeling is to enable accurate automated decision-making. The move to real-time interactions with customers, increasing demands for mobile and self-service access as well as a desire to more explicitly manage recommendations and decisions are all driving increases in automated decision-making. Automated decision-making means that more automated processes, processes that run straight through become possible. Without such automated decision-making every process must stop each time a decision is required so that a human can make the decision.

To deliver this automation organizations must fully understanding their decisions and it is hard to do this without extricating it from the process and explicitly modeling it. A combination of explicit decisions and process management keeps transactions moving with only exceptions ending up on worklists or in an inbox. With human experts expensive and hard to scale, capturing the know-how of experts in explicit decision logic and making it available everywhere focuses scarce expert resources on exceptions and high-value cases and customers. Staff can then focus on value-add activities that require their expertise, adding further value.

The number of exceptions can also be systematically reduced by developing new rules for the decisions as process execution is observed—observing process performance, identifying new rules to handle particular cases, and adding those rules to the automated decision results in continuous improvement and process optimization.

Effective Application of Big Data Analytics

Organizations are increasingly investing in data-driven analytics, encouraged by trends in Big Data and Big Data analytics, in an effort to improve their business results, deepen customer understanding and better manage risk. The value of these analytics lies in improving decision-making—unless a decision is improved as a result of analytics it is hard to argue that the analytics have any value.

When analytics are applied to business processes modeling without explicit decisions the result is a set of graphs or visualizations about the process—which steps execute most often, where are the delays, which steps could perhaps be omitted. While this information is useful it only scratches the surface of what is possible with analytics.

In contrast almost any explicit decision can be improved using analytics. If the decision is identified, modeled and understood then the potential for analytics to improve it is much clearer. Particularly as the details of the decision are broken down into more atomic, simpler elements as described below, the role of analytics in improving some part of the decision making can be documented. This more specific role for analytics increases the potential for using Big Data and the analytics that result to improve decision-making and thus the processes that rely on that decision-making.

Making decision-making explicit and modeling it simplifies processes, increases agility and alignment, allows for more automation and straight through processing and focuses analytics effectively. Effectively defining decisions involves business-friendly approaches to both modeling them and representing detailed decision logic.

3. DECISION REQUIREMENTS MODELING

DMN provides two distinct but interconnected levels of constructs for modeling decision-making: the decision requirements level, and the decision logic level.

Decision Requirements Level

The decision requirements level of DMN allows a domain of decision-making to be modeled at a high level of abstraction, using only four types of elements, corresponding to commonly-used business concepts: decision, input data, business knowledge model and knowledge source.

Input data elements correspond to the business concept of data. They are data structures whose values describe the case about which decisions are to be made. They typically group data into high-level concepts of business significance, e.g. "Application Form", "Claims history" or "Invoices". Input data are notated in DMN using the shape in Figure 1:

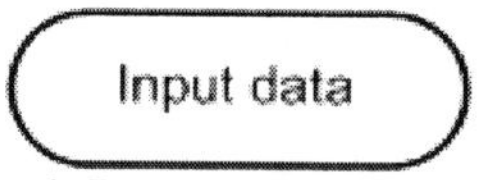

Input data

Figure 1 Input Data Notation

A *decision* element corresponds to the business concept of an operational decision. It is the act of determining an output value (a data structure) from a number of input values (also data structures), using some decision logic. The inputs to a decision may be input data elements or the outputs of other decisions. The decision logic may include the invocation of one or more business knowledge models. A decision is notated in DMN using the shape in Figure 2:

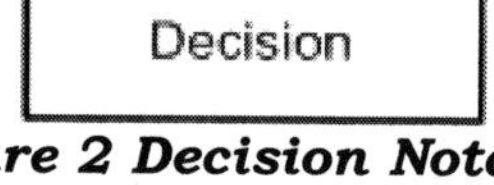

Decision

Figure 2 Decision Notation

A *business knowledge model* corresponds to business concepts such as "expertise", "know-how" or "policy". It is a function which encapsulates an area of business knowledge as executable decision logic, possibly expressed as business rules, an analytic model, or an algorithm. One important form of decision logic specifically supported by DMN is the decision table (see 4. Modeling Decision Logic In Decision Tables). The business knowledge model is parameterized, and is therefore a reusable component that may be called from multiple decisions, or from other business knowledge models. A business knowledge model is notated in DMN using the shape in Figure 3:

Business
knowledge

Figure 3 Business Knowledge Notation

A *knowledge source* defines an authority for decisions or business knowledge models, for example a manager responsible for a decision, a policy manual, or a piece of legislation with which a set of rules must comply. A knowledge source is notated in DMN using the shape in Figure 4:

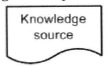

Figure 4 Knowledge Source Notation

These four elements are interdependent, and the interdependencies are characterized in DMN as *requirements*:

- A decision requires all the inputs used in its decision logic: these are called *information requirements*, which are notated as solid arrows
- Decisions may require the invocation of business knowledge models (and business knowledge models may require the invocation of other business knowledge models): these are called *knowledge requirements*, which are notated as dashed arrows
- Decisions and business knowledge models may require sources of authority: these are called *authority requirements*, which are notated as dashed lines with filled circular heads.

When DMN elements are drawn connected by their requirements, the result is a *Decision Requirements Diagram* (DRD) such as Figure 5. A DRD shows the high-level structure of a domain of decision-making, revealing the relationships between a number of decisions, areas of business knowledge, areas of data and responsible authorities.

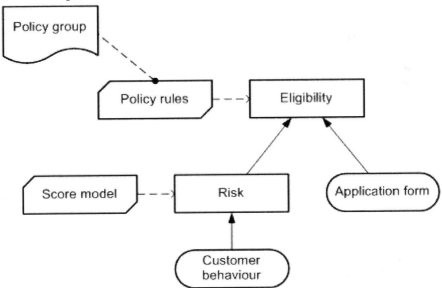

Figure 5 Decision Requirements Diagram

In this simple example, a corporate **Policy group** (a knowledge source) is responsible for defining a set of **Policy rules** (a business knowledge model), which is invoked to make an **Eligibility** decision whose output is (e.g.) ELIGIBLE or INELIGIBLE. The Eligibility decision uses input data from an **Application form**, and the results of another decision: **Risk**, whose output is a risk score. The Risk decision invokes a **Score model** to calculate the score from input data describing past **Customer behavior**.

Decision Logic Level

The decision logic level of DMN provides an expression language (called FEEL) for specifying detailed decision logic, and a corresponding notation (boxed expressions) which allows such expressions to be associated with elements in the decision requirements level.

FEEL – the Friendly Enough Expression Language – is a simple language with inspiration drawn from Java, Javascript, Xpath, SQL, PMML, Lisp, and others. In particular, FEEL extends JSON (JavaScript Object Notation) objects: A JSON object is a number, a string, a context (JSON calls them maps) or a list of JSON objects; FEEL adds date, time, and duration objects, functions, friendlier syntax for literal values, and does not require the context keys to be quoted.

The syntax and semantics of FEEL are defined using grammar rules that show how complex expressions are composed of simpler expressions, and semantic rules that show how the meaning of a complex expression is composed from the meaning of constituent simper expressions. As a result, DMN completely defines the meaning of FEEL expressions (provided they do not invoke externally-defined functions). There are no implementation-defined semantics. FEEL expressions have no side-effects and have the same interpretation in every conformant implementation.

Boxed expressions allow the decision logic to be decomposed into small pieces that can be notated in a standard way and associated with elements at the decision requirements level. A DRD plus its boxed expressions form a mostly graphical language that completely specifies a decision model.

For example, the simple boxed expression in Figure 6 might be associated with the Eligibility decision in the DRD above. It first defines the applicant's age by reference to Application form input data, then calls the Policy rules, providing Age and the results of the Risk decision as parameters. The result forms the output of the Eligibility decision.

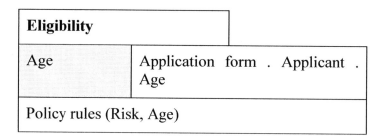

Figure 6 Boxed Expression

One form of boxed expression which is particularly important in DMN is the decision table (described in detail in the next section). The simple example in Figure 7 might be associated with the Policy rules business knowledge model in the DRD above. It represents a set of rules for determining Eligibility from Risk and Age parameters.

Policy rules			
UC	Risk	Age	Eligibility
			"INELIGIBLE", "ELIGIBLE"
1	>=650	< 18	"INELIGIBLE"
2		>= 18	"ELIGIBLE"
3	< 650	-	"INELIGIBLE"

Figure 7 Decision Table

Decision Models

The two levels of DMN—decision requirements and decision logic—together provide a complete *decision model*. At the decision requirements level, the notation of the DRD is simple enough to make the structure of the model immediately apparent, yet the decision logic level provides a specification of the decision-making which is precise enough to allow automatic validation and/or execution.

Figure 8 summarizes the relationship between the levels of a decision model in DMN, and one possible relationship of the decision model with a business process model in BPMN. Decision models are complementary to business process models, and may be used to specify in detail the decision-making carried out in process tasks. This is discussed in more detail in *5 .The Context For Decisions In BPM*. Here it can be seen that the Decision Requirements Diagram is able to form a bridge between a business process model and decision logic expressed (for example) as a decision table.

One of the most common ways to represent decision logic in decision modeling is using a decision table.

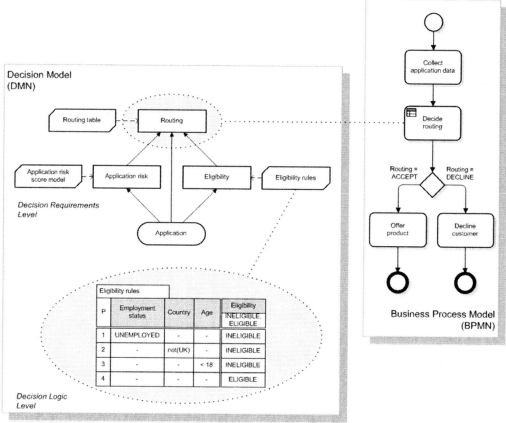

Figure 8 The Relationships Between Decision and Process Models

4. MODELING DECISION LOGIC IN DECISION TABLES

Determining the appropriate outcome value for a number of input values is a central purpose of decision logic. The decision logic for operational decisions is specified in policy documents, scenarios, decision manuals, instructions, reports, all describing what the decision outcome should be for certain value combinations of input conditions. This logic can be discovered and described using a complex analytical model, a simple mathematical function, a list of decision rules, and a variety of other formats. Decision tables traditionally allow the visualization of these input-outcome combinations in a concise tabular format, such that it is easy for business users to specify and maintain business logic in a complete and consistent way, ready for automation or human decision making. DMN provides a standard notation and semantics for decision tables.

Decision logic is built from simple sentences, e.g.:

**The decision outcome for A is a when B (and C, or D, ...)
have a certain value.**

Other values for B or C might lead to a different outcome for A. These are simple statements, or decision rules, all concluding something about A, depending on some conditions. A group of such rules about A is listed in a tabular format: the decision table.

Structuring Decisions and Subdecisions in Tables and Subtables

In real life, the simple sentences are not simple. They are usually disguised and spread out over a more complex document. Structuring the decision therefore requires the grouping of sentences (or rules) according to the decision (or subdecision) they are referring to. Every group of rules can be combined into a table concluding something about the decision (or subdecision) and using the results from other decision tables.

Structuring decisions into a network of decision tables is common practice in decision tables. In Figure 9, in order to know the outcome for A, we need information about B. This information might be readily available or in its turn, B might be concluded from some other elements (E and F). In the latter case, B is a subdecision. It is again represented using a group of rules, now concluding something about B. The structure indicates which subdecisions are required for a decision, and which subsubdecisions are required for every subdecision, and so on.

Figure 9 A Decision Table Network

The fact that B is a subdecision is clear from the observation that sometimes B is used as a *condition* in a statement concluding about A, and sometimes it is used as a *result* in a statement concluding about B.

This concept of decision table networks is further elaborated in DMN by extending the table network into a decision requirements model (see 3. Decision Requirements Modeling above).

Representing The Rules For A Decision

Decision tables are a powerful and proven technique for representing and validating a set of related rules in the form of a table. They have proven a useful aid in modeling complex business decisions and are easy to check for consistency, completeness and correctness.

Because of these interesting properties, decision tables are an important part of DMN. Throughout the years, however, the concept has often been reinvented, renamed or misinterpreted. One of the aims of DMN is to clearly define different types of decision tables, such that there is a common level of understanding and possible exchange when working with decision tables.

A decision table is a tabular representation used to describe and analyze situations where the value of a number of evaluation terms (conditions) determines the value of a set of outcomes. The tabular representation of the decision situation is characterized by the separation between conditions and outcomes, on one hand, and between names and entries (for conditions or outcomes), on the other. In this representation all rules are shown as rows (or columns depending on orientation) in a table. Each column (or row) refers to one condition or outcome.

The fact that in a decision table, conditions and outcomes are recorded in the same order for every rule has a number of advantages over just listing a group of rules:

- Well-designed decision tables avoid common anomalies in rule systems, such as redundant rules, conflicting rules, subsumed rules, unnecessary conditions, circular rules, and missing rules or combinations.
- The acquisition process is well served through the overview and communication abilities of well-structured decision tables.
- When modeling and representing the complex decision logic of real business situations, we want to ensure the quality of the set of rules from the start. Also, because maintaining the rules. by end user domain experts is not a trivial task and often introduces unnoticed anomalies, it is important that this quality is maintained so that the rules remain correct, complete, consistent and simple. Decision tables, with their fixed condition ordering, help with both these qualities.

Decision Table Types

Even though decision tables have been established for some time, and best practices have been defined decades ago, there is still a lot of variation in business practice. DMN will not prescribe a single best format (because it is methodology independent), but will clarify and standardize a number of decision table formats such that exchange is possible and the meaning is clear.

A distinction will be made between tables that return the outcome of one rule and tables that return multiple outcomes. Tables returning one outcome select the appropriate outcome value from the group of rules in the table. Tables returning multiple outcomes select all matching rules in the table and then perform an additional operation, such as adding the outcome values (as in a scorecard).

Tables Returning the Outcome of One Rule

Tables returning one rule outcome select the appropriate rule with its outcome value from the group of rules in the decision table. This may look straightforward (and it usually is), but there can be different rules matching a given set of input values and then a choice has to be made. A distinction is made between tables where (a) there can be only one match, or (b) there can be multiple matches, but with the same outcome, or (c) multiple rules with different outcome can match and a selection has to be made.

DMN therefore distinguishes different table types, identified by the first letter:

- unique hit tables: every input case is included in one rule only. There is no overlap between rules.
- any hit tables: every input case may be included in more than one rule, but the outcomes are equal. Rules are allowed to overlap.
- priority hit tables: multiple rules can match, with different outcome values. This policy returns the matching rule with the highest output value priority (e.g. highest discount).

- first hit tables: multiple (overlapping) rules can match, with different outcome values. The first hit by rule order is returned (and evaluation can halt). This is a common usage, because it resolves inconsistencies by forcing the first hit. It is important to distinguish this type of table from others because the meaning depends on the sequence of the rules. Because of this sequence, the table is hard to validate manually and therefore has to be used with care.

Tables Returning the Outcome of Multiple Rules

Tables returning the outcome of multiple rules collect the outcome value of all matching rules in a list and then return the list or the result of an operation on the list (e.g. the sum of scores). These tables are called multiple hit tables.

DMN distinguishes several forms of multiple hit tables, based on the order of or the operation on the resulting list:

- no order: returns all hits in a unique list in arbitrary order.
- output order: returns all hits in decreasing order of output value priority.
- rule order: returns all hits in rule order. Note: the meaning will depend on the sequence of the rules.
- sum: a common table form, returning the summed output value of all matching rules (a scorecard).

The Advantages Of Well-Defined Decision Tables

Although DMN will allow multiple forms of decision tables, different table types have different properties in terms of validation abilities, ease of construction, etc. This is a modeling issue and not in the scope of DMN. Because various modeling methods exist it is important to recognize and standardize these different forms, and so allow interchange.

Completeness

Not every list of rules in a tabular format represents a complete picture of the decision logic. Completeness means that every possible combination of input values will result in an outcome value (no missing rules). Different table types offer different opportunities to ensure or check completeness.

Exclusivity

Not every tabular representation offers equal opportunities for validation. Validation however is important for the quality of the decision logic. As indicated in the CODASYL report on decision tables (Codasyl 1982), a complete table with mutually exclusive columns offers a number of advantages. This means that each possible combination of conditions can be found in exactly one (one and only one) row (or column). A rule however may include multiple single cases and is then called a contracted rule. Rules are mutually exclusive: no condition combination occurs in more than one rule. If the rules are not exclusive at least one combination of conditions is present in more than one rule. This may look like a harmless redundancy but it opens the door to (future) inconsistencies. Only an exclusive table allows easy checking for consistency and completeness (as in Figure 7).

5 . THE CONTEXT FOR DECISIONS IN BPM

Decisions Within BPM

BPM has become the main focus for a large majority of business IT, centering as it does on the process tasks carried out by the business in its day-to-day operations. Organizations and departments in those organizations typically describe themselves by the work they do—the business processes they carry out to achieve the goals of their remit. The discipline of Business Process Management helps to achieve efficient and controlled business processes through its coverage of processing modeling, testing, governance, and management and control or process execution, either by the organizations' staff or through automation and Straight Through Processing. The focus of DMN is on modeling the business decisions that are made alongside, associated with, driving or being driven by the business processes themselves. So it is no surprise that there is a related discipline of "Decision Management" that covers the same aspects of decision modeling, testing, governance, and execution management and control.

History of Decisions and BPM

It is important to understand that, from a BPM perspective, there has always been a close relationship between "process" and "decision." Workflow and early BPM tools in the 1990s usually provided a means of scripting decision logic (sometimes referred to as "business logic" or "business rules"). By the 2000s there was an increasing trend to link to BRMS (Business Rule Management Systems) to provide this logic, relying on these vendors to provide the modeling, vocabulary handling and runtime capabilities. With the increase in vendor consolidation there has been continued integration of "decision technologies" —especially decision table representations and engines—into BPM tools, albeit without the modeling standardization seen by BPMN.

Anyone familiar with BRMS tools would note that these often provide an orchestration mechanism for defining what is effectively, but never called, a "decision process" —the terms used are "decision flow" or "ruleflow". Nonetheless such processes are used to model some fixed, ordered sequence of decisions— ordered to ensure that subdecisions are available for subsequent decisions— until some primary decision is made whose results are used directly in some business process or processes. Most BRMS tools are of course primarily concerned with rule execution, together with providing content management for the rules and decisions that are to be executed—very little attention is generally made to the aspect of "modeling" these subdecisions or their dependencies per se outside of providing decision representations like decision tables and trees. Ruleflows are a half-way house between a DMN Decision Requirements Diagram (see above) and a BPMN Process Model.

It is worth noting that the importance of decision logic was noted even during the formative days of BPMI during the creation of BPMN—a Business Rules Task Force was even planned, and BRMS vendors participated in BPMI knowing that the success and adoption of BPM would also drive the success and adoption of decision technologies. This has led to the BPMN 2.0 definition of "business rule task" to specify a work task to make decisions.

Decisions in Process Design

Processes are designed with respect to process goals; the effect of DMN on process designers is to encourage them to identify the business decisions that occur in their processes up front, and how their processes relate to these decisions.

For example, the process for Order Processing may include the decision DecideToAcceptOrder which may be the first task. There may be associated decisions at other stages in the process called DecideToRevokeOrder, based on additional information derived during processing as the process proceeds.

Some process designs will need to be reassessed as decision designs. For example, a process called AllocateCallCenterGroupToCall is really a decision based on the attributes of the caller and attributes of the available Call Center groups. Once this is realized some decision analysis methodology can be applied.

Decisions in Process Models

DMN is mostly related to the "modeling" aspect of BPM—indeed the term DMN covers "Decision Model and Notation" in a directly equivalent way to BPMN covering "Business Process Model and Notation". The main observation for process modelers is that decision modeling is *not* a subset of process modeling but an entirely separate discipline: they are usually related of course, as processes refer to decisions and decisions can require processes. However, both are "first class" models from the business modeling perspective.

To demonstrate this, consider that some decision results can be re-used across processes: one might assess the CreditWorthinessDecision of a loan applicant and then for any co-applicant—two instances of the same decision. This decision may of course need to be made at some point in a LoanApplicationProcess, and may need to be remade at different parts of the customer case such as when there is a subsequent re-application or application for a change in the loan. Note the inherent applicability of decisions in Case Management too!

It is worth noting that Process Gateways may or may not signify a business decision: some such gateways are purely related to the management of the process, while others will rely on some business decision—a Business Rule Task containing decision logic that can then be used in the Process Gateway.

Business Process Models Versus Decision Models

It is certainly not the intent of DMN to replace in any way the need for creating process models: on the contrary it is the experiences of many process modelers in accidentally embedding decision designs in process models that has led to the realization for the need for DMN. It is also the case that a common notation for describing decisions—just as BPMN provides for process orchestrations—would be useful for all the business analysts moving between tools in their job.

Decisions Role in Case Management and "Dynamic Intelligent Processes"

It may seem to some that the compartmentalization of decisions in DMN and processes in BPMN runs contrary to the concepts of Case Management and other types of BPM; "Dynamic Intelligent" processes and so forth. However this is not the case; the recognition of specialization in models and execution is key to understanding how to achieve and deliver on these.

In Case Management, there is a new OMG standard called CMMN Case Management Model and Notation, which is expected by its authors to utilize DMN to represent case decisions in a future version.

For "Dynamic Intelligent Processes" there are several considerations. Firstly the "dynamic" aspect implies ability to change and adapt—effectively to make decisions about which processes and process tasks apply on a continuous or near-continuous fashion, responding rapidly to changing events as required. The "intelligent" aspect implies good performance in its decision making that in turn implies advanced decision technologies. Some would argue that the best platform today for implementing dynamic intelligent processes would be the rules engines of the decision technology vendors, using declarative rules to organize decisions and process tasks... but a discussion of that is beyond the remit of this paper!

6. CONCLUSION AND NEXT STEPS

The Decision Model and Notation standard is expected to be submitted to the Object Management Group for approval in 2013 with publication expected in 2014. In the meantime the core elements of the standard—a focus on decisions as peers to process, the value of modeling decisions, the power of decision tables to describe decisions and the use of a simple language to specify decision logic—can be put to work today. Identifying, modeling and describing decisions alongside your business processes helps you manage complexity, drive alignment and improve your business. Adopting the key elements of the standard as part of your approach to intelligent business processes offers tangible, immediate benefits that will only increase in value as the standard is published and adopted.

REFERENCES

(Taylor 2011) James Taylor. Decision Management Systems: A Practical Guide to Using Business Rules and Predictive Analytics. New York: IBM Press, 2011.

(Fish, 2012) Alan Fish. Knowledge Automation: how to implement decision management in business processes. New York. Wiley, 2012

(Codasyl 1982) Codasyl. A Modern Appraisal of Decision Tables. Report of The Decision Table Task Group, ACM, New York, 1982.

A Reliable Methodology for BPM Project Implementation

Josip Brumec and Slaven Brumec, KORIS d.o.o., Croatia

Introduction

Contemporary managers and business experts are mainly familiar with the semantics of the BPMN 2.0 specification and use recommendations for business process modelling and management. These topics are extensively covered in literature; whereas the outstanding book by Silver (2011) is an excellent source concerning the development of a good business process model, business process management has been discussed in several very useful monographs (e.g., Jeston 2008). However, the knowledge of the subject, though indispensable, is not, by itself, sufficient to guarantee that a BPM project will be successfully implemented in practice. Therefore our paper does not deal with the issue of developing a good process model but rather focuses on managing a business process modelling project. We believe that the prospects for successful implementation of BPM projects can be greatly improved if the efforts of all the participants (i.e. management, business experts, business process architects, software engineers) are coordinated and in accordance with a reliable methodology, such as the one proposed in our paper, which we entitled **B**usiness **P**rocess **M**odelling **M**ethodology (**BP2M**).

Business process management as framework for BP2M

A point of departure in devising an unambiguous definition of a business domain that BP2M is applicable to is the concept of business process management system. In our approach business process management (BPM)[i] refers to a well-elaborated set of interlinked procedures through the execution of which an organization accomplishes its mission and realizes its business goals. Such a system can be represented by extending the general PDCA (*Plan, Do, Check, Act*) model by W. E. Deming. The extended Deming cycle, adapted to business process management, which can also be interpreted as a business process life cycle, consists of eight phases that are shown and briefly described in *figure 1*. Drawing on our definition of business process management, it is evident that the BP2M methodology comprises the first three phases of the extended Deming cycle (i.e. Recognize, Model and Improve phases represented in the white segment in *figure 1*). The development of process-oriented applications (Start phase) is beyond the scope of our paper.

Business processes are investigated and modelled to systemize the knowledge of an organization (business, public service or state administration) concerning its operation and allow for its activity to be improved. Consequently, the basic purpose of business process management is the improvement of overall organizational performance, to be measured by means of adequate Key Performance Indicators (KPI), in other words, by monitoring changes in those indicators during implementation (Execute and Monitor phases in *figure 1*).

If at a certain point the performance of new business processes does not meet the predefined values (determined in the Analyze phase), the resources that are available for process execution need to be reallocated (Optimize phase) or a new reengineering and improvement cycle needs to be initiated.

Accordingly, our methodology has been devised with the aim of harmonizing each business process reengineering and improvement project with the organization's (profit organization, public service) strategy and ensuring that such a project is economically justified.

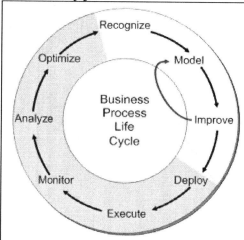

Recognize. Form an expert team. Compose a list of existing business processes.

Model. Define activities, events and business rules, model As-Is mode of process execution in accordance with BPMN 2.0 and document it.

Improve. Plan business process reengineering (BPR) and improvement (BPI) and create the To-Be process model. Assess BPI effects by simulation on the business process diagram (BPD) and calculate return ROI. Repeat it until the agreement on the possibility of implementation is reached.

Deploy. Develop process-oriented applications (POA) on the basis of service-oriented architecture (SOA) and Web technology, and install them in the work environment.

Execute. Operationally execute BPR and introduce process-oriented applications. Train participants for working with improved processes and performing operations in a new way.

Monitor. Track the activity execution by Business Activity Monitoring (BAM) and measure the KPI of new business process. The BAM module needs to be an integral part of a process-oriented application.

Analyze. Compare the actual KPI of the new processes against those projected on the basis of simulation. Determine points in the process that require intervention in order to achieve expected effects.

Optimize. Reallocate the available resources for achieving maximum effects. For external users of business processes these are manifested as shorter process duration and quality improvement, whereas for the organization that owns the processes they refer to reduced resources consumption.

Figure 1: Business Process Life Cycle

The responsibility for strategy selection undoubtedly pertains to the domain of the organization's management. It is the duty of business process analysts and architects to (in cooperation with business experts) propose a business process reengineering and improvement model the effects of which can be calculated and proved exactly. The goals that have been generally formulated as *'BPM resulting in cheaper processes that are executed faster and yield higher quality'* need to be proved by figures based on the mathematical processing of expected improvement results by simulation run on the process model (shown as iteration of Improve and Model phases in *figure 1*).

Business process reengineering and improvement can be motivated by changes in the environment in which the organization operates, introduction of new technologies (including ICT), redesign of particular working steps, or by a combination of all the three factors. Considering that process reengineering and improvement is a costly endeavour, their expected effects need to be compared against necessary investment. According to our methodology, project justifiability can be assessed by calculating Return on Investment (ROI), following the expression *ROI=(Benefit-Cost)/Cost*. As a rule, ROI is calculated for a three-year period, which amounts to the time after which the technology that is being used should be replaced. An improvement project is considered effective if $ROI_3 > 0.5$, although in certain projects executed by the authors of this paper $ROI_3 > 1.0$ was obtained. It should be noted that variables for assessing ROI in public services and state administration are calculated in a somewhat different way than those in profit organizations since the cost and benefit need to be calculated on the service provider's side as well as on that of the user, who needs the required service in shortest possible time and with minimum costs. In our methodology this means that the effect of BPI in public institutions ROI will be calculated for a complex system constituted by the service provider *and* the user.

Description of BP2M methodology

Based on the BPMN 2.0 specification, experience from working in the field and our own research, we devised a comprehensive **B**usiness **P**rocess **M**odelling **M**ethodology (BP2M), so far verified on multiple occasions in projects we participated in. To our knowledge, no similar methodology has previously been described in literature, including online sources. This methodology was grounded on the following assumptions:

- In every organization or company it is the duty of the management and business experts to undertake BPR and BPI. They need to be well familiar with BP2M and cooperate during its implementation to ensure that the developed process model is informed by their knowledge of business processes in their organization and of the business segment in which their organization operates.
- However, when operational use of the methodology is concerned, the management and business experts mainly do not have sufficiently broad knowledge and skills required for business process modelling that would enable their organization to yield a maximum effect facilitated by this modelling technique. The management will therefore hire specialized consultants (business process architects) that possess such knowledge and skills, and cooperate with them by also engaging their best business experts in the BPM project.
- Consultants need to have a good understanding of the domain for which business processes are modelled, but in general do not possess specific knowledge about the business practice in a particular company and are not authorized to operationally implement the improved business process. Reliable process models can therefore only be modelled by consultants cooperating with business experts.

A business process modelling project can only be successful if cooperation on the project is established in a way that the management and the business experts determine **what** a particular model should represent and the consultants provide a modelled solution for **how** that objective can be optimally achieved. Such interaction between the beneficiaries and the designers constitutes the core of BP2M, represented in *figure 2*.

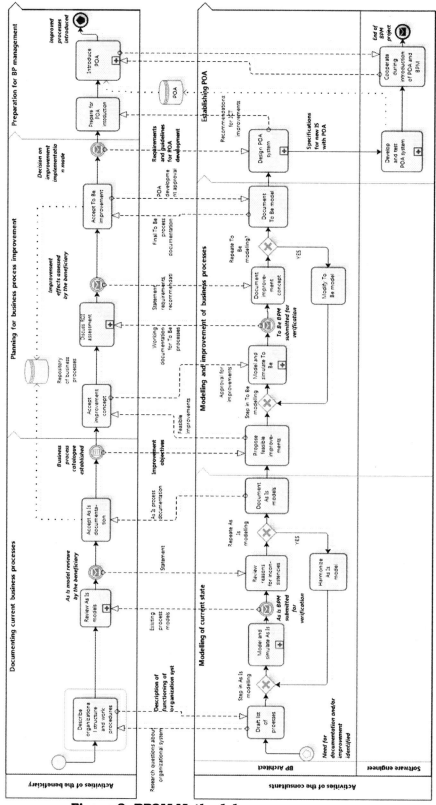

Figure 2: BP2M Methodology as a process

The methodology is defined as a complex business process model executed in accordance with the BPMN 2.0 specification. It is first represented graphically in *figure 2* as a model of collaborative processes that are executed by the beneficiary (Activities of the beneficiary) and the consultants (Activities of the consultants). The activities of the consultants are realized through two roles: the business process architect's role and the software engineer's role. Taking into consideration the aim of this paper, the process-oriented applications (POA) development procedure is not further elaborated. Instead, it is represented as a sub-process.

In addition to the graphical representation, the entire methodology is textually exemplified in *table I*. Each item in the table describes a particular activity that is performed during business process modelling, including the explanations of corresponding events and gates.

Table I: Activities of the beneficiary as part of BP2M

Process name: Activities of the beneficiary	
The term 'beneficiary' refers to any organization (company, institution, public service, state administration body) for which a BPM project is executed. The BPM project is executed through collaboration of processes that are run by the beneficiary on the one hand and by the consultants on the other. In course of that collaboration content is exchanged that is represented as notifications (16 in total). The most important notifications are Description of organizational system functioning, Improvement objectives and Requirements and guidelines for POA development, which therefore need to be documented separately. It is through these documents that the beneficiary, for which the BPM project is executed, can influence the design of a correct model of current processes, and, above all, the reengineering, development and design of improved future processes. The process represents the segment of the BP2M in which business experts or the management of the organization that aims to improve its business processes (beneficiary) are engaged, cooperating with business process architects and software engineers. From the perspective of the beneficiary, a BPM project consists of three phases (modelled as milestones) that refer to the level of business process maturity that the organization desires to achieve. They are: Documenting current business processes, Planning for business process improvement, and Preparation for business process management.	
Name of element	**Process element description**
◯	The initial event of an indefinite type since the beneficiary can have a large number of reasons for initiating a BPM project.
▢ Describe organizational structure and work procedures	On the basis of the targeted research questions provided by the consultants the beneficiary needs to describe their organizational structure, workplaces, way in which processes are conducted, bottlenecks, possible improvements etc. This activity will be performed through several appointments between business process architects, management and the organization's leading business experts. A manager needs to participate in the interview on behalf of the organization: in case the entire organization is encompassed by the BPM project, the CEO acts on behalf of the organization. The output of this activity is the document Description of organizational system functioning, in which all business processes need to be identified. To be prepared for the interview, the business process architect needs to be well-familiar with the organization, its mission and way of functioning in the business area as well as with its processes. This knowledge can be obtained from the organization's internal documents or public documents that regulate its

	activity (laws, professional norms). All business processes need to be briefly described according to a unified schema.
⊞ Review As-Is models	On the basis of the previously described process elements the consultants will model current business processes. A simulation is run on the model to verify its correctness by comparing the actual and simulated values of the selected KPI. After being discussed by business experts, As-Is models are either verified or errors concerning the actual work procedures or discrepancies between simulated and actual KPI values are indicated. This action depends on the organization's internal decision-making procedures and is therefore represented as a sub-process in model.
✉ As-Is model reviewed by the beneficiary	The project is continued after the beneficiary has verified As-Is processes in terms of their structure and correspondence between the actual KPI values and those obtained by simulation. Eventual remarks regarding the presented process model draft or correspondence between the simulated and actual KPI will be submitted by the beneficiary to the consultants in written form. In our process model this is marked as a notification labelled Statement.
Accept As-Is documentation	The beneficiary accepts documentation on the current business processes as correct and in correspondence with the actual state. The documented processes thus serve as the Business process catalogue. If this procedure has been conducted for the entire organization, it can be considered that it has reached the second level of business process maturity.
Business process catalogue established	The beneficiary has received completed and previously approved Business process catalogue. In order to improve their business processes, the beneficiary will send the consultant a specification of Improvement objectives that they desire to achieve by BPR and BPI as well as target values of specific KPI by means of which they aim to measure the effectiveness of the project of reengineering and improvement of their business processes.
Accept improvement concept	On the basis of the received Improvement objectives the consultants will propose organizational, technological and ICT procedures for reengineering and improvement of business processes. The beneficiary will consider the proposal, assess its feasibility in their organization (using SWOT analysis and other methods) and reach a consensus concerning feasible improvements with the consultants. In this way the beneficiary confirms their readiness to conduct the planned modifications in future business processes once the processes have been modelled in detail. On the other hand, the consultant guarantees that proposed measures will be technically feasible with the equipment that is either commercially available or can be purchased under standard commercial terms.
⊞ Discuss ROI assessment	After the consultants have designed To-Be models (into which the previously agreed improvements have been incorporated) and calculated the effects of modifications, the management and business experts will consider the proposal of new business processes, their feasibility and expected cost-effectiveness. The expected cost-effectiveness of a BPM project is obtained by calculating ROI, wherein all the effects and costs of reengineering and improvement are taken into consideration. For this procedure, which is represented as a sub-process, other strategical analysis methods (SWOT, BCG, Value Chain etc.) also need to be used.
✉ Improvement effects assessed by the beneficiary	The project is continued after the beneficiary has accepted all the proposed improvements (represented in To-Be models) and the costs of conducting the planned improvements. Remarks by the

	beneficiary or their request for ROI verification for processes variants will be submitted to the consultants in written form.
Accept To-Be improvement	The beneficiary accepts To-Be processes and expected improvement effects, whereby the Business process catalogue is updated. If this procedure has been conducted for the entire organization, it can be considered that the prerequisites for business process management have been fulfilled, which will be realized only after POA have been implemented. In that sense, the organization will grant (or refuse to grant) its approval for POA development.
Decision on improvement implementation made	The organization has accepted To-Be processes and decides whether to proceed with implementation of accepted solutions through the development of process-oriented applications. In case they decide to continue with implementation, the organization submits the Requirements and guidelines for POA development, in which priorities and additional POA functionalities are specified.
Prepare for POA introduction	During the development of new POA, organizational (reengineering), technical (new SOA-based ICT) and educational (training for new business processes) preparations are undertaken by the beneficiary concerning the implementation of new business processes. Those changes are conducted according to the consultants' instructions, in correspondence with To-Be models.
Introduce POA	Introduction of process-oriented applications is a technical prerequisite for business process management. The implemented POA provide insight into each process instance, identification of bottlenecks, reallocation of resources and measurement of achieved KPI. Those functionalities are an integral part of business process management.
Improved processes introduced	From the organization's perspective, the BPM project has terminated. However, if market or technical conditions in accordance with which new business processes were designed change, or if during business process management new possibilities for improvement are identified, a next phase in the business process life cycle can be initiated (figure 1).
Documenting current business processes	First phase of the BPM project that is aimed at documenting business processes in accordance with the BPMN 2.0. In practice this phase is referred to as Business process catalogue development. Although this phase is itself beneficial in a certain sense, the primary goal of the organization is to acquire the highest level of business process maturity, that is, to proceed with the execution of the second and third phase of the BPM project.
Planning for business process improvement	On the basis of As-Is business processes and the consultants' proposal of possible improvements the organization decides which improvements it is capable of conducting. Based on the organization's decisions the consultants develop To-Be models of new business processes and calculate economic benefits that can be expected if improvements are implemented.
Preparation for BP management	Third phase of the organization's BPM project that is aimed at ensuring the prerequisites for business process management. Technical, organizational and educational activities for POA introduction are practically conducted in this phase leading to facilitation of effective management of new business processes.

The Activities of the consultant's process, which collaborates with the Activities of the beneficiary process in accordance with BP2M, is described in *table II*.

Table II: Activities of the consultants *as part of BP2M*

Process name: Activities of the consultants

This part of BP2M comprises activities that are conducted by the consultants (business process architects and software engineers) but are executed in intense cooperation with the organization's management and its business experts.

From the perspective of the consultants, a BPM project consists of three phases modelled as milestones. They are:

Modelling of current state,

Modelling and improvement of business processes, and

Establishing POA.

This process is conducted by business process architects and software engineers, defined as swimlanes in the model in figure 2.

The BPM project is initiated if one or more of the initial events has occurred.

Name of element	Process element description
⬠ Need for documenta-tion and/or improvement identified	A BPM project can be initiated for the purpose of: documenting the existing processes in order to acquire the second level of business process maturity according to the Business Process Maturity Model (BPMM), improving business processes without providing computer support in business process execution, or improving business processes by providing computer support in the execution and monitoring business Processes (BAM).
▭ Draft list of processes	The goal of this step is to obtain a list of processes in the organiza-tion for which the BPM project is executed, verify the completeness of that list and briefly describe each business process according to a unified schema. For the processes to be identified all external documents (e.g. laws) relevant for the organization's activity and internal documents that determine its work procedures (document and data lists, business rules etc.) need to be analyzed using appro-priate methods (Value Chain and/or Decomposition Diagram) need to be used. The data for these methods is gathered by interviews with the management and the organization's business experts. To prepare themselves for the interview, the consultants are supposed to analyze all the available documents and independently draft the first version of the list of processes. It is essential that the CEO of the organization for which business processes are modelled is present in the interview. Drafting the list of processes should be in strict accordance with the business process definitionii.
◇ Step in As-Is modelling	The subprocess that follows is either performed for the first time or is repeated in case the beneficiary has expressed remarks concerning the correctness of the existing process model.
⊞ Model and simulate As-Is	Modelling is performed in accordance with the BPMN 2.0 by using the appropriate software tool. This complex procedure is further explained by a subprocess. In this phase a Business Process Diagram (BPD) is designed in one of the two following ways: as a collaboration diagram, for a small number of participants. The activities of each participant are placed as a private non-executable process model, while collaboration between them is modelled as the exchange of notifications between activities and events occurring between private processesiii; as a set of BPD's, if there is a large number of participants in a complex process. In that case a private non-executable process model is designed for each participant, while their collaboration with other participants is modelled as messages between activities

	and events in the main process and with each pool representing one of the participants. The selection of the content to be represented by BPD should be in strict accordance with the business process definition. A single project (which will encompass several different BPD) must contain all the processes of an organization. Logical consistency of the designed BPD needs to be verified by using simulation software, which may be incorporated in some BPM tools. The simulation is run for a statistically relevant number of business cases with a 95% reliability. The model is adequate if all the business cases are passed from start to end event, if all the paths were active, and if the KPI's in the original process are statis-tically equal to the KPI's determined by the simulation. KPI typically include the average process duration and the resources usage.
As-Is BPM submitted for verification	The designed process models, along with model adequacy (conducted by statistical comparison between the selected KPI in the real process and the values of those KPI obtained by the simulation), are submitted by the consultants to the beneficiary's business experts and management for adequacy verification.
Review reasons for inconsistencies	The received notification (or the Statement of the beneficiary) can be interpreted as the beneficiary's acceptance of the designed pro-cess models, so next activity is proceeded with. On the other hand, if in their statement the beneficiary has indicated inconsistency be-tween the actual and simulated KPI, the lack of correspondence between the real process and its model needs to be analyzed.
Repeat As-Is modelling?	The procedure of modelling the existing business process is repeated as long as it has been confirmed (in the Statement of the beneficiary) that the process model corresponds with the actual process performed in the organization.
Document As-Is models	Each business process needs to be documented to determine the following attributes: short name, detailed description, KPI concer-ning process performance, start and end event, process inputs and outcomes, activities and decisions within the process, required resources (by type and amount), causes of insufficient process efficiency as well as reasons for improvement and expected benefits it could yield. The names of processes and their related activities need to be brief (15-40 characters), but specific enough to describe their essence. Therefore they should be formulated according to a neutral grammar pattern: 'Predicate object (adverbial phrase)'. The performer is not specified in the name of the activity (since it is determined by the position of the activity on the swimlane), adverbial phrases are to be used only when they are necessary for the understanding of the activity content, whereas appositions and attributes are to be avoided. Examples of activity names are: 'Issue invoice', 'Send goods to customer' etc. The process execution will be exemplified in detail in the description, which, though extensive, needs to be succint and avoid redundant words and phrases. The documentation, completed in accordance with the aforementioned guidelines, is submitted to the beneficiary.
Propose feasible improvements	Consultants, who have familiarized themselves with the organization's business processes during As-Is modelling, propose improvements that are in correspondence with the organization's goals and are feasible in practice. Possible improvements can be grouped into four categories: effects to be achieved by implementing contemporary ICT,

	effects to be achieved by changing the order of execution of activities (elimination of certain activities, changes from serial to parallel execution), that is, by changing model topography, effects to be achieved by organizational changes, rearranging the portfolio of the products and services and a reengineering without changing the organization's legal position, and improvements encompasses by the previous category, which, however, imply a change in the organization's legal position (changes in the portfolio, laws or statutes, etc.) In practice, combined improvements are most common. Moreover, it has to be noted that: all changes must be accepted by consensus between the beneficiary and the consultants, and in case of the improvements described in the fourth category above, changes in the organization's legal position need to be incorporated in the BPM project. In proposing improvements, the current level of the organization's business process maturityiv needs to be taken into consideration.
◇ Step in To-Be modelling	The subprocess that follows is either executed for the first time or is repeated in case the beneficiary has submitted remarks regarding the correctness of the To-Be process model.
⊞ Model and simulate To-Be	The consultants develope To-Be models by incorporating changes adopted by consensus between the beneficiary and the consultants, in other words, anticipates their impact on the process structure, activity duration and the range of required resources. In terms of activity execution, all the explanations provided for the 'Model and simulate As Is' subprocess are applicable here. The integral part of the subprocess is calculating the effects of reengineering on reducing process duration and consumption of required resources. The improvement of business processes is a business venture for which ROI needs to be calculated. In calculating ROI for service providing companies, benefits and costs for the process owners, as well as for all the users of services, need to be included.
✉ To-Be BPM submitted for verification	The designed To-Be process models, along with model adequacy verification (conducted by comparison between the selected KPI in the real process and the values of those KPI obtained by the simulation), are submitted by the consultants to the beneficiary's business experts and management for verification.
☐ Document improvement concept	The received Statement of the beneficiary can be interpreted as the beneficiary's acceptance of the new models, so the procedure is continued by documenting the To-Be state. On the other hand, if beneficiary has indicated issues regarding improvements feasibility, excessive costs or insufficient effects (ROI), additional improvement possibilities are analysed and other To-Be process variants are explored that will subsequently also need to be verified.
◇ Repeat To-Be modelling?	The procedure of To-Be modelling is repeated as long as the beneficiary has confirmed that the process model is satisfactory and feasible, and expected effects correspond with the predefined goals.
☐ Document To-Be model	In terms of documentation content, all the explanations given in the 'Document As-Is models' are applicable, bearing in mind that all the modifications with regards to the As-Is state need to be specified in the documentation.

⊞ Design POA system	Refers to the complex task of designing process-oriented applications (POA) according to structure- and object-oriented methods for information systems design. This implies: designing an executable model for all processes, developing a database, and creating web forms, since POA function as web applications.
⊞ Develop and test POA	Refers to the developing and testing POA, which need to operate in a web environment, running on service-oriented architectures (SOA). The developed process-oriented applications are submitted by the consultants to the beneficiary following ITIL specifications.
Cooperate during introduction of POA and BPM	Business process architects and software engineers cooperate with the beneficiary during POA introduction and the establishment of the Business Activity Monitoring (BAM) system. This cooperation, conducted during the 'Introduce POA' subprocess, is interactive and encompasses, among others, practical training of end-users that will work with the new process-oriented applications.
✉ End of BPM project	The end event in the implementation of BP2M that needs to coincide with the termination of the activity on the beneficiary's side.
Modify To-Be model	If the beneficiary has indicated that the expected effects of BPI are not sufficient and has documented that in Statement, requirements and recommendations, the consultants will explore other improvement possibilities and implement changes in the model to be verified by rerunning of the 'Model and simulate To Be' subprocess.
Harmonize As-Is model	If the beneficiary has indicated any differences between the process model and actual procedures, or between simulated KPI values and real KPI values, the model will be modified by the consultants. These changes will lead to a process model which corresponds more accurately to reality, which needs to be verified by rerunning of the 'Model and simulate As Is' subprocess.
BP architect	Consultant well-familiar with methods and style of business process modelling in accordance with the BPMN 2.0 as well as in correspondence with the business domain for which the BPM project is executed. Their responsibilities include modelling business processes, assessing expected improvements, assisting the beneficiary increasing the business process maturity level and preparing the process model that will serve as a starting point for POA development and business process management, all of which should be done in cooperation with the beneficiary's business experts. Furthermore, the business process architect works closely with software engineers in designing executable business processes.
Software engineer	Consultant with expert knowledge of BPMN 2.0 and effective use of ICT in a given business and technological environment. A software engineer is responsible for designing executable process models and translating them into a process-oriented application to be executed on a SOA platform. In POA development and implementation, the software engineer works closely with the business process architect and jointly participates in training end-users for POA, its implementation and test run.
Modelling of current state	First phase of the BPM project from the consultants' perspective. The output of this phase (or the first partial delivery) is complete documentation on the As-Is business process models developed in accordance with the BPMN 2.0 and verified so as to represent the real current state. Such documentation constitutes the Business process catalogue. This phase does not yield direct benefits for the

	beneficiary (except for the fact that during it the organization's business processes have reached the second level of maturity according to BPMM) unless it is used for the improvement and management of business processes. As-Is models provide a starting point for the development of improved To-Be processes, whose implementation can lead to certain economic benefits.
Modelling and improvement of business processes	Second – creative – phase of the BPM project. On the basis of knowledge about the organization's existing business processes obtained in the previous phase, the consultant proposes improvements, coordinates them with the beneficiary and incorporates them in order to the improve business processes. The To-Be model is used for calculating expected improvement effects, measured by selected KPI (most notably, those that refer to resources, costs and added value of the process as well as process duration from the user's perspective). The output of this phase (or the second partial delivery to the beneficiary) is documented model of future business processes and calculation of ROI that is expected to be obtained by implementation of those processes. In this phase the expected effects are estimated by using simulation on the process model before investments into reengineering and improvement are made.
Establishing POA	Third phase of the BPM project. On the basis of the To-Be model, whose benefits were estimated in the previous phase, POA are developed in order to enable monitoring of each particular business case. Since POA support process execution in strict accordance with the process model they represent a new knowledge-based type of applications. To fulfil that function, POA are running on service-oriented architecture (SOA). The ultimate goal of the BPM project is to reach this phase, since POA implementation implies that the prerequisites for business process management (that is, acquiring a high level of business process maturity) have been met. This should to be the goal of every BPM project.

AREA OF IMPLEMENTATION OF BP2M METHODOLOGY

Business Process Model (BPM) is not a uniform concept. The BPMN 2.0 specification comprises four BPM types: Business Process Diagram (BPD), Collaboration Diagram, Choreography Diagram and Conversation Diagram. BPD, being the most detailed among them, is the one most commonly used in practice, while other three diagrams can be considered synthetic representations of specific knowledge about business processes and/or transitional forms that are used in transforming a verbal business system description into a detailed BPD. Our methodology refers to the BPM execution project and is thus applicable regardless of the diagram type to be used. Still, the methodology steps are arranged so as to support BDP as the most detailed process model type.

The BPMN 2.0 specification defines that in BDP each business process can be represented in three ways: as Public (abstract) process, Private (internal) non-executable process and Private (internal) executable process. On the other hand, from the perspective of the model purpose, Silver (2011) proposes systemization of BDP into Descriptive, Analytic and Executable. In addition, if we consider that a model can refer to the existing (As-Is) or future (To-Be) process and that it can be designed by business or IT experts, it is evident that doubts can ensue over which type of process diagram is most adequate for a given purpose. To address that issue, we developed a model taxonomy that relies on the following three criteria: purpose, development phases and predominant user, shown in *figure 3*.

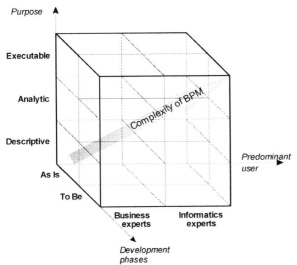

Figure 3: Taxonomy of Business Process Diagrams

In terms of its purpose, a BPM can be *descriptive* (drawn with a basic set of symbols), *analytical* (drawn with a complete set of symbols, intended for process investigation, improvement and simulation) and *executable* (very detailed, aimed for the development of the process-oriented application). In terms of development phases, a BPM can represent the *existing* process (As-Is) or the *improved* process that the organization intends to introduce (To-Be). The predominant user can refer to either *business* or *informatics* experts. By combining these classifications it is possible to recognize 12 BPD types. Each model type M_s is unambiguously defined by values at the axes of the taxonomy space, which can be expressed as $M_s \rightarrow \{x_i, y_j, z_k\}$. Some of them can only appear in theory: for example, $M_s \rightarrow \{'Business', 'Executable', 'To-Be'\}$ will very rarely be developed. Some of them are fairly common, as in the examples: $M_s \rightarrow \{'Business', 'Analytical', 'As-Is'\}$, which enables detailed understanding of existing processes and represents a starting point for their reengineering and improvement, or $M_s \rightarrow \{'Informatics', 'Executable', 'To-Be'\}$, which provides a basis for the development of process-oriented applications to support future business processes. The general direction of process model development and improvement is determined by the main diagonal of the parallelepiped in *figure 3*, extending from $M_0 \rightarrow \{'Business', 'Descriptive', 'As-Is'\}$ to $M_n \rightarrow \{'Informatics', 'Executable', 'To-Be'\}$.

Such a three-dimensional classification will be useful for the management in defining BPM project goals, correct selection of the consultant team members and required competencies that team members need to demonstrate, as well as in estimating project duration and costs.

Our BP2M methodology is applicable to any of the 12 BPD types.

In practice, business process modelling can be aided by the so-called reference models. Some consulting firms provide verified reference models, usually accompanied by software solutions for particular business areas, with the aim of initiating such reengineering of clients' business processes that would allow for applications to be introduced faster. The access to reference models is also possible through non-profit organizations, with the aim of supporting public service companies in optimization of their processes[v].

RECOMMENDATIONS FOR BP2M IMPLEMENTATION

An extensive bibliography on business process modelling – itself a very broad topic – also includes references which represent an outstanding source on the topic. This section contains a list of recommendations that will facilitate more successful management of a BPM project using BP2M:

- Business processes are the only original mechanism that an organization can use to improve its performance only with own resources.
- Processes are subject to change. Owing to developments in the business environment and the increasing potential of contemporary ICT, business processes constantly need to be improved in accordance with principles exemplified in relation to *figure 1.*
- Business goals are achieved by executing processes. If an organization does not manage its processes and does not measure their performance, it can hardly know whether its efforts are headed in the right direction.
- Management is possible if a process as the object of management is clearly defined, which is achieved by modelling business processes using a norm-based procedure that can be understood by all the participants in the BPM project.
- Since modelling presupposes systematic consideration of activities, their purpose and performances, required resources, roles and organizational units responsible for their execution, it cannot be simply restricted only to 'model drawing'.
- A business process model is not supposed to serve its own purpose since it: (a) comprises the organization's entire technological knowledge, (b) enables the assessment of the effects of investments into reengineering and improvement and (c) serves as the basis for the development of process-oriented applications.
- Service Oriented Architecture (SOA) is a platform for the development of process-oriented applications (POA) which connect all activities and participants in a complex process in a way that business experts modelled as optimal in given circumstances.
- Process maturity phases evolve over time. However, maturation will not occur automatically and needs to be motivated by carefully elaborated actions of the management. The understanding of the business process maturity model is helpful in defining adequate actions.
- All the key procedures in business process management are encompassed by professional norms (BPMN, BPMM), which are based on sound theory and have been verified in best practice worldwide.
- Well-structured business processes cannot be bought. Instead, they can only be improved by the organization's business experts led by the management and assisted by experienced consultants. Frameworks are not 'ready for use' solutions; they can only provide guidelines to finding the best solution for each particular organization, enabling it to avoid lengthy distractions.

Modelling and reengineering of business processes in public services needs to be conducted in accordance with legal norms, while also anticipating the potential of contemporary ICT. Consequently, it is an informatics, as well as a business and legal venture.

Process modelling will lead to simpler procedures, make the public sector more capable of providing quality services to individuals and organizations, enable the development of process-oriented applications and create preconditions for business process management.

Business process modelling and reengineering in profit organizations will reduce resources consumption for each unit of the delivered product and thus make them more competitive in the market.

PRACTICAL EXPERIENCES IN IMPLEMENTING BP2M

The BP2M methodology constitutes our synthesis of knowledge and experience regarding business process modelling that has undergone multiple verifications through projects we conducted. Four of them are described below:

Analysis, improvement and reengineering of business processes (*Croatian Institute for Pension Insurance – CIPI, 2009*). A complex project in which, apart from 15 members of the consultants' team, about 40 business experts from CIPI also participated. Around 300 business processes (both in the CIPI headquarters and over 70 of its branch offices) were modelled in the As-Is version, then optimized and modelled in the To-Be version, using BPMN 1.1 notation and IBM WebSphere Business Process Modeler. Reengineering and improvement effects for all business processes were calculated using simulation, with estimated cost reduction for CIPI resources amounting to about 30% and reduction of service time for the end-user amounting to about 46-67%. ROI for the entire project was also calculated. Terms of Reference (TOR) specifications for the new process-oriented system were drafted. A generic ICT infrastructure based on SOA was proposed.

Supervision of business and ICT integration (*Plinacro – Gas Transmission System Operator, 2010*). Modelling harmonized business and gas transportation processes (using BPMN 1.2 and IBM WebSphere Process Modeler) to verify effects of implementation of a new information system. Improving the business processes for gas transportation control and aligning them with the management information system. Testing the software supplied in accordance with ISO/IEC 9126 standard and advising the client on the organization of ICT operations in accordance with ITIL.

ICT strategy for process-oriented Document Management System (*Croatian Employment Service – CES, 2011*). Content and workflow analysis for more than 500 documents which enter CES, are created by CES or are sent to clients (unemployed persons and employers) was performed. A strategy for a new process-oriented Document Management System (pDMS) was established. All business documentation was classified into 14 basic types. Developing As-Is flows of documentation for all these types in accordance with the process approach and drafting To-Be models in accordance with BPMN 2.0. The existing DB was expanded and all new program procedures were designed. Expected effects and cost savings were obtained by simulation and ROI for the entire project was calculated. TOR specifications for the development and implementation of the new pDMS were drafted.

Process model of the University (*University of Zagreb, 2012*). Analysis and modelling of all academic, teaching, research and student As-Is processes at Croatian universities. Reengineering and improvement of processes by using contemporary ICT, modelling To-Be processes, simulation on the process model and calculation of expected effects. All business processes were modelled in accordance with the BPMN 2.0 specification. For several processes new process-oriented applications were developed using BizAgi Studio, which were deployed for execution on the process engine.

Conclusion

In this paper our methodology for BPM project implementation is shown as an array of interlinked activities executed by business experts, business process architects and software engineers, who cooperate during BPM project execution. Each participant has a particular role. Business experts are responsible for As-Is modelling, defining key performance indicators for measuring the reengineering effects, validating To-Be models and making the company ready for implementation. Business process architects' job is to define optimal solutions regarding To-Be business processes and to prove that their performance has indeed been enhanced using predefined KPI on the one hand and to define software and ICT for BPM on the other.

Finally, developing and testing process-oriented applications, as well as preparation for their implementation is the responsibility of software engineers.

The methodology itself is defined as a business process comprising 21 acti-vities and subprocesses organized in two pools and three lanes. Procedures for each participant are defined by sequence flows, events and decisions, whereas collaboration between participants is shown by message flows. The methodology has been graphically designed in accordance with the BPMN 2.0 specification, with the description of all steps provided separately.

The proposed methodology has been verified in practice on several real-life projects, wherein it has proved to be an invaluable tool for the management in supervising BPM projects.

References

(Silver 2011) Bruce Silver. BPMN Method & Style with Implementer's Guide. Aptos, CA: Cody-Cassidy Press, 2011.

(Jeston 2009) John Jeston and Johan Nelis. Business Process Management: Practical Guidelines to Successful Implementations. Oxford UK: Elsevier 2007.

(Allweyer, 2010) Thomas Allweyer. BPMN 2.0-Introduction to the Standard for Business Process Modelling. Norderstedt: Books on Demand 2010.

(Panagacos, 2012) Theodor Panagacos. The Ultimate Guide to Business Process Modelling. Copyright © 2012 Theodore Panagacos.

---

[i] The acronym BPM stands for 'Business Process Management' as well as for 'Business Process Modelling'. The former meaning of the acronym is the one most commonly used in articles on management, with the assumption that 'Modelling' represents the first phase without which 'Management' cannot be accomplished. The term 'Business Process Management' thus comprises all the 8 phases of the business process life cycle (*figure 1*).

[ii] Several different definitions of the business process are provided in literature. Having synthesized various sources we propose the following definition: *A business process is an elaborately interlinked set of activities and decisions which is executed upon an external inventive in order to accomplish a certain measurable organizational goal, and for which time and resources are spent while converting input values into specific products or services significant for the buyer or user.*

[iii] This is how the methodology proposed in this paper is also presented.

[iv] Further information on measuring the business process maturitiy level in accordance with the BPMM is provided in the standard that can be downloaded at http://www.omg.org/spec/BPMM/1.0/PDF.

[v] Highly abstract standard process models devised by APQC (American Productivity & Quality Center) can be downloaded at http://www.apqc.org.

Composing Services in the Future Internet: Choreography-Based Approach

Marco Autili, University of L'Aquila, Italy
Amira Ben Hamida, Linagora GSO, France
Guglielmo De Angelis, CNR-ISTI, Italy
Darius Silingas, No Magic Europe, Lithuania

INTRODUCTION

In this chapter, we will discuss emerging technology that enables intelligent business processes enacting services based on choreography specifications. This technology was produced by CHOReOS research project funded under European research program FP7 (CHOReOS 2013).

Today service-based software engineering is heavily based on service orchestrations that can be specified in various formats, such as BPEL (OASIS 2007) or BPMN 2.0 (OMG 2011). Service orchestration is a centralized approach to composing multiple services into a larger application. It works well in static environments where services are predefined and environment changes are minimal. Alas, this is a wrong assumption for the Future Internet, which envisions an ultra large number of diverse service providers and consumers that are impossible to coordinate using centralized manner.

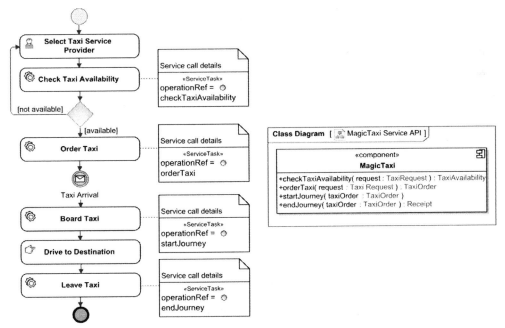

Figure 1. Service Orchestration in BPMN 2.0

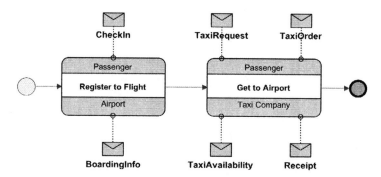

Figure 2. Service Choreography in BPMN 2.0

Service choreography is a decentralized approach, which provides a looser way to design service composition by specifying participants and message protocol between them but not coupling choreography tasks to concrete services. The need for service choreography was recognized in BPMN 2.0, which introduced choreography modeling constructs. However, until now service choreographies were solely used for design purposes only as there was no technology support for enabling a smooth transition from service choreography design to execution.

LEVERAGING SERVICE CHOREOGRAPHIES FOR THE FUTURE INTERNET

During the last years a growing interest has been rising around the elicitation of new requirement, and the development of new ideas envisioning how both Internet, and the services it is offering will change. The buzzword "Future Internet" (FI) (ECRIM 2009) has been introduced and it became the main focus of several initiatives all over the world, e.g.:

- FI initiative in the EU: http://www.future-internet.eu
- FI initiative in the USA: http://www.nets-find.net
- FI initiative in China: http://www.cstnet.net.cn/
- FI initiative in Korea: http://fif.kr
- FI initiative in Japan: http://akari-project.nict.go.jp/

However, as often happen with buzzwords the adoption of a single precise definition it may result limiting; in particular when they are adopted in order to push new research across several orthogonal domains. Thus also the definition of "Future Internet" as been identified as the union and cooperation of other more specific class of the Internet of Content, Internet of Services, Internet for People, and Internet of Things (EC 2009).

Specifically, with respect to the Internet of Services, many research communities refer to the well-founded Service-Oriented Computing (SOC) as the reference paradigm for Future Internet computing (Papazoglou 2012). SOC promotes the idea of assembling application components into a network of services that can be loosely coupled to create flexible, dynamic business processes and agile applications that span organizations and computing platforms.

Service choreographies (Peltz 2003) will certainly have an important role in shaping the SOC within the vision of Future Internet. Contrary to the centralized approach taken in service orchestration, choreographies aggregate services in a decentralized way. Specifically, service choreographies model peer-to-peer communication. It uses a loose design of service compositions, focused on the specification of the participants (i.e., roles) and the messaging protocols between them, but decoupling choreography tasks from the concrete services performing them.

Choreography defines a multi-party protocol that, when put in place by the cooperating parties, will permit to reach the overall choreography objectives. In this sense, modeling service choreographies is quite different from modeling service orchestrations in which a single stakeholder centrally plans and decides how an objective should be reached through the cooperation with other services.

Within a Future Internet context, we imagine the establishment of service federation in which different providers and users interact, following specific rules established to foster and simplify inter-organization integration according to the requirements coming from a specific context (e.g., high security guarantees). However, service choreographies will contribute to the SOC vision within the Future Internet only if supported by suitable design and development environments, as well as a set of infrastructural services.

Among the others, one of the main issues putting service choreographies in place often occur due to parties that intend to independently refine the abstraction specified by the choreography. Usually this step is done through the independent coding of services without any concrete interaction with the implementations provided by other providers.

Thus, a resulting challenge is investing on a quality assurance process putting in place mechanisms aiming at ensuring that unspecified events, leading to undesired interactions, do not happen, or that the probability they can happen is minimized (Crnkovic, 2011). Different kind of strategies can be pursued in order to achieve this goal. As detailed in the following the CHOReOS project tackled this issue by a combination of both model-to-code synthesis procedures, and the adoption of governance infrastructures and policies. The former proposal enables the automatic generation of code-based artifacts supporting the distributed integration of heterogeneous business services as specified in a model of service choreography. The latter proposal is meant as the act of administering the whole lifecycle of service choreography, and it refers to all measures, rules, decision-making, information, monitoring, and enforcement that ensure the proper functioning and control of the governed system.

The research on choreographies and SOA governance can stimulate interesting aspect of the Future Internet meant as an open world (Baresi 2006), in which pervasive software-intensive systems evolve only abiding by abstract specifications, but with no single organization controlling the whole. Specifically, they can leverage the progressive shifting of traditional Software Engineering activities from only the pre-runtime phases also towards "at run-time", during normal operation of deployed services (Ali 2013), (Bertolino 2012).

Finally, in addition to the modeling of the functional specification, the non-functional properties gain importance with respect to the service orchestration paradigm as seen in the literature (Calinescu 2011). Researchers are also starting to debate that in case of service choreographies. The non-functional properties exposed by a choreographed service can be at-least as important as its functional behavior (Bartolini 2013). Therefore, both the definition and the realization of resilient choreography would also count on means for specifying and assessing non-functional properties that the composition must abide by.

CHOREOGRAPHY-BASED SERVICE COMPOSITION: THE CHOREOS APPROACH

We will discuss the choreography-driven approach, which addresses service oriented computing challenges presented in the previous section. This approach was proposed in CHOReOS project and is driven by an innovative development process, which integrates design and runtime activities, and an associated Integrated Development and Runtime Environment (IDRE), which supports this process.

The Future Internet envisions a dynamic (from design- to run-time) and user-centric development process that, spanning all the software lifecycle, considers the user as an active part of the choreography. Within a specific domain, it should be possible for users, even when they are not expert of the technical aspects of service choreography, to specify the service coordination required to achieve their domain (business) goals. This asks for the definition of a domain-expert specification framework with its associated modeling language and tools to support the development of adaptable choreographies including quality of service (QoS) properties. Since in the Future Internet it is unreasonable to a priori specify what services must be actually used to achieve the choreography goal, from the functional and non-functional choreography specification, we must be able to understand how to actually coordinate the discovered services so to realize the specified choreography. This asks for automatic choreography synthesis algorithms that consider dynamically discovered services and decide which services to use for choreography fulfillment at runtime.

In this direction, the core objective of CHOReOS is to leverage model-based methodologies and relevant SOA standards, while making choreography development a systematic process to the reuse and the assembling of services discovered within the Future Internet. CHOReOS revisits the concept of choreography-based service-oriented systems, and introduces a model-based development process, and associated synthesis methods and middleware for choreographing services.

The CHOReOS solution is based on an innovative model-driven engineering process supporting a complete lifecycle of a service choreography, which is depicted in diagram below.

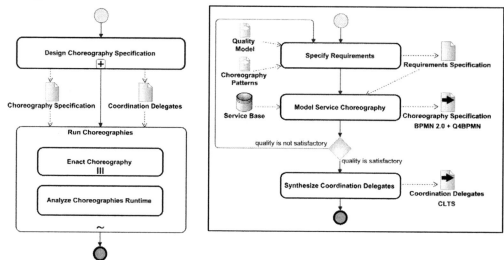

Figure 3. CHOReOS process for overall choreography lifecycle and a sub-process for designing service choreography specification

Specifying Requirements

In order to enable a domain expert-centric approach to specify QoS-aware choreographies, as well as taking an adaptive approach based on the needs of end-users, CHOReOS leverages an approach that enables domain experts and service consumers, rather than requirements analysts, to express functional and quality requirements (e.g., accuracy, reliability, security) on a service-based system and to transform them into a first cut choreography specification. Considering the large scale of the Future Internet, there might be a large number of requirements concerning a particular service domain to be managed. CHOReOS provides a domain expert tool supporting clustering similar requirements and mapping them to choreography patterns. For a given domain, the latter include knowledge of codified workflows (tasks) and natural language terms describing service classes. The result of this process is requirements specification based on task models, which can be imported via transformation into the choreography-modeling tool.

Modeling Service Choreography

After specifying requirements the transformation into the BPMN 2.0 choreography model can be undertaken. The clustered requirements are imported into modeling tool supporting BPMN 2.0 and requirements (CHOReOS is using MagicDraw–http://www.magicdraw.com/) along with additional properties, for example, the levels of quality that have been specified and a logical ordering of the groupings.

While BPMN 2.0 language focuses on functional aspects it is not designed to handle non-functional requirements or quality of service (QoS). In service choreographies this important issue rises at significant heights as choreography is made up of services that are generally not under the control of a single entity. If one of the services fails or does not provide required QoS, the entire choreography might suffer. Therefore, it is important that the choreography designer would be able to describe what he/she expects the services to do and the expected quality level. In order to enable choreography designer to specify non-functional requirements, CHOReOS proposed Q4BPMN, an extension to BPMN 2.0, which supports specification of non-functional constraints for choreography participants and tasks (Bartolini 2012). The aforementioned non-functional requirements annotations have been successfully applied to a BPMN 2.0 model inside MagicDraw. The current implementation of Q4BPMN is a UML profile that defines a set of stereotypes and tags for decorating choreography tasks with non-functional requirements.

Once choreography model is specified taking into account both functional and quality requirements, the business services suitable to play the participant roles, as specified by the modeled choreography, have to be discovered based on service descriptions. The searching criteria concern the functional and/or the non-functional properties of the desired services. The discovery process enabled by CHOReOS middleware is based on the provided searching criteria and finally, the abstractions that satisfy the criteria along with their represented services are returned. CHOReOS process foresees a task to perform a quality assessment using automated tools as some choreography modeling activities such as specifying QoS properties are rather complicated and error prone. In case choreography specification quality issues are identified, choreography designer will need to perform another iteration of choreography design starting from requirements refinement, e.g., setting lower QoS requirements.

Synthesizing Coordination Delegates

When choreography specification is assessed as well formed, and sufficiently detailed to support automation, it can be used for automatically synthesizing further code-based artifacts that are used by the runtime environment. Before describing the approach that CHOReOS is proposing to the automatic choreography synthesis, it is worth to briefly discuss what are the problems usually addressed when considering a choreography-based specification of the system to be realized:

(a) *realizability check* – whether the choreography specification can be realized by implementing each participant service conforming to the played role; and (b) *conformance check* – whether the set of services satisfies the choreography specification or not. In the research literature many approaches have been proposed to address these problems, e.g., (Poizat 2012), (Calvanese 2008), and (Pathak 2008).

When actually realizing service choreographies by possibly reusing (third-party) services, a further problem is *automatic choreography realizability enforcement* – external coordination of existing services discovered as suitable choreography participants. This requires extracting from the choreography specification the global coordination logic to be distributed and enforced among the participants. The general problem here is that, although services may have been discovered as suitable endpoints to realize all the choreography participant roles, their composite interaction may prevent the choreography realizability if left uncontrolled (or coordinated in a wrong way). CHOReOS proposes a model-driven synthesis approach to generate based on a BPMN 2.0 choreography model an automata-based specification (called CLTS) of the coordination logic "implied" by the choreography. A CLTS provides an explicit description of the allowed sequences of In/Out service operation calls and, as such, represents an intermediate representation of the choreography that facilitates the extraction of the complex coordination logics "hidden" in BPMN 2.0 choreography specifications (Autili 2013). Basically, a CLTS is an extended Labeled Transition System (LTS) that allows handling complex constructs of BPMN 2.0 Choreography Diagrams such as all types of gateways and loops. For the choreography to be externally enforced, the coordination logic modeled by the CLTS is distributed between additional software entities, whose goal is to coordinate (from outside) the interaction of the participant services in a way that the resulting collaboration realizes the specified choreography. The synthesis processor automatically derives these software entities, called Coordination Delegates (CDs), and interposes them among the participant services according to the CHOReOS architectural style.

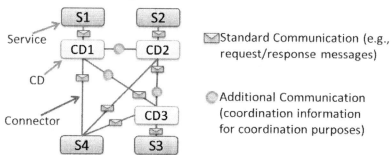

Figure 4. CHOReOS architectural style

CDs perform pure business-level coordination by intercepting/proxifying the services' interaction (i.e., standard communication in the figure), and by mediating it in a way that the resulting collaboration realizes the specified choreography. To this purpose, the CDs exchange the coordination information (i.e., additional communication in the figure) contained in the coordination models to mediate the interaction of the services participating to the specified choreography in order to prevent possible undesired interactions. The latter are those interactions that do not belong to the set of interactions allowed by the choreography specification and can happen when the services collaborate in an uncontrolled way. The generated coordination delegates code is able to properly access and coordinate the discovered services relying on the communication facilities provided by the CHOReOS middleware. A detailed approach to service discovery for preparing service base, selecting and binding services to choreography specification, performing quality assessment, and synthesizing coordination delegates is yet under research in CHOReOS project. However, prototypes for supporting the whole choreography lifecycle have been already implemented and show promising results demonstrating the feasibility of CHOReOS process.

IMPLEMENTING THE CHOReOS APPROACH

The CHOReOS project addresses the raised challenges presented in the previous section by investigating the following middleware domains: the Service Discovery, Service Composition, Service Access, and Cloud & Grid Middleware. The CHOReOS Project addresses the Future Internet challenges by dealing with both Business-based and Things-based Services. In this chapter, we will only describe the features related to the business-based services.

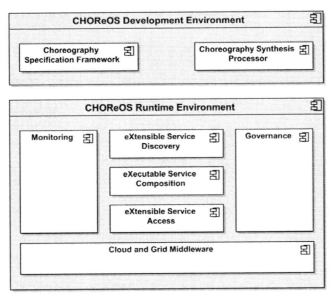

Figure 5. CHOReOS implementation architecture (simplified)

Retrieving Relevant Services and Choreography

Typically, in a service-oriented environment the publication and discovery of services is facilitated via service registries that collect published service descriptions and allow their querying by interested users. Still, how can we cope with the vast amount of available services and be able to work with them even though they come in different kinds and by different providers? Both the vast amount of available services in the Future Internet and their heterogeneity require sophisticated structuring of the traditional-style services (e.g., like the ones available information in order to address the users' information needs. To resolve the mass and heterogeneity problems and facilitate effective and efficient discovery of services, CHOReOS provides an eXtensible Service Discovery (XSD) component providing multi-protocol layer for both services and choreography.

More precisely, the eXtensible Service Discovery middleware relies on a service base that stores and classifies in a suitable way an important amount of services data. Within the project, this platform is called Abstraction-oriented Service Base Management (AoSBM). It provides advanced features for (a) retrieving service descriptions from the surrounding environment and storing them in a local registry,

(b) organizing them in groups of similar services and (c) allowing the user to retrieve services appropriate to his needs efficiently and effectively. To this end, it facilitates the retrieval of information about available services from multiple sources in order to organize them with respect to functional and non-functional abstractions. Functional abstractions consist of collections of services comprising services of similar functional and syntactic characteristics (i.e., the members of the same collection comprise services that implement the same functionality and share common operation signatures). The non-functional abstractions comprise services that are characterized by similar QoS characteristics (i.e., they are similar in terms of response time, cost, reputation, availability, etc). Both kinds of abstractions can come in hierarchies: a high-level abstraction is the union of several lower level abstractions with the benefit of broader coverage and the price of cohesion of the collection of services. Once the services are organized in such abstractions, then the users can use these structures to retrieve the services they are interested in, either via Browsing (greatly simplified by the concise nature of abstraction) or via Querying for services.

The service base is populated by a sophisticated plugin-based mechanism that retrieves services from heterogeneous sources. The plugin mechanism unifies the access to several service discovery protocols and makes it possible to extend the discovery to new protocols if the needed plugin interface is implemented. We consider that the existing service infrastructures do not adequately support the challenges identified at Section 2, especially with respect to those activities dealing with the governance and the lifecycle of both services and choreographies.

In our research we identified that a choreography registry (i.e., Governance Registry for Business Services) could efficiently support the choreography life-cycle and constitute a real meeting point among all the stakeholders involved in the provisioning and usage of a service based application. For example, a choreography registry could be the guarantor for the good behavior of the involved services (i.e. their compliance with what is established in the specification) by monitoring and checking the occurring interactions with suitable mechanisms such as in (Decker 2009) and (Bertolino 2012). It could also support features for estimating the trustworthiness of the items it indexes (i.e., both services and choreographies).

Within the CHOReOS project, we developed ServicePot (Ali 2013) as reference implementation for such a choreography registry. Specifically, ServicePot relies on an increased information model for a classical service registry. In particular, on one side it permits to store and retrieve choreography specifications, while on the other side it assumes that a service willing to be indexed in the registry can specify which roles it is able to play within one or more choreographies. Obviously, more advanced techniques can be used to match services with roles in choreography specifications. In this first implementation we decided to take the simplest path and ask for explicit role identification. More complex functionality can be implemented using extension mechanisms.

Composing Services within Choreographies

If no single service satisfies the specific request of a user, it may be necessary to compose existing services. Resulting composite services can be used as basic services in further hierarchical service compositions or offered as complete applications to service clients. Briefly stated, the process of (automated) service composition is as follows. The service requester defines the requirements (in a specification language) and the service composition engine (based on the requirements, the services available and their current state) generates the composition, which is deployed in the execution engine of the middleware.

In the last few years, building upon the wide acceptance of the service-oriented architecture paradigm, there is a growing interest in choreography as a key concept in forming complex service-oriented systems. Choreography is put forward as a generic abstraction of any possible collaboration among multiple services, and integrates previously established views on service composition, among which service orchestration. The CHOReOS project investigates the Choreography paradigm for addressing highly challenging issues in the Service Composition domain. Still, the Future Internet raises additional challenges for service composition, especially with respect to handling the scale and heterogeneity of the target networking environment although, related issues are partly covered by the underlying middleware functions for service discovery and access.

Within the CHOReOS project, we provide a sophisticated engine that fulfills the composition of choreographies involving services. Namely, the eXecutable Service Composition (XSC) middleware is dedicated to deal with Ultra Large Scale choreographies of services. As described earlier in the choreography development process, we base upon a model-driven top-down approach, for capturing the user requirements, generating the choreography model in BPMN 2.0 with some extensions and enacting the choreography of Business Services based on Coordination Delegates. After assigning the candidate services thanks to the discovery facilities, the Coordination Delegates are deployed on top of the EasyESB bus. Specific components of the bus are dedicated to the distributed management of the Coordination Delegates, namely the Coordination Delegates Components. The CHOReOS Composition layer benefits from the Service Discovery previously described and Service Access middleware presented hereafter.

Accessing Services

The major issue for service access towards dealing with the Future Internet challenges is to be able to cope with the heterogeneity of interaction protocols employed by Business Services. More specifically, the problematic of integration several services coming from different sources is exacerbated by the Future Internet requirements. Within the CHOReOS Project, we propose a unified approach to access services, both Business and Things services. In the following we will only describe the facilities implemented to access the Business services. The Service Access layer mainly relies on the Enterprise Service Bus (ESB) technology. The ESB solutions bring interesting features of extensibility and scalability, which enable dealing with the interaction protocol diversity.

In general, ESB leverages best practices from EAI (Enterprise Application Integration) mechanisms and the Service Oriented Composition paradigms. ESB is based on an open, standard message bus dedicated to enable the implementation, deployment and management of service-oriented applications. It exploits Web Services, Message Oriented Middleware, smart message routing, and transformation mechanisms. ESB supports systems that involve a large number of services and high distribution, and thus provides a scalable and manageable integration infrastructure. ESB acts as a mediator between service providers and consumers.

We build upon the facilities brought by the ESB technology and provide a unified layer for dealing with high-level generic application paradigms and business services. The Service Access middleware mainly relies on the EasyESB platform and implements above an abstract layer providing generic interaction semantics. This upper layer aims at enhancing EasyESB for covering a much larger interaction protocol diversity, including the typical client/server interactions, publish/subscribe and tuple space, or streaming, etc. Meanwhile, being fully based on advanced SOA paradigms, EasyESB can be easily exploited and integrated to existent interaction technologies. More precisely, it offers a backbone middleware that hosts the components taking in charge the enactment of the choreographies. Moreover, it offers useful functionalities for monitoring the services involved into choreographies. The monitoring aspects are useful for following the respect of the BPMN 2.0 process depicted at the beginning of the development steps. Achieved details of achieved results are described in (Ben Hamida 2012), (Zribi 2012), and (Lesbequeries 2012). Furthermore, EasyESB benefits from a flexible and dynamic topology that enables the automatic discovery of neighbor bus nodes and services. We enhance these aspects and exploit them to leverage the bus deployment on top of an elastic cloud and grid infrastructure. Taking benefit from the hardware resources afforded thanks to existent cloud solutions, we make a step forward for the enhancement of the ESB technologies towards Future Internet complex environments. We break up the orchestration philosophy that relies on a single composition engine to a distributed topology where services and their coordinators are available regardless of their real locations.

Considering Clouds and Grids

With respect to ensuring scalability in dealing with user load, paradigms for high-performance computing and computing based on resources retrieved on demand, such as Grid and Cloud computing, seem to be very promising to be employed by SOM. Hence, there has been research for many years on Grid middleware solutions to enable the execution of computationally-intensive applications on sets of geographically distributed clusters of machines. Originally targeting the scientific community with their large data processing needs, Grids can provide solutions to any computing-intensive application. Cloud computing is a more recent paradigm providing virtualization mechanisms for supporting elastic and on-demand provision of remote networked resources at different levels, such as infrastructural resources (Infrastructure as a Service—IaaS), higher-level service components for building applications (Platform as a Service—PaaS), or even complete applications (Software as a Service—SaaS). This enables the support of everyday Web applications that are used by hundreds of millions of users. While Grids and Clouds have proved their ability to scale, the Future Internet introduces such unique scalability requirements that new Service Oriented Middleware solutions need to be devised. Besides employing the pool of Grid and Cloud computational resources for covering demanding service loads, some of the high processing needs of a global-scale ESB middleware could also be served in the same way.

In order to fulfill this, we abstract different Infrastructure as a Service (IaaS) implementations in a common interface, providing a more high-level API for the instantiation of choreographies. Thus, CHOReOS will act as a Platform as a Service (PaaS) system, enabling the enactment of choreographies that, if desirable, can work in the Software as a Service (SaaS) model.

We provide a novel solution for the execution of complex services on the Cloud. Current Cloud Computing technologies focus on the allocation of virtual machines and on low-level resource management. CHOReOS platform, on the other hand, will raise the level of abstraction by providing the means to specify sophisticated distributed systems composed of multiple heterogeneous services in the end-user application level. The CHOReOS infrastructure will then map this specification to a real, large-scale distributed system that will be validated, automatically deployed and executed on cloud machines, monitored, verified, and dynamically adapted. If services require high computational power, the CHOReOS middleware will adapt to allocate grid nodes to avoid violations of QoS requirements.

CONCLUSIONS

Service choreography provides a decentralized contract-based approach for composing services in order to support a specific business process, which satisfies user needs/requirements. Emerging modeling and service middleware technologies will enable a smooth transition from service choreography design to runtime and minimize the barriers to practical use of service choreographies, which in turn will enable many useful applications and business processes composed from numerous and heterogeneous services offered by the Future Internet. These applications and business processes will be more intelligent, mobile and adaptive to their context as they will be able to select the best from the available services and maintain expected quality contracts based on the runtime analysis. CHOReOS research project produced the initial technology (concepts, process, and integrated development and runtime environment) to support the innovative choreography-based approach to distributed service composition. For more detailed information about CHOReOS and the use cases demonstrating how CHOReOS is applied in real-world scenarios, we kindly invite reader to visit http://www.choreos.eu . CHOReOS project source code is open source; integrated and published on the publicly accessible software forge of the OW2 Consortium.

ACKNOWLEDGEMENTS

This work is supported by the European Community's Seventh Framework Programme FP7/2007-2013 under grant agreement number 257178 (project CHOReOS—Large Scale Choreographies for the Future Internet— www.choreos.eu). We would like to thank all the members of CHOReOS project for their contributions, as this chapter is based on the collaborative work done during the project.

REFERENCES

(CHOReOS 2013). CHOReOS: Large Scale Choreographies for the Future Internet. FP7 integrated research project. http://www.choreos.eu

(EC 2009). Future Internet 2020 : Visions of an Industry Expert Group. Bruxelles: Commission européenne, 2009. ISSN 978-92-79-11320-8.

(OASIS 2007) Web Services Business Process Execution Language (BPEL), version 2.0. OASIS, 2007. http://docs.oasis-open.org/wsbpel/2.0/wsbpel-v2.0.pdf

(OMG 2011) Business Process Model and Notation (BPMN) version 2.0. Object Management Group (OMG), 2011. http://www.omg.org/spec/BPMN/2.0/

(Bartolini 2012) Cesare Bartolini, Antonia Bertolino, Andrea Ciancone, Guglielmo De Angelis, and Raffaela Mirandola. Quality Requirements for Service Choreographies. In Proc. of WEBIST 2012.

(Crnkovic, 2011) I. Crnkovic, "Predictability and evolution in resilient systems," in Proc. of SERENE 2011, ser. LNCS, vol. 6968. Springer, 2011, pp. 113–114, – Invited Talk.

(Baresi 2006) L. Baresi, E. Di Nitto, and C. Ghezzi, "Toward Open-world Software: Issue and Challenges," Computer, vol. 39, pp. 36–43, 2006.

(Ali 2013) M. Ali, G. De Angelis, and A. Polini. ServicePot – an Extensible Registry for Choreography Governance. In Proc. of the 7th International Symposium on Service Oriented System Engineering (SOSE 2013), IEEE-CS (2013), pp 113-124.

(Bertolino 2012) A. Bertolino, G. De Angelis, S. Kellomaki, and A. Polini. Enhancing Service Federation Trustworthiness through Online Testing. Computer, vol.45, no.1, pp.66-72, 2012.

(Calinescu 2011) R. Calinescu, L. Grunske, M. Z. Kwiatkowska, R. Mirandola, and G. Tamburrelli, "Dynamic qos management and optimization in service-based systems," IEEE Trans. Software Eng., vol. 37, no. 3, pp. 387–409, 2011.

(Bartolini 2013) C. Bartolini, A. Bertolino, G. De Angelis, A. Ciancone, and R. Mirandola. Apprehensive QoS monitoring of Service choreographies. In Proceedings of the 28th Annual ACM Symposium on Applied Computing (SAC '13). ACM, New York, NY, USA, 1893-1899.

(Peltz 2003) C. Peltz: Web Services Orchestration and Choreography. IEEE Computer (COMPUTER) 36(10):46-52 (2003)

(Decker 2009) G. Decker, O. Kopp, F. Leymann, and M. Weske, "Interacting Services: From Specification to Execution," Data & Knowledge Engineering, vol. 68, no. 10, pp. 946 – 972, 2009.

(Baldoni 2008) C. Baroglio, A. Martelli, V. Patti, and C. Schifanella, "Service selection by choreography-driven matching," in Emerging Web Services Technology, Vol. II, T. Gschwind et al., Eds. Birkhäuser Basel, 2008, pp. 5–22.

(ECRIM 2009) ERCIM News, "Special Theme: Future Internet Technology". Number 77, April 2009.

(Poizat 2012) P. Poizat and G. Salaün, "Checking the Realizability of BPMN 2.0 Choreographies," in Proc. of SAC 2012, 2012, pp. 1927–1934.

(Calvanese 2008) D. Calvanese, G. D. Giacomo, M. Lenzerini, M. Mecella, and F. Patrizi, "Automatic service composition and synthesis: the roman model," IEEE Data Eng. Bull., vol. 31, no. 3, pp. 18–22, 2008.

(Pathak 2008) J. Pathak, R. Lutz, and V. Honavar, "Moscoe: An approach for composing web services through iterative reformulation of functional specifications," International Journal on Artificial Intelligence Tools, vol. 17, pp. 109–138, 2008.

(Autili 2013) M. Autili, D. Ruscio, A. Salle, P. Inverardi, and M. Tivoli, "A model-based synthesis process for choreography realizability enforcement," in FASE, Lecture Notes in Computer Science, 2013, vol. 7793, pp. 37–52.

(Ben Hamida 2012) Amira Ben Hamida, Antonia Bertolino, Antonello Calabrò, Guglielmo De Angelis, Nelson Lago, Julien Lesbegueries: Monitoring Service Choreographies from Multiple Sources. SERENE 2012: 134-149

(Zribi 2012) Sarah Zribi, Frédérick Bénaben, Amira Ben Hamida, Jean-Pierre Lorré: Towards a Service and Choreography Governance Framework for Future Internet. I-ESA 2012: 281-291

(Lesbequeries 2012) Julien Lesbegueries, Amira Ben Hamida, Nicolas Salatge, Sarah Zribi, Jean-Pierre Lorré: Multilevel event-based monitoring framework for the petals enterprise service bus: industry article. DEBS 2012: 48-57

(Papazoglou 2012) M. P. Papazoglou, P. Traverso, S. Dustdar, and F. Leymann. Service-Oriented Computing: State of the Art and Research Challenges. IEEE Computer, 40(11):38–45, 2007.

Making SOA Work—
a Practice-Oriented Overview

Gerhard Rempp and Martin Löffler, MID GmbH, Germany

INTRODUCTION

Services represent the pivotal feature of service-oriented architecture.

This paper highlights how a service evolution can take place within a SOA service lifecycle, from the specialized process and defining business services all the way to technical service implementation.

THE KING IS DEAD – LONG LIVE THE KING!

SOA has often been declared a failure. But, in fact, we can see that SOA use has now become a reality! After all, those who have been declared dead often live the longest, and many prophets are later revealed to be naysayers.

There are active SOA projects in every large company, and SOA-ification is forging ahead. Still, there is no longer any huge hype surrounding it. And that's a good sign! SOA and the associated standardization has become part of our everyday lives.

Still, there are some unresolved issues. These issues have less and less to do with technology, because there are plenty of platforms available – from open-source platforms with MuleESB, JBoss and jBPM to others from the Apache universe, and commercial platforms from the usual suspects like Oracle and IBM. In addition, there are more and more cloud services, for instance from Amazon, Google and Microsoft. The technical platforms are available, in other words, and people can make choices based on their preferences or a strict catalogue of criteria.

The evolution in modeling languages is also helping to bring together specialized areas and IT; the often-cited IT alignment between business and IT is increasingly becoming a reality. BPMN 2.0 has also broken through as a standard language for process modeling.

Then, everything's just great, isn't it?

Well, in the last few years we have learned not to view this issue just through a technical lens. Because, if the development of SOA services is seen only in terms of technology, it often doesn't produce the desired results. Why is that?

The miraculous promise of SOA was, and still is, something like this: "And lo, it shall come to pass that your processes shall be automated and implemented even more quickly than your thoughts! Truly there shall be joy and celebration. Milk and honey shall flow, and there shall be eternal jubilation among the management." At least that's what the marketing pitches tell us!

All right, so it wasn't always completely true, but nowadays no one would doubt that we're on the right path!

So what is really important if we want to explore a meaningful way to find services?

TWO'S A CROWD

In order to lay the right foundations for a successful SOA project, services need to be developed on the basis of specialized knowledge. In the last few years, modeling has emerged as a useful and necessary way to provide the ideal support for business/IT alignment. BPMN models are playing an increasingly important role in this. A business process analysis allows us to achieve multiple quality goals for a SOA project.

For SOA, the highest priority is given to optimal service profile. Modeling business processes is an important requirement, because we can only prevent services from overlapping if we use suitable, specialized business process models. By defining various domains and assigning services, we can eliminate overlaps and achieve loose coupling. It is worth noting that we are just talking about the specialized aspect for now, and not dealing with any technical details – after all, what are generators for? If a model establishes the relationship between service, processes, any applications, data, responsible parties, stakeholders and users, that's a huge step toward governance already! After all, the following questions will always come up in the SOA environment:

- Who is responsible for a service?
- Who uses a service?
- Who needs to be involved in decisions about creating and making later changes to a service?
- Which processes and applications will use a service?
- What data is needed by a service, and what data will it provide?
- Which services will a domain provide, and which ones will be assigned to a domain?

This is also associated with a high level of reusability for services.

PLANNING IS HALF THE SERVICE

In order to make sure that SOA Service Lifecycle Management (SOA SLM) isn't left to chance, it is a good idea to plan the process in advance and answer the following questions: What exactly does the service development process look like? Which roles will be involved and when? What expertise is needed, and which tools will be used?

SPEM[1] stands for Software & Systems Process Engineering Meta-Model, and the M³ Process Engineering Framework provides all of the necessary resources for defining a new process or adapting an existing process, along with the methodology. M³PEF uses BPMN 2.0 for the simple, fast implementation of SPEM.

The central aspects of this meta-model are consecutive activities, work results, roles, milestones and tools. The activities use work results from previous activities, and they can produce work results themselves. By defining milestones and the roles assigned to activities as well as the tools they will use, you can create an image of the overall process. Figure 1 shows an excerpt from a model structure.

---

[1] http://www.omg.org/spec/SPEM/2.0/

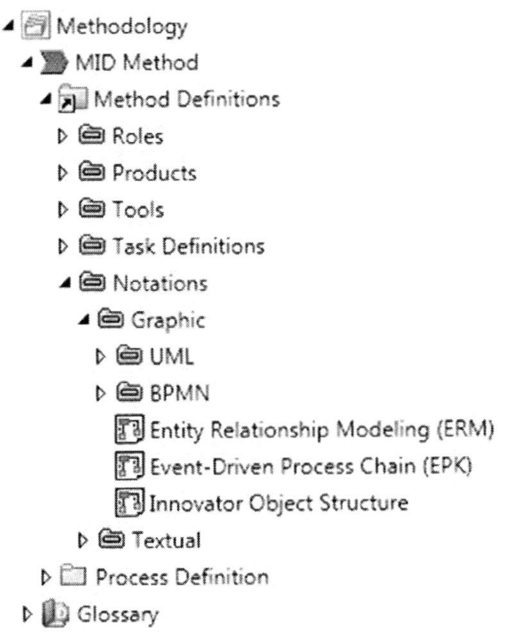

▲ 📇 Methodology
  ▲ 📜 MID Method
    ▲ 🔳 Method Definitions
      ▷ 📁 Roles
      ▷ 📁 Products
      ▷ 📁 Tools
      ▷ 📁 Task Definitions
      ▲ 📁 Notations
        ▲ 📁 Graphic
          ▷ 📁 UML
          ▷ 📁 BPMN
          📄 Entity Relationship Modeling (ERM)
          📄 Event-Driven Process Chain (EPK)
          📄 Innovator Object Structure
        ▷ 📁 Textual
    ▷ 🗀 Process Definition
  ▷ 📖 Glossary

Figure 1: Model structure for M³PEF using SPEM

In addition to a clearer understanding for all of the participants, this provides another important building block for SOA governance! Figure 2 shows a sample initiation phase for Model-Driven SOA (MDSOA[2]), which was modeled with M³PEF on the basis of SPEM.

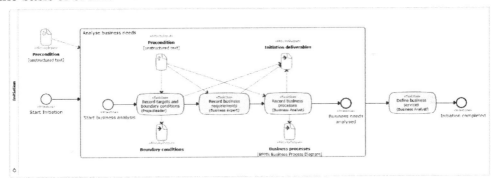

Figure 2: MDSOA phase initiation modeled with M³PEF

LOOK BEFORE YOU LEAP!

In the first phase, the specialized department is highlighted as a key contact partner. It provides as much information as possible about the specialized process, which is compiled as an initial business process model by the department itself or by a business analyst. Typically, important information can be derived from specialized concepts, workshop results, existing models and information about the en-

---

[2] The "Model Driven SOA" method, from the book with the same name; see [MDSOA]

terprise architecture, or by using investigation techniques from Requirements Engineering.[3] This step intentionally avoids developing the model in too much detail in order to take advantage of the quick process recording without a large training effort. The first priority is to acquire the appropriate specialized knowledge.

Once the processes have been recorded, they are analyzed. This analysis includes identifying service candidates and service operations, defining business services and assigning services to domains. Fundamentally, candidates for service include:

- Tasks or processes that need to be automated
- Reading, modifying, creating and deleting business objects
- Interfaces between processes and organizational units

Figure 3 shows a typical decision tree that is used to find a candidate for service.

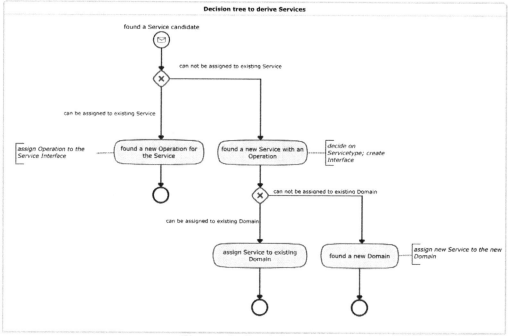

Figure 3: Decision tree

Also included in the considerations:

- existing services and applications
- existing databases and/or their models (conceptual or logical DB models)

SERVICE TYPES LOVE COMPANY

In order to derive the corresponding technical processes from the specialized processes, various requirements need to be taken into account. Are there any technical processes or partial processes that can be reused? Can costs or processing times be optimized? Is the specialized process defined in enough detail to derive the technical implementation? When deriving technical services and the technical processes that will use these services, the services and processes can often be optimized. It is important to remember that all of the technical services and processes must meet the specialized requirements.

---

[3] Typical techniques in RE are: document analysis, questioning techniques, interviews, observations, brainstorming, mind maps, rapid prototyping.

As an example of generalization, the creation of an email in the specialized process could be used to derive a notification service, which would not only send an email, but could also address groups or send a text message.

Designing the technical processes goes hand in hand with defining the technical services. The requirements for technical services can be roughly described as follows:

- A technical service functionally represents a closed unit.
- A service is provided via one or more interfaces.
- One service cannot overlap with the performance of other services.
- Services can be assigned to a specialized domain.
- Each service can be used by a wide variety of consumers.
- A service provides a business-administration-related, meaningful and high-value benefit.
- Processes use technical services to perform their functions. Processes themselves can be considered services.

In our experience, it is very helpful to work with service categories right from the start. Fundamentally, we can identify the following types:[4]

Service type	Description
ProcessService	A process service is distinguished by its potential longevity. It has an asynchronous character and is often status-related. A process service, as the name indicates, covers entire processes or partial processes. Process services have a controlling function.
ActivityService	An activity service encapsulates a specific smaller part of a functionality. It is usually used synchronously, and is not usually status-related—or only during short periods while it is executing its own process. It is similar to a façade;[5] in other words, it hides a certain complexity from the client who is using it.
RuleService	A rule service encapsulates one or more business rules, and thus it includes a decision-making or evaluation logic. By nature, it is not status-related, and it is used synchronously.
DataService	A data service is responsible for the consistency and correct persistence of a quantity of data that may be related. It provides the typical operations to create, read, update and delete items.[6]

Modeling BPMN collaborations makes it possible to orchestrate and choreograph technical processes and services. Since the participants have a connection with the services they are representing and the respective tasks also represent operations

---

[4] The classification of service types is taken from the article series [JMSOA].

[5] A façade is an object that provides a simplified interface to a larger body of code and promotes loose coupling (see also: http://en.wikipedia.org/wiki/Facade_pattern).

[6] Also known as CRUD: Create, Read, Update, Delete

for services, these diagrams can be used to create standard artifacts from the SOA world, such as WDSL and BPEL or BPMN-XML. Figure 4 shows what we call a service collaboration, with a black box representation of the other participants.

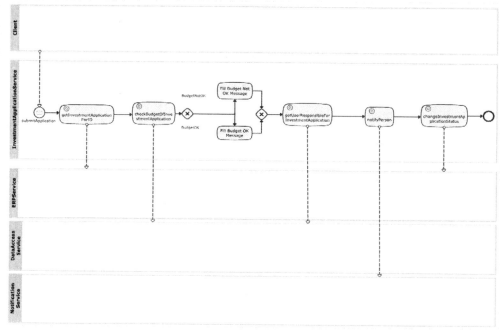

Figure 4: Service collaboration

MOVING AHEAD!

As already mentioned, the service collaboration can be used to create a derivation according to either BPEL or BPMN-XML. These outputs ultimately stand for various process services. The corresponding artifacts can be created for each participant here, in order to import them into a process engine and execute them.

The technical interface definition in the model can be used to generate corresponding WSDL and XSD artifacts.

The interactions between the individual services, their interfaces and the messages exchanged are thus largely specified, and are used to derive standards from the model. Many execution platforms can simply use these directly.

LAST BUT NOT LEAST...

But that's not all! If each defined service already has an existing implementation, we're in luck. Otherwise, we still need to take care of the implementation of the services. Fortunately, we have already gathered quite a bit of information in our model, which allows us to automatically derive suitable model artifacts.

The technical services can be transferred to a UML representation, where further technology-specific information can be added (e.g. the use of the Java type system, adding JPA properties, etc.). The messages exchanged between services can now also be defined in more detail, for instance in class diagrams. Generators provide the option of translating the implementation-specific model contents into target languages like Java or C#.

In addition, most execution platforms provide their own implementation technology. For instance, the business logic for the individual service operations is also formulated and directly executed in BPEL, BPMN, UML or a proprietary graphics language and does not need to be implemented manually.

AT A GLANCE

- SOA starts with specialized knowledge
- SOA is not just about technology
- Meaningful business services come from a specialized process analysis
- Technical services are derived from business services
- Service categories help with the service profile
- Assigning domains, responsibilities, stakeholders and users helps you find (and retrieve) services, both for operations and for maintenance

REFERENCES

(JMSOA) Maier B, Normann H, Trops B et al. SOA aus dem wahren Leben. JavaMagazin, 11/2008 ff.

(MDSOA) Rempp G, Akermann M, Löffler M, Lehmann J. Model Driven SOA – Anwendungsorientierte Methodik und Vorgehen in der Praxis, Heidelberg, Springer Verlag 2011. http://www.springer.com/978-3-642-14469-1.

Smart Tools and Visual Analytics

Hartmann Genrich, Process Analytica, Germany
Robert Shapiro, Process Analytica, USA

INTRODUCTION

Smart tools of *PA Optima* support fast optimization by simulation and analysis using only that subset of the analytics required by the particular optimization technique. They are rather 'autistic' and focus on efficiency rather than interaction and generality.

So far two such tools are available: *Smart Resource Allocation* and *Smart Productivity Improvement*. We briefly describe Smart Allocation because the optimization algorithms in it are also used in Smart Productivity.

SMART ALLOCATION

Once started, the *Smart Resource Allocation* tool allows in a quick 'assess, change and try' iteration the changing of the number of copies ('clones') of each resource, simulation of the given set of work item arrivals and assessing the results in terms of resource idleness (upper chart), cycle times (lower chart).

Figure 1

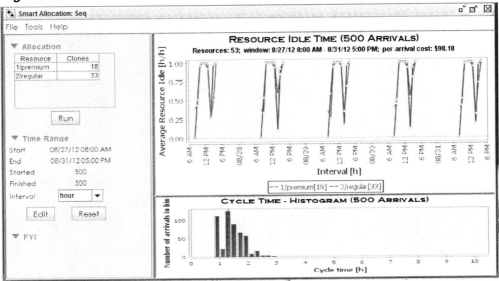

Approach

The approach of *Smart Resource Allocation* is to support a quick iteration of 'assess, change and try' steps. In addition to changing the allocation manually there are two automatic allocation modes: *initial allocation* and *idleness reduction*.

An *idleness* chart, and a *cycle time* chart support assessment.

Assessment

The tool allows the assessment of a particular allocation in several respects.

1. The *per-arrival costs* appear in the title of the resource idle time chart (upper pane) and on top of the FYI text field. The costs are calculated on the basis of the times the resources are on shift (scheduled) during the given time window (default: simulation period) and their respective salaries, divided by the number work items that finish in that window.

2. The idle time chart (upper pane) plots idleness of every resource over the time axis.

3. The FYI text shows a simple characterization of *idleness distribution*. The plot is virtually divided into three bands (*upper, middle* or *lower*) of equal width and for each resource the percentage of idle time in each band is listed.

4. The *cycle times* are plotted in the lower pane of the window, optionally as histogram or scatter plot.[2] They allow a quick assessment of performance under the chosen allocation.

The initial example was created by initial resource allocation with maximum hourly workload (see *Initial Resource Allocation* below). It obviously gives high performance at a high cost. In the sequel we lower the performance to a tolerable level (work item finished within one workday) in order to lower the costs.

Resource Idleness

A *resource idleness* chart shows for every period of selected length (full hour | full day) and every resource an *average idleness* between 0 and 1. These values are calculated as follows by *resource utilization* analysis.

Let:

res be a resource,

$R_{res} = (res.clones + 1)$ be its capacity (the number of copies),

$schd = res.schedule$ be its schedule,

prd be a period of the x-axis[1].

The algorithm calculates variables

$busy_{res,prd}$: the sum of times some copy of res spent processing a task during period prd,

$onshift_{res,prd}$: the time period prd intersects with the times that resource res is scheduled to work.

It takes the set of all occurrences occ of tasks in all histories (see [1]) where the resource field of occ denotes a copy of res; it adds to $busy$ the sum of the time occ spent processing during period prd. This requires splitting the processing period of occ into pieces belonging to shift instances of schedule $schd$ and add the intersections of those pieces with period prd.

The results are stored in maps

$OnShift : res \times prd \rightarrow onshift_{res,prd}$

$Busy : res \times prd \rightarrow busy_{res,prd}$

---

[1] The x-axis starts with the period that contains the simulation start time and ends with the period that contains the simulation end time.

The variable $idle_{res,prd} = (onshift_{res,prd} * R_{res} - busy_{res,prd}) / onshift_{res,prd} * R_{res}$ is the *average idleness* of (the copies of) *res* relative to the time *res* is on shift during period *prd*. It is plotted in the idleness chart.

Initial Resource Allocation

Initial resource allocation uses a two pass approach.

First, the workflow is simulated with a *'universal'* resource, a special device of the simulator providing unlimited resource capacity for any performer. The *universal* resource can perform any role and work concurrently on multiple tasks. It allows the simulation to generate the 'ideal' workload drivers. The business schedule determines when the business is 'open'. The resulting simulation produces the fastest end-to-end cycle time as if we were willing to schedule enough resources to handle the sharpest peak loads.

In a variation of the resource utilization algorithm above, the *Busy* map becomes the set of workload drivers for each performer. Depending on the selected option the demand per hour for each performer is determined. Then a resource is defined for each performer with the default salary and performance defined for the performer and the number of clones determined by the workloads and the selected options.

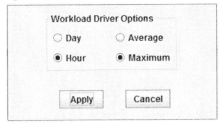

Example: if option *hour&max* is selected and the peak hourly demand of performer *premium* is 20 hours, then a resource is created that plays role *premium* and has 20 copies (19 clones).

With the resulting resource allocation the workflow is simulated again. The results of the second pass are then loaded into a new copy of the allocation tool.

Idleness Reduction

The idleness reduction algorithm, too, uses the results of the *resource utilization* algorithm above. For each resource it removes clones one by one as long as its remaining average idleness does not fall below 20%; this lower limit 0.2 of idleness is a wired-in heuristic constant that prevents the resources from being maxed out.

We started with the initial allocation created above, see Once started, the *Smart Resource Allocation* tool allows in a quick 'assess, change and try' iteration the changing of the number of copies ('clones') of each resource, simulation of the given set of work item arrivals and assessing the results in terms of resource idleness (upper chart), cycle times (lower chart).

Figure 1. After two applications of idleness reduction – the first one leaves a little room for a second and final round – we get an allocation with clone counts considerably reduced; see Figure 2 and Table 1. The cost per arrival goes down from $98.18 to $24.44 and the work is still finished within one work day (the outliers are due to the weekend).

Figure 2

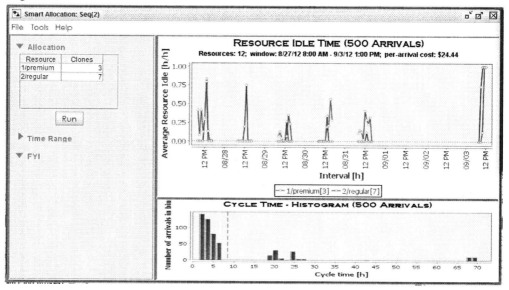

Table 1

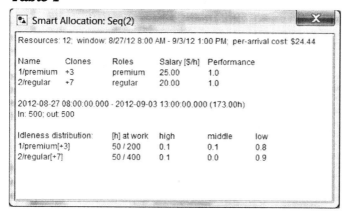

The idleness distribution given in the text window confirms the visual impression of the idleness chart that for both resources their idleness is in the lower sector most of the time. Further manual reduction may push the per-arrival costs further down but the cycle times will go up drastically.

SMART PRODUCTIVITY

In some way all components of *Optima* are concerned with productivity improvement. This productivity tool, however, is different and novel. It goes one step beyond identifying potential improvement; it facilitates *Cost/Benefit* and *Return-on-Investment* analysis of *proposed improvement* measures.

Our running example is once more the somewhat superficial view (expressed in BPMN [3]) of a workflow handling the applications for a bank account of type *regular* or *premium*; see Figure 3 and Figure 4. We will see how different proposals can be assessed with respect to their costs and benefits and to the return on the necessary investments.

Figure 3
A workflow (top-level process, sub-processes collapsed)

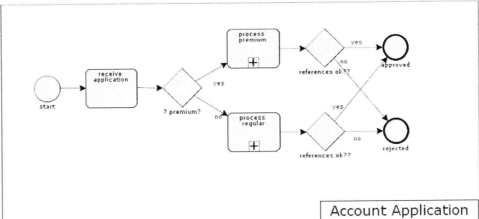

Figure 4
Sub-process details

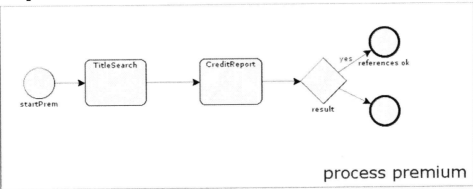

There are two types of windows in the *Productivity Improvement* tool. The primary window, the *project* window (see Figure 5), is opened for a loaded scenario via the *Tools* menu of *OPTIMIZE* or the respective scenario button in *ANALYZE* (chart, table and tool browser). It has three major panes, the *Parameter Setting* pane, the *Return-on-Investment* prediction pane and a tabbed pane with two auxiliary charts, *Workload* and *Cycle Time*, for a quick assessment of performance. An optional text window, *FYI*, presents additional information in textual or tabular form.

The secondary, auxiliary windows (see Figure 6) present the details of the *Cost/Benefit* analysis that populates the ROI prediction. It is started by a right-click on the *As-Is* or some *To-Be* column.

Project Window

Figure 5
The Productivity Improvement Window

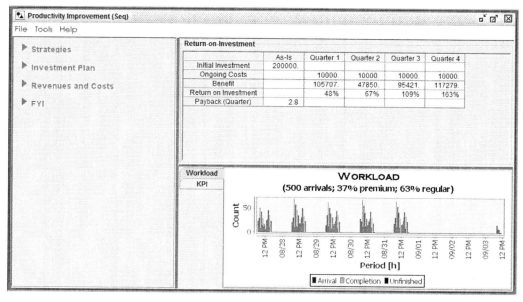

Cost/Benefit Window

A window with detailed *Cost/Benefit* analysis, of the *As-Is* scenario or of any of the *To-Be* intervals, is started by a right-click on the respective column of the ROI table. The tool

- depicts various details of the run for the respective interval,
- allows a quick series of 'fine tuning' experiments with changed resource allocation and/or task simulations details.

Figure 6
Cost/Benefit Details

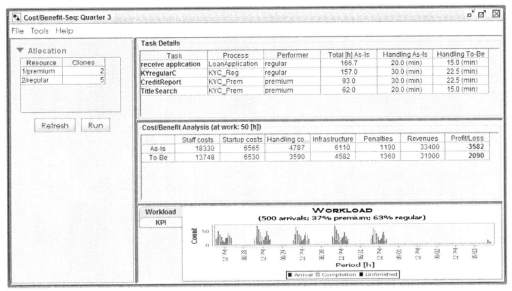

Functionality, Modes of Operation

Auto-Allocation

In order to make resource costs comparable the resource capacities (numbers of copies/clones for each resource) are re-calculated with the same rules for each step. The algorithm is a simple version of initial resource allocation (see *Smart Resource Allocation* [1]).

For every performer the total workload entailed by the set of arrivals is calculated.

Then a resource is constructed with a capacity (number of copies/clones) sufficient to accomplish this work load during the same number of workdays as work items arrive (principle *of balanced load and capacity*). The assumption here is that
- distribution and period of arrivals is representative,
- task performers are chosen such that resources don't have to wait for work.

Example:

arrival period:	*5 workdays*
workday (business schedule):	*8 hours*
total workload for performer *regular.*	*300 hours*
resource capacity required for *regular.*	*300 / (5 * 8) = 7.5*
resource[2] :	*'2/regular'* with *7* clones

WorkLoad Growth

If we set the growth parameter of the strategies group to a percentage ≠ *0* we expect the workload, the collection of work item arrivals, to grow (or to shrink, for that

---

[2] The resource is created and named by the auto-allocation algorithm. Its name consists of a sequence number (id) and the first characters of the performer.

that matter). Arrivals are specified as *batches* with a *start* date/time, a *size*, a *recurrence pattern* and value assignments for *data fields* (process properties). These batches are expanded by the simulator into collections of *data field inputs* (often called arrivals, too) at the start of a simulation.

Applying a growth ≠ *0%* must only change the *size* of batches which is an *integer* number > *0*. If the sizes are big enough we can just add or subtract the specified amount without much loss of precisions. If some sizes are too small, however, this might change the character of the workload too much.

An alternative approach might be to pick at random the required number of data field inputs (batch instances) and remove them or add a copy. However, it is the arrival batches that belong to the scenarios and they cannot be abstracted from the list of individual batch instances.

Hence the growth is applied by a combination of the two ideas.

Let *G* be the growth *factor*, *G* = *1* + *growth/100%*.

Let *delta* be a variable that holds the accrued rounding errors; it is *0* initially;

In a first pass, for each batch with size S and recurrence count R,

the size is set to *S'* = *round(S * G)*,

the error *(S' − S * G) * R* is added to *delta*.

In a second pass, repeatedly,

a batch is selected at random,

its *size* is increased respectively decreased by *1*,

delta is reduced by the batch's recurrence count, *R*,

until *delta* is exhausted.

Return-on-Investment Prediction

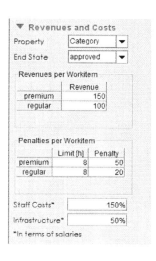

STRATEGIES

The tool offers three options for improving the productivity.

1. Invest in training to improve staff performance.
2. Invest in reducing the handling time at tasks.
    a. Tasks are ranked according to their total handling time. You can choose to invest in the top n %.
3. You can import a separate To-Be model with its own simulation details.

    a. If you check 'import' the import button becomes enabled.
    b. If you start a run with import checked and no To-Be imported yet you will be asked to do so.
4. If you plan the investment to prepare for more business you can set the growth per interval to the expected percentage – to be applied from the second interval on.

REVENUES AND COSTS

The assumption is that work items that *end* 'successfully' yield *revenues* and that the amount depends on a data field denoting a certain *kind* of work item. Similarly, work items that take too long to finish may result in some loss that can be quantified by a *penalty*.

In our example,

- revenues are specified for work items that finish with an *approved* state and the amount depending on the values *premium* or *regular* of process property *Category*.
- similarly, penalties have to be experienced if the cycle times exceed 8 hours.

For the operating costs it is assumed that they consist of staff costs (salaries plus benefits etc.) infrastructure costs (e.g. office space, equipment) and can be expressed in proportion to the costs for staff salaries. In our example, the total costs of operation are assumed to be twice the costs for salaries

CONCLUSION

The *Smart Productivity Improvement* tool is novel and different from all other components of *Optima*. It goes one step beyond identifying potential improvement. It combines functionality of existing applications for cost/benefit and return-on-investment analysis with the *Visual Analytics* power of *PA Optima*; it facilitates the quick assessment of *proposed* improvement measures.

The tool is still in the state of a prototype rather than a full-fledged return-on-investment application. However, it demonstrates the feasibility of the approach as well as the power of *PA Optima* in general.

REFERENCES

[1]   *Workflow Histories in Optima.* Technical Report. Process Analytica (2013)

[2]   *The JFreeChart Class Library*, Version 1.0.13. Developer Guide. Object Refinery Ltd. (2009)

[3]   Bruce Silver: *BPMN Method and Style*, 2nd Edition. Cody-Cassidy Press (2011)

[4]   *Smart Resource Allocation.* Technical Report. Process Analytica (2013)

[5]   Robert M. Shapiro and Hartmann J. Genrich: *Optima Visual Analytics.* Process Analytica (In Preparation)

Section 2

WfMC Structure and Membership Information

What is the Workflow Management Coalition?

The Workflow Management Coalition, founded in August 1993, is a non-profit, international organization of BPM and workflow vendors, users, analysts and university/research groups. The Coalition's mission is to promote and develop the use of BPM and workflow through the establishment of standards for software terminology, interoperability and connectivity among BPM and workflow products. Comprising more than 250 members worldwide, the Coalition is the primary standards body for this software market.

Workflow Standards Framework

The Coalition has developed a framework for the establishment of workflow standards. This framework includes five categories of interoperability and communication standards that will allow multiple workflow products to coexist and interoperate within a user's environment. Technical details are included in the white paper entitled, "The Work of the Coalition," available at www.wfmc.org.

Workflow Management Coalition Structure

The Coalition is divided into three major committees, the Technical Committee, the External Relations Committee, and the Steering Committee. Small working groups exist within each committee for the purpose of defining workflow terminology, interoperability and connectivity standards, conformance requirements, and for assisting in the communication of this information to the workflow user community.

The Coalition's major committees meet three times per calendar year for three days at a time, with meetings usually alternating between a North American and a European location. The working group meetings are held during these three days, and as necessary throughout the year.

Coalition membership is open to all interested parties involved in the creation, analysis or deployment of workflow software systems. Membership is governed by a Document of Understanding, which outlines meeting regulations, voting rights etc. Membership material is available at www.wfmc.org.

Coalition Working Groups

The Coalition has established a number of Working Groups, each working on a particular area of specification. The working groups are loosely structured around the "Workflow Reference Model" which provides the framework for the Coalition's standards program. The Reference Model identifies the common characteristics of workflow systems and defines five discrete functional interfaces through which a workflow management system interacts with its environment—users, computer tools and applications, other software services, etc. Working groups meet individually, and also under the umbrella of the Technical Committee, which is responsible for overall technical direction and co-ordination.

Achievements

The initial work of the Coalition focused on publishing the Reference Model and Glossary, defining a common architecture and terminology for the industry. A major milestone was achieved with the publication of the first versions of the Workflow

API (WAPI) specification, covering the Workflow Client Application Interface, and the Workflow Interoperability specification.

In addition to a series of successful tutorials industry wide, the WfMC spent many hours over 2009 helping to drive awareness, understanding and adoption of XPDL, now the standard means for business process definition in over 80 BPM products. As a result, it has been cited as the most deployed BPM standard by a number of industry analysts, and continues to receive a growing amount of media attention.

Workflow Reference Model

The Workflow Reference Model was published first in 1995 and still forms the basis of most BPM and workflow software systems in use today. It was developed from the generic workflow application structure by identifying the interfaces which enable products to interoperate at a variety of levels. All workflow systems contain a number of generic components which interact in a defined set of ways; different products will typically exhibit different levels of capability within each of these generic components. To achieve interoperability between workflow products a standardized set of interfaces and data interchange formats between such components is necessary. A number of distinct interoperability scenarios can then be constructed by reference to such interfaces, identifying different levels of functional conformance as appropriate to the range of products in the market.

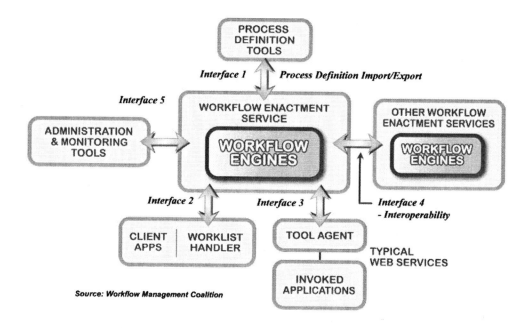

WORKFLOW REFERENCE MODEL DIAGRAM

XPDL (XML Process Definition Language)

An XML based language for describing a process definition, developed by the WfMC. Version 1.0 was released in 2002. Version 2.0 was released in Oct 2005. The goal of XPDL is to store and exchange the process diagram, to allow one tool to model a process diagram, and another to read the diagram and edit, another to "run" the process model on an XPDL-compliant BPM engine, and so on. For this reason,

XPDL is not an executable programming language like BPEL, but specifically a process design format that literally represents the "drawing" of the process definition. Thus it has 'XY' or vector coordinates, including lines and points that define process flows. This allows an XPDL to store a one-to-one representation of a BPMN process diagram. For this reason, XPDL is effectively the file format or "serialization" of BPMN, as well as any non-BPMN design method or process model which use in their underlying definition the XPDL meta-model (there are presently about 60 tools which use XPDL for storing process models.)

In spring 2012, the WfMC completed XPDL 2.2 as the *fifth* revision of this specification. XPDL 2.2 builds on version 2.1 by introducing support for the process modeling extensions added to BPMN 2.0.

BPSim

The Business Process Simulation (BPSim) framework is a standardized specification that allows business process models captured in either BPMN or XPDL to be augmented with information in support of rigorous methods of analysis. It defines the parameterization and interchange of process analysis data allowing structural and capacity analysis of process models. BPSim is meant to support both pre-execution and post-execution optimization of said process models. The BPSim specification consists of an underlying computer-interpretable representation (meta-model) and an accompanying electronic file format to ease the safeguard and transfer of this data between different tools (interchange format).

Wf-XML

Wf-XML is designed and implemented as an extension to the OASIS Asynchronous Service Access Protocol (ASAP). ASAP provides a standardized way that a program can start and monitor a program that might take a long time to complete. It provides the capability to monitor the running service, and be informed of changes in its status. Wf-XML extends this by providing additional standard web service operations that allow sending and retrieving the "program" or definition of the service which is provided. A process engine has this behavior of providing a service that lasts a long time, and also being programmable by being able to install process definitions.

Awards

The Workflow Management Coalition sponsors three annual award programs.

1. The **Global Awards for Excellence in BPM & Workflow**[1] recognizes organizations that have implemented particularly innovative workflow solutions. Every year between 10 and 15 BPM and workflow solutions are recognized in this manner. WfMC publishes the case studies in the annual Excellence in Practice series.

2. WfMC inaugurated a Global Awards program in 2011 for **Adaptive Case Management**[2] case studies to recognize and focus upon ACM use cases. Adaptive Case Management, also known as Dynamic or Advanced Case Management, is a new technological approach to supporting knowledge workers in today's leading edge organizations. These awards are designed to highlight the best examples of technology to support knowledge workers. In 2012 nine teams were awarded top honors at the ACM Live Event and are featured in the book, "How

---

[1] www.BPMF.org

[2] www.adaptivecasemanagement.org

Knowledge Workers Get Things Done.[3]" In 2013, WfMC updated the program to "WfMC Awards for Excellence in Case Management" to recognize the growing deployment of Production Case Management.

3. The **Marvin L. Manheim Award For Significant Contributions** in the Field of Workflow is given to one person every year in recognition of individual contributions to workflow and BPM standards. This award commemorates Marvin Manheim who played a key motivational role in the founding of the WfMC.

WHY YOU SHOULD JOIN

1. Gain Access to Members-Only Research and Q&A Forums
2. Participate in Members-Only "Brown Bag" Networking Sessions and Industry Speaker Series
3. Receive Free Admission to Business Process Focused Events and Programs (a Benefit Worth $1,000s Annually)
4. Access to the Industry's Largest Research Library on Business Process Modeling, Workflow, BPMS
5. Assistance in Product Certification and Conformance, as well as Requirements Analysis and Procurement Strategy

Being a member of the Workflow Management Coalition gives you the unique opportunity to participate in the creation of standards for the workflow industry as they are developing. Your contributions to our community ensure that progress continues in the adoption of royalty-free workflow and process standards.

BENEFITS OF MEMBERSHIP

Membership offers exclusive visibility in this sector at events and seminars across the world, enhancing your customers' perception of you as an industry authority, on our web site, in the Coalition Handbook and CDROM, by speaking opportunities, access to the Members Only area of our web site, attending the Coalition meetings and most importantly within the workgroups whereby through discussion and personal involvement, using your voting power, you can contribute actively to the development of standards and interfaces.

Full member benefits include:

- Web Visibility: your logo on WfMC pages, inclusion in the WfMC web banner network, a detailed company profile in online member directory as well as in all WfMC publications.
- User RFIs: (Requests for Information) is an exclusive privilege to all full members. We often receive queries from user organizations looking for specific workflow solutions. These valuable leads can result in real business benefits for your organization.
- Publicity: full members may choose to have their company logos including collaterals displayed along with WfMC material at conferences /expos we attend. You may also list corporate events and press releases (relating to WfMC issues) on the relevant pages on the website, and have a company entry in the annual Coalition Workflow Handbook
- Speaking Opportunities: We frequently receive calls for speakers at industry events because many of our members are recognized experts in their fields. These opportunities are forwarded to Full Members for their direct response to the respective conference organizers.

---

[3] *How Knowledge Workers Get Things Done.* Published 2012 by Future Strategies Inc. http://www.futstrat.com/books/HowKnowledgeWorkers.php

ASSOCIATE MEMBERSHIP

Associate and Academic Membership is appropriate for those (such as IT user organizations) who need to keep abreast of workflow developments, but who are not workflow vendors. It allows voting on decision-making issues, including the publication of standards and interfaces but does not permit anything near the amount of visibility or incentives provided to a Full Member. You may include up to three active members from your organization on your application.

INDIVIDUAL MEMBERSHIP

Individual Membership is appropriate for self-employed persons or small user companies. Employees of workflow vendors, academic institutions or analyst organizations are not typically eligible for this category. Individual membership is held in one person's name only, is not a corporate membership, and is not transferable within the company. If three or more people within a company wish to participate in the WfMC, it would be cost-effective to upgrade to corporate Associate Membership whereby all employees worldwide are granted membership status.

HOW TO JOIN

Complete the form on the Coalition's website, or contact the Coalition Secretariat, at the address below. All members are required to sign the Coalition's "Document of Understanding" which sets out the contractual rights and obligations between members and the Coalition.

THE SECRETARIAT

Workflow Management Coalition (WfMC)

Nathaniel Palmer, Executive Director,

+1-781-923-1411 (t), +1-781-735-0491 (f)

nathaniel@wfmc.org

Author Appendix

ROY ALTMAN

CEO, Peopleserv, Inc., USA

Roy Altman founded Peopleserv, a New York-based software/services company, in 2003. Over a multifaceted career, Altman has a history of delivering business value to well-known companies in the financial services industry and beyond. He has published extensively and has contributed to three prior books in the Future Strategies BPM Workflow series. Altman frequently presents at conferences and on webinars, including the inaugural bpmNEXT conference, and has taught at Columbia University and other institutions.

MARCO AUTILI, PH.D.

Department of Information Engineering Computer Science and Mathematics – University of L'Aquila, Italy

Marco Autili is an Assistant Professor. His main research areas are Software Architectures with particular reference to Service Oriented Architectures, application of Formal Methods to the Verification, Analysis and automatic Synthesis of complex systems, Component Based Software Engineering, and Context-Oriented Programming. He is (has been) involved in a number of European and Italian projects and initiatives in the above areas. Currently, as WP Leader of the CHOReOS – IP EU FP7 project (Oct, 2010 – Sep, 2013), he is working on a systematic approach to the automatic realizability enforcement of choreography-based service-oriented systems: from the choreography specification to the synthesis of coordination code, to the actual deployment on grid/cloud middleware. Further information about Marco's research interests and his publications can be found at http://www.di.univaq.it/marco.autili/

AMIRA BEN HAMIDA, PH.D.

R&D Engineer, Linagora GSO

Ms. Amira Ben Hamida received her Ph.D. in 2010 in Computer Science from the National Institute of Applied Sciences of Lyon (INSA Lyon) and is currently a research and development engineer at Linagora GSO firm. Her research interests relate to middleware, Service Oriented Architectures, and choreographies of services over Enterprise Service Bus technologies. She is currently involved in the works around the design and implementation of innovative solutions towards choreography design, enactment and runtime governance.

GIANPIERO BONGALLINO

Project Manager, Senior Software Engineer, Researcher and Analyst, openwork, Italy

Gianpiero Bongallino graduated in IT, specialized in Intelligent Systems, Artificial Intelligence and Software Engineering. Since 2005, he contributed to the development of Web-based and Server-side tools for an Italian BPM company (openwork). Those activities included image recognition & processing, automation, digital sign, client/server integration and enterprise application developments, also involving him as BPM Consultant for processes related to document processing and digital sign, for technical and legal matters. He coordinates teams in different projects and acted as a tutor for innovation internship and theses, collaborating also with Universities in multi-company research projects.

Gianpiero is now BPM, Complex Event Processing, SOA Specialist, Software Architect, Researcher, Developer and member of Artificial Intelligence, Project Management and Agile teams.

JOSIP BRUMEC, PH.D.

University of Zagreb, Croatia

Prof. Josip Brumec, Ph.D., is CEO of the consulting firm Koris based in Zagreb (Croatia) and a full professor at the University of Zagreb. His research interest is focused on strategic planning of information systems, business process modelling and management, ERP systems and business performance measurement. He has published over 80 scientific papers and led several research projects. Before his teaching career at the university, he had spent over 25 years in the industry. He is a member of AIS, ACM, IEEE and the Croatian Academy of Engineering.

SLAVEN BRUMEC, PH.D.

University College for Applied Computer Engineering, Zagreb, Croatia

Slaven Brumec, Ph.D., is the development manager at the consulting firm Koris and a lecturer at the University College for Applied Computer Engineering in Zagreb (Croatia). He received his doctoral degree with a thesis entitled "Computing Clouds as a Part of Service-Oriented Architecture".

He has worked as a member of a project team, as well as a researcher or a manager in several projects in the field of mobile information systems, cloud computing and BPM. He is also a certified specialist in Microsoft technologies (MCSD) and business process management (OCEB).

STEINAR CARLSEN

Chief Engineer, Computas AS, Norway

Dr. Steinar Carlsen is a recognized Norwegian expert within business processes and workflow technology. He is a senior advisor specializing in adaptive case management, business process management, knowledge management, social technologies, with more than 20 years of experience in different approaches to the modelling of work processes. His focus is on realizing work support systems, as well as baselining "organizational implementation/enactment". Steinar has a background from applied research within business process modelling, enterprise modelling, enterprise architecture and requirements engineering. Steinar is the product owner of FrameSolutions™ - Computas AS' framework for realizing operational ACM solutions.

GUNNAR JOHN COLL

Senior Advisor, VP, Computas AS

Gunnar John Coll represents a behavioural approach to technology, organization and knowledge. He assists customers in corporate process initiatives, including knowledge management and organizational learning. His main area of work is where business process and human competence meet with new technology, to answer the need for change. He provides perspectives, facilitates and manages initiatives in close cooperation with customer's key personnel. Gunnar has more than 25 years of experience in IT projects related to organizational processes. Due to his combined background as a psychologist and an IT professional, he provides a complementary perspective on system development and organizational adoption.

GUGLIELMO DE ANGELIS, PH.D.

Technologist, ISTI-CNR, Italy

Guglielmo De Angelis received a first-class honors degree in Computer Science in 2003 from University of L'Aquila and a PhD in Industrial and Information Engineering from Scuola Superiore Sant'Anna of Pisa in 2007. Currently, Guglielmo is a technologist at ISTI-CNR. His research mainly focuses on Model-Driven Engineering and on Service Oriented Architectures. In particular, he is studying approaches for: the generation of environments for QoS testing, the generation of adaptable monitoring infrastructures for QoS, analytical prediction of performance parameters, empirical testing of performance parameters, and testing online QoS parameters such as trustworthiness.

DIRK DRAHEIM

CIO, Head of IT Division, University of Innsbruck, Austria

Dirk Draheim holds a Diploma in computer science from the Technische Universität Berlin and a PhD in computer science from the Freie Universität Berlin. Since summer 2006 until autumn 2008 he was area manager for database technology at the Software Competence Center Hagenberg. Since autumn 2008 he is head of the IT service management division of the University of Innsbruck. Dirk Draheim is Adjunct Reader in software engineering at the University of Mannheim.

LAYNA FISCHER

Publisher, Future Strategies Inc., USA

Ms Fischer is the CEO of Future Strategies Inc., the official publishers to WfMC.org. She was also Executive Director of WfMC and BPMI (now merged with OMG) and continues to work closely with these organizations to promote industry awareness of BPM and Workflow.

Future Strategies Inc. (www.FutStrat.com) publishes books and papers on business process management and workflow, specializing in dissemination of information about BPM, workflow technology and electronic commerce. As such, the company collaborates with individual authors and corporations worldwide and also manages the renowned annual Global Awards for Excellence in BPM and Workflow and the new annual WfMC Awards for Excellence in Case Management.

Future Strategies Inc., is the publisher of the business book series New Tools for New Times, the annual Excellence in Practice series of award-winning case studies and the annual BPM and Workflow Handbook series, published in collaboration with the WfMC. Ms. Fischer was a senior editor of a leading international computer publication for four years and has been involved in international computer journalism and publishing for over 20 years.

ALAN FISH

Principal Consultant Decision Solutions, FICO

Alan Fish has been building decision-making systems for 30 years. He has worked in many diverse domains over this time, including defense, robotics, industrial process control, government, utilities, asset management, insurance, and retail credit. As a result he has always been interested in generic techniques for decision modeling, and is the originator of the Decision Requirements Diagram (DRD). Alan is currently Principal Consultant in Decision Solutions with FICO (Fair, Isaac Corporation), working in Europe, Middle East, and Africa. Previously, he ran a small consultancy specializing in applications of artificial intelligence and data mining. He holds a BSc in psychology and a PhD in neural networks, and is the author of "Knowledge Automation: how to implement decision management in business processes" (Wiley).

HELLE FRISAK SEM

Chief Architect, Computas AS, Norway

Dr. Helle Frisak Sem is a Chief Architect in Computas, specializing in solution architecture and requirements engineering. With more than 20 years of experience, Helle leads functional teams towards the realization of operational ACM solutions, in collaboration with customer and user. She is a senior advisor in knowledge management, work process support, enterprise modelling, estimation of software projects and user interface design. From a background in research and education, Helle combines deep technical knowledge with experience on how customers' problems may be met by an operational solution. Helle is the functional architect behind the MATS solution described in this book, and over the last 15 years she has been a main contributor to FrameSolutions™ - Computas AS' framework for realizing operational ACM solutions.

HARTMANN GENRICH

Hartmann Genrich worked for Gesellschaft für Mathematik und Daten verarbeitung (GMD), the German National Research Institute for Information Technology. He holds a Dr. rer. nat. in Mathematics from University of Bonn and published various papers on the mathematics of Petri Nets. Later he got involved in the modeling, simulation and analysis of workflow systems. He retired from GMD in 2001 and works as a consultant to North American and German companies.

SETRAG KHOSHAFIAN

Chief Evangelist BPM Technology, Pegasystems Inc., USA

Dr. Setrag Khoshafian is one of the industry´s pioneers and recognized experts in BPM. He has been a senior executive in the software industry for the past 25 years, where he has invented, architected, and led the production of several enterprise software products and solutions. Currently, he is Pega's Chief Evangelist and strategic BPM technology thought leader involved in numerous technology, marketing, alliance, and customer initiatives. Prior to Pega, he was the Senior VP of Technology at Savvion, He is a frequent speaker and presenter in international workshops and conferences. He is the lead author of 10 books. Dr. Khoshafian holds a PhD in Computer Science from the University of Wisconsin-Madison.

THEODORICH KOPETZKY

Project Manager, Software Competence Center Hagenberg, Austria

Theodorich Kopetzky is a researcher and project manager at the Software Competence Center Hagenberg. His research interests include software development processes and formalization of business processes. He has led many large software development projects in different domains and is a lecturer with the University of Applied Sciences at Hagenberg. He received his diploma in computer sciences from the Johannes Kepler University Linz, Austria, in 1993.

JOSEF KÜNG

Consultant, FAW GmbH, Hagenberg, Austria

Josef Küng is associate professor for applied computer science at Johannes Kepler University Linz and consultant at FAW GmbH in Hagenberg, Austria. His core competencies in research and development cover Information Systems, Knowledge

Based Systems and Business Process Modeling. Among other scientific service activities he was Board Member of GI-Chapter 2.5.2 EMISA (Development Methodologies for Information Systems and their Application) and has been manager of several successful research projects.

MARTIN LÖFFLER

Senior Consultant, MID GmbH, Germany

Martin Löffler has worked for MID GmbH since 2009. In his role as Senior Consultant, he supports official agencies and large companies in various industries. His work focuses on the model-driven creation of software systems. He designs, automates, implements and performs quality assurance for customer-specific development processes, and he also frequently speaks about these topics at conferences.

NATHANIEL PALMER

Executive Director, Workflow Management Coalition, USA.

Nathaniel Palmer is Executive Director of the Workflow Management Coalition (WfMC). In addition he was recently appointed Editor-in-Chief of BPM.com–the BPM market's most-trafficked destination site. He is also the founder and chairman of the successful Transformation and Innovation event series, widely regarded as the leading conference on business transformation. Previously he was Director, Business Consulting for Perot Systems Corp, where he worked for business process guru Jim Champy. He spent over a decade with Delphi Group as Vice President and Chief Analyst. The author of over several dozen research studies as well as co-author of the critically-acclaimed management text "The X-Economy" (Texere, 2001) and the "BPM and Workflow Handbook" (FSI, 2007), Nathaniel has been featured in numerous media ranging from Fortune to The New York Times. He is on the advisory boards of many relevant industry publications, as well as the Board of Directors of Association of Information Management (AIIM) NE, and was nominated to represent the Governor of Massachusetts on the Commonwealth's IT Advisory Board.

THOMAS BECH PETTERSEN

CTO, Computas AS, Norway

Thomas is an experienced information system architect and knowledge management specialist with an emphasis on active business process and case management systems; i.e. adaptive case management systems that go all the way to knowledge supported business process execution in the daily workplace. "Why be satisfied with just mapping business processes? Go all the way to activate the processes for each individual employee and associate!" Thomas is a Division Director in Computas with more than 20 years of experience with workflow technology, process-based and rule-based solutions. He has worked with clients such as the Norwegian courts and the police and prosecuting authority, and served also as a functional adviser on the NFSA MATS project. Thomas has been a key player in the Computas FrameSolutions initiative, that has brought forward FrameSolutions as an ACM framework product. He has also spoken at OOPSLA and several national conferences.

GERHARD REMPP

Project Manager, MID GmbH, Germany

Gerhard Rempp is Project Manager at MID GmbH based in Stuttgart, Germany. His major topics include the Innovator Modeling Platform and the Methodology M3, as well as BPM, EAM and SOA. He has successfully worked for many years in complex IT projects in the private and public sector. He has been a speaker at several conferences and events. He is coauthor of the book "Modeldriven SOA – Anwendungsorientierte Methodik und Vorgehen in der Praxis" (Springer Verlag).

DON SCHUERMAN

Senior Director of Solution Architecture, Pegasystems Inc., USA

Don Schuerman is Senior Director of Solution Architecture for Pegasystems. He joined Pegasystems fifteen years ago in the Solution Delivery team, spent five years working for Pega Engineering, and has spent the past eight years running the architecture and engineering functions within the Solutions Consulting and Frameworks team. In these roles, Don has led enterprise software implementations and provided technology and architecture consulting to Senior Business and Technology Executives from Fortune 500 organizations, including American Express, Citibank, JP Morgan Chase, and BP.

ROBERT SHAPIRO

SVP Research: OpenText

Robert Shapiro is SVP: Research for OpenText and chairman of ProcessAnalytica. He founded CapeVisions and developed Analytics and Simulation software used by FileNet/IBM, Fujitsu, PegaSystems and Global360/OpenText.

Prior to CapeVisions, he founded Meta Software Corporation and developed graphical modeling and optimization tools for business process improvement. These tools were used by BankAmerica, Wells Fargo, JPMChase and other banks to optimize check processing and LockBox operations.

As Technical Committee chair of the WfMC, he plays a critical role in developing international standards for workflow and business process management. He has been instrumental in the creation and evolution of XPDL and BPMN. He is currently co-chair of The Business Process Simulation Working Group developing standards to support sharing of simulation input and output data for process models based on BPMN and XPDL.

In his recent work he has created a workbench for process optimization, using Visual Analytics and 'hypergraphics' to integrate process modeling, simulation, analytics and optimization.

DARIUS SILINGAS, PH.D.

Head of Solutions Department, No Magic Europe, Lithuania

Dr. Darius Silingas has been working in software engineering domain since 1998. Currently, Darius is a Head of Solutions Department at No Magic Europe, a vendor of a popular modeling platform MagicDraw. His main responsibility is helping No Magic customers to establish efficient modeling solutions based on MagicDraw. Darius has delivered over 200 training/consulting sessions worldwide, spoken at various conferences and written a number of articles on business and systems modeling. He also plays a role of dissemination and technology transfer leader in a research project CHOReOS, which aims to provide novel technologies for large-scale service choreographies in the Future Internet. Darius is an active evangelist of BPM – he regularly speaks and writes about business process management with a focus on modeling aspects. Darius is the founder and chair of an annual conference BPM in Practice (http://www.bpmpractice.com) and is also acting as a Head of BPM education module in Master of Management studies at ISM Executive School. Darius owns Ph.D. in Informatics and is OMG Certified Expert in BPM.

JIM SINUR

Independent Consultant and Gartner Emeritus

Jim Sinur is an independent thought leader in applying business process management (BPM) to innovative and intelligent business operations (IBO). His research and areas of personal experience focus on business process innovation, business modeling, business process management technology (iBPMS), process collaboration for knowledge workers, process intelligence/optimization, business policy/rule management (BRMS), and leveraging business applications in processes.

When with Gartner, Mr. Sinur was critical in creating the first Hype Cycle and Maturity Model, which have become a hallmark of Gartner analysis, along with the Magic Quadrant. He has been active in the rules, data and computing communities, helping shape direction based on practical experience. Mr. Sinur has vertical industry experience on the investment and operational sides of the insurance and financial services.

Prior to joining Gartner, Mr. Sinur was a director of technologies with American Express, where he worked on a large, industrial-strength, model-driven implementation of a business-critical merchant management system. This system is still active in the merchant retention and support functions for American Express. His responsibilities there included architecture, advanced development technologies and data/database administration.

Before American Express, Mr. Sinur worked for Northwestern Mutual Life, where he was involved in leading-edge projects like the Underwriting Workbench that employed many new and emerging methods and technologies. This was after he was involved with building and re-architecting many major applications on the investment and annuity side of NML's business.

KEITH SWENSON

Vice President of R&D, Fujitsu America Inc., USA

Keith Swenson is Vice President of Research and Development at Fujitsu America Inc. and is the Chief Software Architect for the Interstage family of products. He is known for having been a pioneer in collaboration software and web services, and has helped the development of many workflow and BPM standards. He is currently the Chairman of the Workflow Management Coalition. In the past, he led development of collaboration software MS2, Netscape, Ashton Tate and Fujitsu. In 2004 he was awarded the Marvin L. Manheim Award for outstanding contributions in the field of workflow. His blog is at http://social-biz.org/.

JAMES TAYLOR

CEO of Decision Management Solutions

James is the CEO of Decision Management Solutions. He is a leading expert in how to use business rules and analytic technology to build Decision Management Systems. James is passionate about using Decision Management Systems to help companies improve decision making and develop an agile, analytic and adaptive business. Decision Management Solutions provides strategic consulting to companies of all sizes, working with clients in all sectors to adopt decision making technology. James has led Decision Management efforts for leading companies in insurance, banking, health management and telecommunications.

James is the author of "Decision Management Systems: A practical guide to using business rules and predictive analytics" (IBM Press, 2011). He previously wrote Smart (Enough) Systems: How to Deliver Competitive Advantage by Automating

Hidden Decisions (Prentice Hall) with Neil Raden, and has contributed chapters on Decision Management to multiple books including "Applying Real-World BPM in an SAP Environment", "The Decision Model", "The Business Rules Revolution: Doing Business The Right Way" and "Business Intelligence Implementation: Issues and Perspectives." He regularly speaks, teaches and writes on Decision Management. James can be contacted by email james@decisionmanagementsolutions.com

Pieter van Schalkwyk

CEO, XMPro, USA

Pieter is the CEO of XMPro, a Gartner Cool Vendor for BPM 2012. Pieter has more than 12 years BPMS experience and is an evangelist for Intelligent Business Operations. Pieter holds a Master's degree in IT and is a graduate mechanical engineer. Pieter is also the author of a published academic article. His LinkedIn Profile: www.linkedin.com/in/pietervs/

Jan Vanthienen

Professor, KU Leuven, Department of Decision Sciences and Information Management, Information Systems Group , Netherlands

Jan Vanthienen is full professor of information systems at KU Leuven, Department of Decision Sciences and Information Management, Information Systems Group, where he is teaching and researching on business intelligence, analytics, business rules and processes, business information systems and information management. He has published more than 150 full papers in reviewed international journals and conference proceedings. He received the Belgian Francqui Chair 2009 at FUNDP and an IBM Faculty Award in 2011. He is co-founder and president-elect of the Benelux Association for Information Systems (BENAIS). He is also member of the IEEE task force on process mining, and co-author of the Business Process Mining Manifesto. According to the Web of Science, professor Vanthienen's current H-index is 15, with a total number of citations equal to 937. His top six papers each have more than 50 citations. The areas of business rules modeling, validation and verification, business process management and decision modeling have been his major areas of research and expertise for many years.

Paul Vincent

Event Processing Specialist, TIBCO Software

Vincent is a long-time practitioner of the business rules approach, including R&D into real-time expert systems, working for a decision management company, and now a middleware and event processing specialist TIBCO Software. He has also been involved in W3C RIF and OMG PRR rule standards, and currently event-related and decision model standards.

Paul Vincent is a veteran of the rules industry, having started on Intelligent Systems for Monte Carlo simulation models before moving to C and Java-based business rules engines and BRMS tools, and more recently CEP and the business real-time rule engine TIBCO BusinessEvents. At TIBCO he also works on Monitoring Systems including one of the most widely-deployed rules engines in systems today, TIBCO Hawk. Industry groups he supports include the Event Processing Technical Society Reference Architecture Group and the OMG standards body for the Decision Model and Notation.

CHARLES WEBSTER, MD, MSIE, MSIS

President, EHR Workflow Inc.

Charles Webster, MD, MSIE, MSIS is a prolific thought leader in the health and health IT space, noted by Healthcare IT News as one of the most important bloggers in the healthcare IT community and one of the most active health IT leaders on Twitter. You can read his blogs, EHR Workflow Management Systems at http://ChuckWebster.com, The Healthcare BPM Blog at http://hcBPM.com, and follow him on Twitter at http://twitter.com/wareFLO. With degrees in Accountancy, Industrial Engineering, Artificial Intelligence, and Medicine, Dr. Webster's wide range of expertise gives him a unique and comprehensive view into the healthcare sector. He designed the first undergraduate program in Medical Informatics, was CMIO for an EHR vendor, and wrote the first three award-winning case studies submitted for the HIMSS Davies Award for EHR Ambulatory Excellence. Dr. Webster is a tireless proponent for process-aware information systems in healthcare.

Index

Additional Resources

NEW E-BOOK SERIES ($9.97 EACH)

Download PDF immediately and start reading.

- Introduction to BPM and Workflow
  http://store.futstrat.com/servlet/Detail?no=75

- Financial Services
  http://store.futstrat.com/servlet/Detail?no=90

- Healthcare
  http://store.futstrat.com/servlet/Detail?no=81

- Utilities and Telecommunications
  http://store.futstrat.com/servlet/Detail?no=92

NON-PROFIT ASSOCIATIONS AND RELATED STANDARDS RESEARCH ONLINE

- AIIM (Association for Information and Image Management)
  http://www.aiim.org
- BPM and Workflow online news, research, forums
  http://bpm.com
- BPM Research at Stevens Institute of Technology
  http://www.bpm-research.com
- Business Process Management Initiative
  http://www.bpmi.org *see* Object Management Group
- IEEE (Electrical and Electronics Engineers, Inc.)
  http://www.ieee.org
- Institute for Information Management (IIM)
  http://www.iim.org
- ISO (International Organization for Standardization)
  http://www.iso.ch
- Object Management Group
  http://www.omg.org
- Open Document Management Association
  http://nfocentrale.net/dmware
- Organization for the Advancement of Structured Information Standards
  http://www.oasis-open.org
- Society for Human Resource Management
  http://www.shrm.org
- Society for Information Management
  http://www.simnet.org
- Wesley J. Howe School of Technology Management
  http://howe.stevens.edu/research/research-centers/business-process-innovation
- Workflow And Reengineering International Association (WARIA)
  http://www.waria.com
- Workflow Management Coalition (WfMC)
  http://www.wfmc.org
- Workflow Portal
  http://www.e-workflow.org

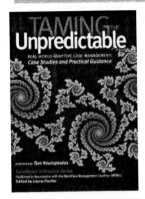

TAMING THE UNPREDICTABLE

http://futstrat.com/books/eip11.php

The core element of Adaptive Case Management (ACM) is the support for real-time decision-making by knowledge workers.

Taming the Unpredictable presents the logical starting point for understanding how to take advantage of ACM. This book goes beyond talking about concepts, and delivers actionable advice for embarking on your own journey of ACM-driven transformation.

Retail #49.95 (see discount on website)

HOW KNOWLEDGE WORKERS GET THINGS DONE

http://www.futstrat.com/books/HowKnowledgeWorkers.php

How Knowledge Workers Get Things Done describes the work of managers, decision makers, executives, doctors, lawyers, campaign managers, emergency responders, strategists, and many others who have to think for a living.

These are people who figure out what needs to be done, at the same time that they do it, and there is a new approach to support this presents the logical starting point for understanding how to take advantage of ACM.

Retail $49.95 (see discount offer on website)

DELIVERING BPM EXCELLENCE

http://futstrat.com/books/Delivering_BPM.php

Business Process Management in Practice

The companies whose case studies are featured in this book have proven excellence in their creative and successful deployment of advanced BPM concepts. These companies focused on excelling in *innovation, implementation* and *impact* when installing BPM and workflow technologies. The positive impact includes increased revenues, more productive and satisfied employees, product enhancements, better customer service and quality improvements.

$39.95 (see discount on website)

DELIVERING THE CUSTOMER-CENTRIC ORGANIZATION

http://futstrat.com/books/Customer-Centric.php

The ability to successfully manage the customer value chain across the life cycle of a customer is the key to the survival of any company today. Business processes must react to changing and diverse customer needs and interactions to ensure efficient and effective outcomes.

This important book looks at the shifting nature of consumers and the workplace, and how BPM and associated emergent technologies will play a part in shaping the companies of the future.

Retail $39.95

BPMN 2.0 Handbook SECOND EDITION

(see two-BPM book bundle offer on website: get BPMN Reference Guide Free)

http://futstrat.com/books/bpmnhandbook2.php

Updated and expanded with exciting new content!

Authored by members of WfMC, OMG and other key participants in the development of BPMN 2.0, the BPMN 2.0 Handbook brings together worldwide thought-leaders and experts in this space. Exclusive and unique contributions examine a variety of aspects that start with an introduction of what's new in BPMN 2.0, and look closely at interchange, analytics, conformance, optimization, simulation and more. **Retail $75.00**

BPMN MODELING AND REFERENCE GUIDE

(Download **two-BPMN book bundle:** Only **$69.95** for both books)

http://www.futstrat.com/books/BPMN-Guide.php

Understanding and Using BPMN

How to develop rigorous yet understandable graphical representations of business processes. Business Process Modeling Notation (BPMN) is a standard, graphical modeling representation for business processes. It provides an easy to use, flow-charting notation that is independent of the implementation environment. **Retail $39.95**

BPM & WORKFLOW HANDBOOK: HUMAN-CENTRIC BPM

http://www.futstrat.com/books/handbook08.php

Human-centric business process management (BPM) has become the product and service differentiator. The topic now captures substantial mindshare and market share in the human-centric BPM space as leading vendors have strengthened their human-centric business processes. Our spotlight this year examines challenges in human-driven workflow and its integration across the enterprise.

Retail $95.00 (see discount on website)

Social BPM

http://futstrat.com/books/handbook11.php

Work, Planning, and Collaboration Under the Impact of Social Technology

Today we see the transformation of both the look and feel of BPM technologies along the lines of social media, as well as the increasing adoption of social tools and techniques democratizing process development and design. It is along these two trend lines; the evolution of system interfaces and the increased engagement of stakeholders in process improvement, that Social BPM has taken shape.

Retail $59.95 (see discount offer on website)

Get 25% Discount on ALL Books in our Store.

Please use the discount code **SPEC25** to get **25% discount** on ALL books in our store; both Print and Digital Editions (two discount codes cannot be used together).

www.FutStrat.com